THE CENTRE COURT STORY

H.R.H. The Duchess of Kent.   President of the All England Lawn Tennis and Croquet Club.

THE
CENTRE COURT
STORY

by

MAURICE BRADY

INTRODUCTION BY
JAROSLAV DROBNY

Published for
THE FIRESIDE PRESS
by
W. FOULSHAM & CO. LTD.
LONDON
NEW YORK . TORONTO . CAPE TOWN . SYDNEY

W. Foulsham & Co. Ltd.
2-5 Old Bond St., London, W.1

DEDICATED TO MY MOTHER

In salutation of her complete understanding of lawn tennis— and her refusals to "come and have tea" while watching the unfolding of the Centre Court Story.

MADE IN GREAT BRITAIN
by C. Tinling & Co. Ltd.
Liverpool, London and Prescot

INTRODUCTION

by Jaroslav Drobny

Wimbledon Singles Champion in 1954

It is with much pleasure that I write this introduction to Maurice Brady's book "The Centre Court Story." Having read, with considerable interest, his articles on lawn tennis personalities, I am not surprised that he has put his efforts into writing this book for I know few who are better qualified to bring out a work of this kind. An immense enthusiast and student of the game, the author has dealt with his subject with remarkable detail and accuracy.

For me, of course, there are parts of particular interest, for it has been my good fortune to play against, and to become acquainted with, several of the players described.

In my opinion, "The Centre Court Story," apart from having an instant appeal to tennis lovers everywhere, provides an invaluable record of the achievements earned by outstanding personalities. It re-produces the colour and liveliness which always exists with the game, but which is lost to many because of the lack of telling.

Presented with light-heartedness and humour, this book brings out the human angle showing the masters, not as machine-like personalities especially endowed by nature for the game, but as ordinary people subject to ordinary set-backs, yet capable of wonderful application for hard work.

I wish "The Centre Court Story" every success.

ACKNOWLEDGMENTS

If, through the medium of this book, I can transmit to others some of the pleasure I have experienced when watching lawn tennis experts in action, I shall be well content. In writing this story of the Wimbledon celebrities I have tried not only to record their successes, but also to recapture the spirit of their personalities. It is this element that plays such a vital part in bringing colour and charm to the Centre Court.

My sincere thanks are due to Jaroslav Drobny who has enhanced my book by adding an introduction. I would also like to express my gratitude to Mrs. L. A. Godfree and to Vic Seixas who were kind enough to lend me photographs.

Finally, I acknowledge, with appreciation, the invaluable assistance given in checking records and scores by C. M. "Jimmy" Jones and Keith Dyer, of "British Lawn Tennis and Squash".

MAURICE BRADY.

CONTENTS

Chapter 1. THE BULLDOG BREED   *page* 11

2. PAVLOVA OF TENNIS   16

3. "MR. TENNIS"   25

4. "LITTLE BILL"   34

5. UNDER THE SHADOW OF SUZANNE   40

6. PETER PAN OF TENNIS   44

7. MONSIEUR LE CROCODILE   50

8. WHERE THERE'S A WILLS . . .   56

9. SPORTSMAN OF DESTINY   65

10. LADY OF SPAIN   74

11. THE YOUNGEST-EVER CHAMPION   77

12. FIVE-FOOT FRAULEIN   82

13. A VOLCANO ARRIVES AT WIMBLEDON   85

14. ONE OF THE CLASSICS   92

15. "DOROTHY ROUNDS UP THE TENNIS"   99

16. BUNNY—BUT NO RABBIT   103

17. BRITAIN'S BLACK PANTHER   108

18. HELEN II   113

19. BEAU BRUMMELL OF TENNIS   119

20. FAMOUS RED-HEAD OF TENNIS   123

21. TRIUMPH AND TRAGEDY   128

22. "BAD BOY OF TENNIS"   132

23. THE TRICOLOUR AGAIN   137

CONTENTS

Chapter 24. "PEERLESS PAULINE"   *page* 141

25. "KING KRAMER"   145

26. "THE WIZARD OF OZ"   148

27. A FALLING STAR   152

28. "FOREVER AMBLING"   156

29. PLAYBOY TURNS CHAMPION   158

30. GREAT GIRL FROM OKLAHOMA   164

31. TOO TOUGH, THIS TENNIS   170

32. FRILLS . . . AND THRILLS   174

33. GOLDEN BOY OF TENNIS   177

34. ADONIS OF TENNIS   181

35. SHE WALKED . . . AND SHE WON   185

36. THE DROBNY SAGA   190

37. TYCOON OF TENNIS   197

38. EMPRESS OF TENNIS   201

39. HURRICANE HOAD   205

40. MUSCLES FROM AUSTRALIA   210

41. THE GIRL WHO CAME BACK   214

42. "I'M OLDER THAN HIS MOTHER"   218

ILLUSTRATIONS

H.R.H. The Duchess of Kent. President of the All England Lawn
Tennis and Croquet Club . . . . *Frontis.*

Between
Pages

Gerald L. Patterson (Australia). Wimbledon Champion 1919 and
1922 16–17

Mlle. Suzanne Lenglen. France's most famous sportswoman . 16–17

William T. " Big Bill " Tilden. Considered the greatest-ever
player 32–33

William M. " Little Bill " Johnston (U.S.A.) 32–33

Mrs. L. A. Godfree (Kitty McKane). Recovered to win Wimbldon
in 1924 and 1926 32–33

Jean Borotra (France) making a typical picturesque plunge . . 32–33

15-year old American Sydney B. Wood congratulates René
Lacoste (France) at Wimbledon in 1927 48–49

Mrs. Helen Wills Moody (now Mrs. Roark). Won Wimbledon
eight times 48–49

Frenchman Henri Cochet, Wimbledon Champion in 1927 and 1929 48–49

Comtesse De La Valdène (Lili D'Alvarez). Wimbledon finalist in
1926, 1927 and 1928 48–49

Contessa Della Corte Brae (Cilly Aussem). Won Wimbledon in
1931 64–65

H. Ellsworth Vines. Became the Champion of 1932 . . . 64–65

Australian Jack Crawford who won a spectacular victory over Vines 64–65

Mrs. L. Little (Dorothy Round). Won the Championship twice
for Britain (1934 and 1937) 64–65

H. W. " Bunny " Austin, the Englishman who introduced shorts to
the Centre Court 80–81

Frederick J. Perry whose overwhelming attack gained great glory
for Britain 80–81

Two famous Californians, Miss Helen Jacobs (Champion in 1936)
and Miss Alice Marble (Champion in 1939) 80–81

The last meeting . . . the battle of the " Helens " . . . 80–81

Baron Gottfried Von Cramm magnificent but unlucky . 96–97

ILLUSTRATIONS

Between Pages

Crimson-haired and very popular, Donald Budge (U.S.A.) . . 96–97

Robert L. Riggs the wily little American who was never beaten at Wimbledon 96–97

The Tricolour again! Yvon Petra, giant Frenchman 96–97

Mrs. Robert Addie (U.S.A.). As Pauline Betz, she took everything in her stride at Wimbledon in 1946—even the net! . . 112–113

Jack Kramer, Champion in 1947 112–113

Names that have become world-famous. Miss Louise Brough and her fellow American Mrs. Margaret Osborne Du Pont . . 112–113

Robert Falkenburg, a fiery American whose amazing victory at Wimbledon in 1948 caused an uproar of comment . . . 112–113

Partners at Wimbledon in 1949. Frederick R. " Ted " Schroeder (U.S.A.) and American Doubles star Gardnar Mulloy . . 128–129

Budge Patty. Elegant, economical, popular American . . 128–129

Dick Savitt (U.S.A.) secured the Wimbledon crown at his first appearance 128–129

Miss Gertrude Moran, America's much publicized " Gorgeous Gussy " 128–129

Frank Sedgman, Australia's " Golden Boy " of Tennis . . 144–145

Vic Seixas (U.S.A.). His own favourite photograph . . 144–145

Miss Doris Hart. Became Wimbledon Champion in 1951 . 144–145

Formerly a Czech, now an Egyptian, Jaroslav Drobny has a huge following on the Centre Court 144–145

The end of one of the greatest dramas staged on the Centre Court. Drobny and Patty exchange weary smiles . . . 160–161

Tony Trabert who captured the Wimbledon title in 1955 . 160–161

Mrs. Norman Brinker (Maureen Connolly). America's fabulous " Little Mo " 192–193

Lew Hoad (Australia) whose power tennis won Wimbledon in 1956 192–193

Ken Rosewall. His enchanting tennis took him to the Wimbledon Finali n 1954 and in 1956 208–209

Miss Shirley Fry (U.S.A.) who made a great come back to capture the Wimbledon crown in 1956 208–209

The Bulldog Breed

THE man who had never seen a game of tennis was taken by a friend to witness the world champion in action. But it was not one of the latter's best performances. Fearsome and flamboyant, he had offered a freakish mixture of winners and losers. "Well, what do you think of him?" the man was asked by his friend, anxious to ascertain a newcomer's reaction.

"He hits very hard," was the reply, "but I should imagine he usually plays on a bigger court."

Australia gleefully circulated this story about her popular Melbourne-born champion Gerald Patterson. If out of form, Patterson was wont to lose accuracy entirely.

Bulky and burly, this likeable six-footer received the Military Cross in World War I. He started tennis on his parents' court in Melbourne and was the favourite nephew of Dame Nellie Melba who was also his most ardent supporter.

To Lacoste, Patterson's service was "the most perfect ever executed." About a meeting in 1925 he wrote "I hardly saw the ball pass . . . needless to say I did not often return it." This tribute came from a man capable of handling Tilden's thunderbolts.

The Australian had a habit of gearing himself up into the sky for his smash which was virtually untakeable. In his forehand driving and volleying lay great power, but the balance of Patterson's equipment was weakened by an ugly pushed backhand which drew from Tilden "But—his backhand!" The American summed up this shot by adding dryly, "It is all wrong but it gets there."

On form, however, few players were strong enough to probe this deficiency. Most of his rivals were pounded into submission by his service and forehand. Interleaved with all this bludgeoning was a surprisingly delicate stop-volley and a delightful touch on the half-volley.

Patterson came to England in 1919 when aged twenty-four and did not drop a set at Surbiton or Roehampton. At Wimbledon the debut of Melba's nephew caused great excitement—and it was soon evident that 42-year-old Norman Brookes would be matched against his young compatriot in the Challenge Round.

The newcomer opened with a tempestuous attack against C. J.

Gilbert (6-0, 6-4, 6-0)—Roper Barrett made him run but could not get a set (7-5, 6-2, 7-5)—T. Mavrogordato surrendered the first nine games in fifteen minutes (6-0, 6-3, 7-5)—and from 2-all in the first set S. N. Doust collapsed under a rain of terrific aces and smashes, losing eleven successive games (6-2, 6-0, 6-2).

Frenchman André Gobert, possessor of a mighty service and a flighty temperament, was the next obstacle. He surpassed Patterson in style but not in stolidity. Losing the long first set he was never again in the fight (10-8, 6-3, 6-2).

Patterson then lost a set to M. J. G. Ritchie (6-1, 7-5, 1-6, 6-3) but in the final was too powerful for Kingscote (6-2, 6-1, 6-3).

Youth was served against Norman Brookes who could not reproduce those sparkling left-handed volleys that had deprived Wilding of his title in 1914. Patterson won the first set easily. He was thoroughly extended by the "Wizard's" guile in the second, but dominated the third, finishing the tournament with four dynamic aces (6-3, 7-5, 6-2).

From Wimbledon to America where an erratic Patterson clashed with Bill Johnston in the last sixteen. It was an amazing and, at times, amusing spectacle. "Little Bill" undeterred by a big service steered the ball neatly on to Patterson's unreliable backhand and settled down quietly for a winning volleying campaign. Leading two sets to one and 4-1 in the fourth, the match, to him, seemed safe enough. But Patterson under pressure was getting wilder and wilder. At this stage two arching backhands nearly knocked the umpire off his stand. The crowd roared at the Australian's mixture of bad and brilliant shots and Johnston lost his nerve, his concentration and five successive games.

He recovered to lead 5-3 in the final set only to again falter before a succession of drives that raised chalk or else caused officials to duck. He missed his own returns and 5-all was called. Then Johnston pulled himself together and scrambled home somewhat fortuitously, 6-2, 3-6, 6-4, 4-6, 7-5.

In 1920, the Wimbledon entry was much stronger and Tilden came through a brilliant field to fight Patterson. The champion, missing his friend and adviser Norman Brookes, had steadfastly refused tournament play before the Challenge Round—consequently he was in no mental shape to combat the American's attack.

Patterson won the first set—but only nine more games. Tilden dipped his service returns to Patterson's toes causing him to mis-hit many low volleys. The Australian's backhand, too, wilted under Tilden's mixture of power and placement and nearly every rally terminated with a wild loser. It was a disappointing struggle

12

Patterson netting a quarter of his returns on his weaker wing. The American was victorious 2-6, 6-2, 6-3, 6-4.

Nobody accepted defeat more gallantly. Tilden declared "It was a pleasure to play against Gerald." The Australian gained some consolation when he and Suzanne won the mixed doubles from the holders Lycett—Miss Ryan 7-5, 6-3.

Two years later Patterson returned to Wimbledon—and regained his title, a task helped by the absence of Tilden and Johnston. His equipment was smoother and to his repertoire was now added a safer chopped backhand.

Starting with four aces Patterson crushed A. C. Gravem 6-1, 6-1, 6-4. Borotra was hit off court 6-0, 6-1, 6-3, but Kingscote presented a very different problem. The Englishman's elegant game nearly overcame Patterson's power tennis. Unusual double-faults marred the Australian's play and he only scored 173 winners to Kingscote's 171, before triumphing 6-4, 3-6, 5-7, 6-4, 6-3.

At 1-all in the fourth set of the Patterson-Cecil Campbell quarter-final, rain stopped play. On resumption, Patterson unleashed such fury that it was all over in six minutes. Campbell could only win five rallies, whereas Patterson gathered two love games and also scored four aces in the fifth game. This 7-9, 6-3, 6-2, 6-1 victory revealed the biggest hitting yet seen at the new Wimbledon.

Australian Joe Anderson was his next opponent, a man who had won two of their three encounters. In a somewhat uncomfortable rain-interrupted affair, Patterson won 6-1, 3-6, 7-9, 6-1, 6-3. He raised a laugh by bringing on court a toy rabbit in response to Anderson's famous toy kangaroo.

Patterson irritated his opponent by delaying over a handkerchief he wore around his forehead. Trouble with one of his shoes also annoyed Anderson. Patterson's new chopped backhand was a source of profit on the damp grass and the quality of tennis was raised by some wonder volleying and half-volleying on his part.

This was virtually the final. In his last match—which had to be postponed until Monday because of rain—Patterson easily defeated Lycett 6-3, 6-4, 6-2. This was achieved in the presence of Melba and the game was dictated by the winner's tremendous service which forced Lycett to stand well behind the baseline.

Soon afterwards in America Patterson defeated Gobert, Cochet, de Gomar and Manoel Alonso in Davis Cup matches. But although his defence was now sounder, the Australian fell to Tilden 7-5, 10-8, 6-0, and was crushed by Johnston 6-2, 6-2, 6-1. In the U.S. semi-final too, he could do no more than take a set off Tilden (4-6, 6-4, 6-3, 6-1).

The husky Australian seldom scored any stirring success in

13

America—except with spectators who were schooled to admire athletes of the Babe Ruth type. They loved his simplicity, his will to win and his absorption in tennis. He had (to quote Tilden) "gained a permanent place in American hearts."

Patterson re-visited the United States in 1924 as Davis Cup Captain. He lost to Lacoste, but won the Inter-Zone against France, when at his flailing best the Australian overwhelmed Borotra 6-3, 6-1, 6-3.

He failed, however, to make any impression on Tilden or Vincent Richards in the Challenge Round. In the American semi-final he received his greatest defeat when a violent counter-attack from Johnston knocked him off court 6-2, 6-0, 6-0 in forty bewildering minutes.

Next year although France gained a 4-1 revenge, Patterson scored Australia's one victory. He beat Lacoste (Wimbledon champion) 6-3, 6-4, 6-2.

The doubles tie nearly ended in tragedy. Borotra, hampered by an unsteady Lacoste, opposed Hawkes and Patterson—and continually achieved winning volleys by cutting off Hawkes' returns. This was galling to Patterson who suddenly took a violent swipe at the ball hitting Borotra on the temple with a tremendous volley. The Basque collapsed. The first to reach him was Patterson. The crowd panicked but Borotra eventually revived and continued.

On Hawkes' next return he again jumped in. Patterson, guessing his intention, repeated that full-blooded swipe, missing Borotra by inches. The Basque chuckled but some sections of the crowd booed the usually popular Patterson. Eventually France won 6-4, 3-6, 6-4, 1-6, 10-8.

In 1927, the Australian achieved a great ambition when he won his national championship. It took him three hours to overcome the tenacity of Hawkes (3-6, 6-4, 3-6, 18-16, 6-3).

Next year Patterson re-visited Wimbledon. Handicapped by tennis elbow, he survived another tremendous game against C. H. Kingsley (10-8, 9-11, 10-8, 5-7, 6-2). The duration of the match cost the L.T.A. more than £100 in overtime payments. The Australian went out in the fourth round, his backhand giving Brugnon the chance to produce many elegant winning volleys (6-3, 5-7, 6-4, 6-2).

In doubles, however, Patterson reproduced much of his disrupting overhead power. He and Pat O'Hara Wood defeated Borotra-Lacoste and then saved match point against the holders Tilden-Hunter (7-9, 7-9, 6-4, 6-4, 10-8). In the final they succumbed to the mechanical team-work of Cochet-Brugnon (13-11, 6-4, 6-4).

Aged thirty-three, Patterson was now playing much less frequently. Business prevented him from accepting the Davis Cup captaincy in

14

1930, but he was a welcome and interested spectator at the Centre Court in 1934 and 1937.

He came to Wimbledon again in 1946. Apart from very occasional exhibition games, Patterson has abandoned tennis. His weight has increased to eighteen stone. Left a considerable fortune by his parents and his aunt, Patterson lives in luxury in Australia and is now one of the richest men in tennis.

2

Pavlova of Tennis

MOST champions have enriched the history of tennis by their play or their personality. Maurice McLoughlin showed the power of the serve-volley game so popular in the later schools of America . . . Tilden proved it was possible to combat this danger. The daring of Borotra was a model for every would-be net-player . . . the exotic d'Alvarez demonstrated a wonder half-volley.

But surely nobody had as much influence on tennis as Suzanne Lenglen! This young Frenchwoman not only played the game with superb matchless artistry—she revolutionised the entire tennis scene, adding to it glamour and world-wide publicity.

Her parents were poor and soon realised the enormous financial return this prodigy might achieve. To Suzanne, therefore, victory became all-important and tennis became a business. She was born at Compiègne on 24th May, 1899, and as a child spent so many hours perfecting her tennis that it was claimed she could hit a handkerchief placed anywhere on court. Despite this Trojan-like training, however, Suzanne was essentially feminine and never developed into a sporting outdoor Amazon.

She hit her forehand harder than her backhand but was, if possible, even more accurate with the latter stroke. Her smashes frequently raised chalk, her volleys, executed with exquisite delicacy, skilfully wrong-footed the most nimble opponent. But Suzanne preferred to conduct her battles from the baseline, two or three perfect placements usually securing every point. Double-faults were a rarity and, if needed, a service ace could be produced.

Like Laurie Doherty and Tilden, Suzanne always restrained her return of service. Like them again, she seldom was compelled to chase the ball—rather it seemed to find her racket a magnet.

If forced out of position, the French player soon recovered poise, springing through the air like a ballerina. Secure in her equipment, Suzanne concentrated confidently on strategy, knowing instinctively the correct counter to any attack.

Such overwhelming perfection might be considered uninteresting. Far from it—Suzanne's greatest enemy on court was her own temperament. Her genius, her stormy home life (she and her mother quarrelled incessantly) her poor health and her nerves all combined

*Gerald L. Patterson (Australia).   His power and personality won the Wimbledon Champion-
ship in 1919 and 1922.*

Mlle. Suzanne Lenglen. France's most famous sportswoman. Her matchless artistry captured six Wimbledon championships (1919–1923 and 1925).

to make every match a possible dramatic upset. There were innumerable "regrettable incidents" but Suzanne held the public enthralled for many years. She loved to perform before thousands. "I am not nervous. The bigger the crowd, the better."

Never before had tennis provided such box-office attraction. Certainly not beautiful, Suzanne overcame this defect by her grace, her vivacity and her exquisite clothes (soon copied slavishly). She produced glamour, she provided emotion and she presented the beauty of tennis in a manner never equalled again.

Aged fifteen, she won the French Hard Court singles from Mme. Golding 6-2, 6-1, and on the Riviera she encountered the redoubtable Mrs. Lambert Chambers then the greatest player of the day. Mrs. Chambers frequently extolled her young opponent so it was not without some advance publicity that Suzanne arrived at Wimbledon in 1919. France, trampled yet triumphant, was then greatly in the news and Suzanne caused an immediate sensation.

Women then played tennis in long-sleeved blouses, petticoats and skirts to the ankles. Suzanne was clad in a short-sleeved one-piece dress reaching to her knees, minus a petticoat and plus lipstick.

The crowd was shocked—and the queues grew daily!

This was her first appearance on grass. Immediately something unusual was at hand. Mrs. Cobb, Suzanne's opponent, unaware that she was due to play, had arrived without a racket.

Suzanne allowed her first opponent one game, but Charles Lenglen, her staunch adviser, was warned that he must not coach his daughter from "inside" the court.

She then overthrew the famous Mrs. Larcombe (champion in 1912) 6-2, 6-1, and next routed Mrs. Craddock for the loss of one game.

After conquering England's best young player, Miss McKane, 6-0, 6-1, the French girl was nearly halted. Leading Elizabeth Ryan 6-4, 5-2, 40-15 Suzanne wavered before the relentless chopping and chasing of the Californian. Amidst great excitement Miss Ryan pulled up to 5-all, and Suzanne was visibly losing her control. At this stage luckily for France there was a deluge of rain. Miss Ryan's attack was disturbed and unable to get on level terms again, she surrendered the next two games on resumption.

The tireless Mrs. Satterthwaite held no terrors for Suzanne who crushed her 6-1, 6-1 to reach the Challenge Round. Here she met Mrs. Chambers, an opponent of equal calibre. Suzanne after a confident start (she led 5-3) was caught and passed by Mrs. Chambers whose deep devastating drives carried her to 6-5, 40-15. Wonderfully mobile and courageous, Suzanne met the challenge, eventually capturing a brilliant first set 10-8. England then led 4-1, France pulled up to 4-all, but could not save the second set.

17

In the final struggle an inspired Suzanne led 4-1—only to extract the best from her dauntless older opponent, who swept to 6-5, 40-15.

A desperate "wooden" volley saved the first match point, a beautiful backhand secured the second. Mrs. Chambers showed no sign of nerves or fatigue, despite the tremendous pace, but Suzanne finally triumphed in a wonderful victory, 10-8, 4-6, 9-7.

The seal was set on Suzanne's success story. Her ecstatic parents, their finances assured, deluged her with embraces. Max Decugis, the first Frenchman to win an English tournament, did likewise. Mrs. Chambers seemed equally pleased, declaring she had never played better tennis in her life.

1920 revealed a smarter, more sophisticated Suzanne. She was expensively and beautifully gowned, transforming the little French girl into an attractive world personality. Her series of coloured (and later, multi-coloured) bandeaux replaced the floppy white hat of 1919—and were adopted as an essential part of all tennis outfits. A diamond pin kept her headgear in place.

This year she awaited the challenge of Mrs. Chambers, who had crushed Mrs. Mallory and Miss Ryan for the loss of six games.

A fight seemed assured when Mrs. Chambers hit a destructive forehand that left even Suzanne standing, to bring the score to 2-all. But from that stage, Suzanne dictated the pace. Mrs. Chambers was made to run the whole length of the court for every shot and lost her accuracy under such tremendous pressure. From 3-all the champion, alert and artistic, produced an amazing exhibition to win the last nine games.

Suzanne's Continental successes (most 6-0, 6-0 wins) are too numerous to mention. In France she won all three titles from 1919 to 1923. Illness intervened in 1924. In 1925, the championship was thrown up to "foreigners" but Lenglen regained the triple crown, and did so again in 1926.

In the "World's Hard Court" final in 1921 Suzanne encountered, for the first time, the famous U.S. champion Mrs. Molla Mallory. Molla, renowned for her amazing foot-work, recovered most of Suzanne's delicate thoughtful placements. Moreover, after losing the first set, she produced several savage winning forehands and led 3-2, 40-30, in the second.

Unnerved, Suzanne wished to retire. Her feet, she declared, were hurting too much. Svengali (Charles Lenglen) ordered his Trilby back to the baseline. Molla netted the next shot, and this restored Suzanne's equanimity. She won 6-2, 6-3.

The American never played so well again in Europe, but Suzanne scored 77 winners to Molla's 49. These rivals did not like, nor understand, one another. Tilden was Molla's great friend and was, naturally, in her camp. He declared "Suzanne was supreme in victory, regrettable in defeat." This was in the early 'twenties. In 1938 he took a more tolerant view, "Mind you, I really like Suzanne . . . when I met her again after her tennis days were over I found her a witty charming woman."

With many other competitors, however, Suzanne was popular. She was always very close to the "Musketeers" and Lacoste called her "their wonderful comrade and friend." Her partner was masculine Elizabeth Ryan who understood the Frenchwoman thoroughly. She knew how to restore Suzanne's calm and between them lay the deepest affection.

It was Elizabeth Ryan—victor over Mrs. Mallory—who challenged Suzanne at Wimbledon in 1921. She led 2-1 but did not win another game. Unable to fence with Suzanne from the baseline, she tried forcing at the net but floundered against a stream of accurate passing shots and beautiful diagonal lobs. Suzanne met Miss Ryan thirty-eight times, the French player's baseline strength always winning.

The Lenglens were now fêted and entertained by wealthy families all over Europe. But "Papa" was unwell and very disturbed by Suzanne's latest idea—she wanted to visit America on her own. Tilden and Molla Mallory had competed in France that spring, so a courtesy return trip for Suzanne, in order to raise funds for France's war-ruined towns, was suggested. Charles Lenglen demurred but his daughter, asserting her independence for once, agreed with delight.

Suzanne was to team-up with Molla and to partner Bill Johnston in the mixed. What plans! and how fate dealt with them! In those days the draw at Forest Hills was unseeded. Suzanne's first opponent, Eleanor Goss withdrew, leaving her to combat—the holder, Molla Mallory!

Tilden meeting Suzanne before the match was calmly told, "I will beat her 6-0, 6-0." "No woman can beat Molla" he snapped, "least of all, you."

Molla—who had been stimulated by Tilden reminding her of all the characteristics in Suzanne she disliked most—was never more determined. Suzanne, recently ill with asthma, came on court with the word "Poilu" whispered into her ear by M. de Joannis, Vice-President of the French lawn tennis association. He was reminding her of the plight of France's shattered cities.

Suzanne, trying to lure Molla up court, saw her medium-paced returns dispatched for winners. To the gallery's amazement and delight Molla captured the first set, 6-2.

Coughing nervously, Suzanne attempted a harder forcing shot, but aware that for once the crowd was not on her side she lost control of her game. Molla led 2-0 and Suzanne's nerve cracked.

Not even "Poilu" could save the situation. What was needed was Charles Lenglen. His daughter's "I cannot go on, I really am too ill" announced the retirement of the world champion and the ruin of her American tour.

Pandemonium set in as Molla walked swiftly off court alone. Spectators deprived of their money's worth were furious, as Suzanne, leaning on the arm of M. de Joannis, left the arena in tears.

Lenglen supporters deny this was a complete defeat. But early in 1922 after overcoming a spirited Kitty McKane 10-8, 6-2, Suzanne, declaring she was unwell, refused to play Elizabeth Ryan in the final at Brussels. No doctor was willing to declare her unfit, so she played—and won easily 6-3, 6-2. Many people were, however, asserting that the Frenchwoman greatly feared meeting her rivals.

At Wimbledon, however, she was just as great an attraction. English crowds are less blood-thirsty than trans-Atlantic spectators, and Suzanne's exit at Forest Hills was not held against her.

Playing through (the Challenge Round was abolished in 1922) Suzanne reached the final with a 6-4, 6-1 win over Mrs. Peacock. She seemed to have lost a measure of her supremacy, being extended by Miss McKane to 6-1, 7-5, and by Miss Ryan to 6-1, 8-6.

The final, however, against Molla Mallory revealed Suzanne at her zenith. Rain held up the start until 7.0 p.m. and in twenty-six minutes Suzanne had retained her title (6-2, 6-0).

Molla fought frantically—only she could have performed so well under such remorseless pressure. But she was kept racing up and down court whilst her lithe opponent danced on her toes on the base-line. Suzanne employed every stroke in tennis but the shot that brought the Centre Court to its feet was her dazzling backhand down the line, that time and again wrong-footed the swift-moving American.

As they tipped fingers in the most hostile handshake seen at Wimbledon, Suzanne said icily "Now you know I was ill in America"—and received no reply.

Suzanne's superiority was again asserted, when soon after she devastated Molla at Nice 6-0, 6-0, winning the second set in seven minutes. One wonders what Tilden thought!

Suzanne was jealous of her position as champion. At Wimbledon she found unfamiliar clothes in her dressing room. Enraged, she flung them out of the window—only to discover they belonged to her friend Elizabeth Ryan.

She did not lose more than four games in any set while winning the championship again in 1923. In the final she overcame Miss McKane 6-2, 6-2.

That autumn, however, trans-Atlantic tennis provided a shock. Molla Mallory fell at Forest Hills to the mechanical pounding of 17-year-old Helen Wills whom America gleefully announced would be a Lenglen-beater. This match, plus her father's poor health, worried Suzanne. Suffering from jaundice, she was unable to defend her French title in 1924.

Despite medical advice not to compete at Wimbledon, Suzanne appeared in the championship. She seemed well enough and won her first forty games. This took her to 4-0 against Miss Ryan, and she soon pocketed the opening set 6-2.

But Miss Ryan, perhaps sensing that Suzanne's stamina had deteriorated, retrieved gallantly. Suzanne wavered on her forehand—and for once failed to time her opponent's cut shots. To the amazement of the Centre Court, the Californian captured the second set 8-6.

This was only the second set that Suzanne had lost at Wimbledon! Shaken and weary, but remembering the U.S. taunt "Lenglen is a quitter" Suzanne forced herself to continue and won a desperate third set 6-4.

The battle finished her stamina. On doctor's orders, despite some unfavourable comment, the French player withdrew from all events. Later the Wimbledon finalists Miss McKane and Miss Wills competed in the Olympic championship in Paris. Suzanne entered, but subsequently withdrew again causing criticism.

1925 saw her regain her high estate. "My daughter will play better than ever this year" prophesied Charles Lenglen. How right he proved to be!

Helen Wills did not leave America and Suzanne regained her triple crown in Paris. At her greatest Wimbledon she lost five games in five matches overwhelming Miss Goldsack 6-1, 6-0; Miss Ryan 6-2, 6-0; Mrs. Beamish 6-0, 6-0; Miss McKane (holder) 6-0, 6-0, and Miss Fry 6-2, 6-0.

Early in 1926, however, M. Lenglen was seriously ill—and Helen Wills arrived on the Riviera. Both players were accused of avoiding one another in singles unless conditions were favourable. Newspapermen also spread distorted, unfounded tales of hostility. The rivals certainly moved in different circles—Suzanne had plenty of friends on the Riviera while Helen lived quietly with her mother in a hotel—but they were on good terms, if never intimate.

In February with the eyes of the tennis world upon them, Suzanne and Helen met at Cannes. Thousands queued for this relatively unimportant final, gendarmes even chasing would-be spectators off trees.

Suzanne had watched Helen at practice and realised the American made those devastating shots best when standing still. Her plan was, therefore, to keep Helen moving and to hit a medium-paced ball forcing her opponent to make her own speed.

These tactics won Suzanne the first set, 6-3. But tiring against Helen's remarkable relentless driving, she was 4-5 down in the second set. Revived by brandy, Suzanne displayed exquisite control of the half-court shot, won a love game and then reached 6-5, 40-15.

After a long rally, Helen appeared to over-hit a drive and the players shook hands. In fact the American's shot had landed on the line and play was resumed, Suzanne eventually winning 8-6.

Then reaction set in. Amidst flowers and feverish excitement, the Prima Donna of tennis relieved herself by hysterics.

A return match was expected in the French championships but Helen developed appendicitis, and Suzanne swept the board losing four games in ten sets. Her victims were Mme. Peteri 6-0, 6-0; Mrs. Shepherd-Barron 6-0, 6-0; Mme. Mathieu 6-0, 6-0; Miss Fry 6-2, 6-1, and Mary K. Browne 6-1, 6-0.

The excitement of the 1926 Jubilee Wimbledon, the absence of her father and her forthcoming presentation at Court, proved too much for Suzanne's nerves. The French L.T.A. also upset her by pairing her at Wimbledon with Didi Vlasto (Suzanne and Didi were firm friends, but the Lenglen-Ryan team had competed at Wimbledon since 1919). Possibly, too, Suzanne resented the interest in a newcomer, lovely Lili d'Alvarez.

Queen Mary, who greatly admired Suzanne, came down to Wimbledon on the first Wednesday. The French star was due' to play a single and then to partner Didi Vlasto against Elizabeth Ryan-Mary K. Browne.

Resentful at having to appear twice Suzanne arrived very late—and when Mr. Burrow rebuked her tactlessly before the Committee she furiously gave him a violent piece of her mind. Hysterics followed. Borotra, who always had a soothing effect, could do nothing. Weeping and storming, Suzanne soon left the ground leaving him to apologise to Queen Mary. There were scathing press comments, even Suzanne's supporters considering she had been very unwise.

Several competitors thought, however, that Suzanne was justified in refusing to play singles before that important doubles encounter, later won by the Americans, 3-6, 9-7, 6-2. Suzanne and Didi lost three match points but came off court cheerfully arm-in-arm.

But Suzanne's popularity had suffered a severe set-back—and on Saturday the crowd, remembering the Queen's disappointment was distinctly hostile. The former idol of Wimbledon was the victim of a barrage and an unpleasant situation was only saved by some quick-witted tomfoolery from her partner Borotra.

On diplomatic advice, Suzanne retired from Wimbledon and her presentation at Court was abandoned. Soon after, she turned professional and opposed Mary K. Browne in a series of matches. "Suzanne Lenglen" clothes and perfumes appeared on sale everywhere. But although earning 100,000 dollars, Suzanne (still unbeaten), never liked exhibition tennis.

In 1928, following her father's death, Suzanne was reported to be marrying but this proved untrue. Still intensely interested in tennis, she denied in 1930 that she was intending to apply for reinstatement as an amateur.

Simonne Mathieu was now France's No. 1. Suzanne, anxious for a French victory at Wimbledon, coached her in 1932, but she was no match for Helen Wills-Moody. Suzanne then tackled Helen Jacobs, her own close friend. This was more successful as Miss Jacobs improved so much that she overthrew Helen Moody at Forest Hills in 1933. The loser retired with a back injury, and ironically Suzanne had to condone her action so similar to her own withdrawal against Molla Mallory. "Come back?" she snapped at a reporter, "She (Mrs. Moody) hasn't even gone yet!"

Suzanne was called upon to assist René Lacoste in 1933 in the training of young André Merlin, France's "ewe lamb" who replaced Borotra in the "Musketeers'" famous last defence of the Davis Cup. Her efforts were discernible in Merlin's gallant fight against Perry in the deciding rubber.

She took up skating and squash, and was a frequent visitor at Wimbledon where she was greeted with welcome, the past long forgotten. It was obvious with the strain of international competition removed, Suzanne was a likeable talented woman.

She never missed her more hectic glamourous days and was completely content as the head of a successful tennis school in Paris. But in 1938 soon after her thirty-ninth birthday, it was announced that Suzanne was seriously ill with pernicious anæmia.

Her condition deteriorated. Her physique, weakened by her arduous tennis training, was unable to combat the disease. Soon it was evident that Suzanne was fighting her last great battle.

It was the time of the Wimbledon championship and Suzanne lay unconscious dying. Helen Wills-Moody broke all records by her eighth win. Suzanne recovered enough consciousness to be told of her rival's success and whispered, "I'm so glad". On the 4th July, 1938, after undergoing much suffering, she died—France's most famous sportswoman.

The tennis world was plunged in sorrow. Thousands of telegrams reached Mme. Lenglen. France recognised Suzanne's services by posthumously awarding her the Cross of the Legion of Honour.

Amongst the many comments came Mrs. Moody's, "It is regrettable that no complete film of her was ever made, since it would constitute an instruction for all of us". Even an eight-times champion admitted she could learn something from the French star. Jacques Brugnon, Suzanne's favourite partner, declared "She was marvellous—she was always our comrade".

When Borotra said "Her place in French lawn tennis will never be filled" he voiced general opinion. It was Borotra who read an oration at her funeral. With him she had played her last match at that ill-fated Jubilee Wimbledon.

Her funeral was the most impressive seen in sport. Buried with regality, the queen of tennis was laid to rest, thousands coming to pay tribute to a great artist.

Suzanne stays supreme. To those who were lucky enough to see her, she remains the Pavlova of tennis and to others she has become the Lenglen legend.

3

"Mr. Tennis"

THE press named him "Mr. Tennis" . . . the public acknowledged his mastery. But although William Tatem Tilden, stream-lined by nature for athletic proficiency, had a devouring interest in the game, he was too versatile to let it dominate him. Actor and author, playwright and producer, Tilden enjoyed bridge and music—and was enchanted when Nellie Melba, aunt of his friend Gerald Patterson, recognised him at a London party and exclaimed "You're the Blue Grizzly", a reference to his famous cartoon-creating pullover.

"Big Bill" was born in Philadelphia on the 10th February, 1893. His tall attractive physique, slow graceful movements and enigmatic smile—people often compared his looks to actor Herbert Marshall —soon drew attention. This interest was increased by his remarkable mannerisms on court and his eccentricities. For Tilden, life had to be dynamic and dangerous. A chain smoker, who drank very little, he always drove a car at an outrageous pace. The American seldom varied his meals—huge steaks—and was a fanatical film fan.

Early in his career, Tilden's outspoken comments, his dictatorial attitude on court and his intolerance of mistakes, alienated a public once drawn by his youthful attractiveness. A born showman, he possessed a somewhat sardonic sense of humour. Nevertheless, Tilden had many sincere friends who realised that genius needs an outlet and that his exhibitions of temper on court were occasions when Tilden felt completely justified.

Besides a service timed at 124 miles per hour, Tilden possessed the best forehand in tennis and an elegantly executed backhand. Allied to these attributes were an acute tennis brain, amazing anticipation, and immense reserves of stamina and self-discipline. In 1922, an operation removed the top of one finger, but Tilden changed his grip and played better tennis after it! A surprising feature of his game was a very light racket—many women players use a heavier one.

Tilden dominated everyone with whom he came in contact—often for their own good. Consequently, his partners had to efface themselves and allow him to conduct a glorified single. Tilden won several international doubles titles, although one critic describing his doubles play declared "He (Tilden) parked his intelligence outside the stadium" much to the latter's delight.

His first cup was won at the age of seven by beating "my hated rival, 6-0, 0-6, 19-17". Despite his physique, Tilden was only accepted for the Pay Corps. Granted leave for the 1918 U.S. championship, he reached the final there to lose to R. L. Murray in straight sets.

It was in 1919 that the famous drama-laden Bill Tilden—Bill Johnston series started. In their first meeting, flying ants invaded the court, postponing play for an hour. They contested the U.S. final and Johnston, then America's best player, triumphed 6-4, 6-4, 6-3 by a vicious volleying offensive on Tilden's backhand.

The loser was so impressed by the ease of his defeat that he devoted a winter's practice to perfect his backhand. The result was one of the best shots of all time, Tilden's driving on the run never having been surpassed.

America invaded Wimbledon in 1920. Patterson was holder and Johnston favourite, but the towering Tilden stole the limelight, even the great Suzanne Lenglen sensing the magnetism of this trans-Atlantic sensation.

With Johnston failing unexpectedly to Parke, Tilden—taken to five sets by A. R. F. Kingscote and extended to 6-4, 6-4, 13-11 by Z. Shimidzu—advanced to the Challenge Round. A record crowd witnessed him lose the first set and then assault Patterson's ungainly backhand so devastatingly that the Australian's game collapsed completely. By winning 2-6, 6-2, 6-3, 6-4, Tilden became the first American to win the Blue Riband of tennis, and immediately refused 25,000 dollars to turn professional.

The tennis world was eagerly anticipating another Johnston-Tilden clash. In the U.S. final of 1920 this was gratified, when in a feverishly dramatic duel Tilden de-throned "Little Bill" 6-1, 1-6, 7-5, 5-7, 6-3, after losing three match points in the fourth set. Rain and an air crash before the gaze of horrified thousands caused delays and panic.

With Johnston scoring wonder volleys, and Tilden achieving priceless passing shots, it was anybody's game until 3-all in the final set. Here Johnston's strength suddenly and dramatically wilted. He could offer no further resistance and had to be helped off court amidst wild excitement.

American supremacy was complete when Tilden and Johnston won the Davis Cup from Australia in December. On their arrival home, the "Bills" were treated like conquering heroes.

Struck down by a weakening illness, Tilden refused a European tour in 1921. But President Harding—for whom Tilden cherished great admiration—persuaded the Philadelphian to change his mind. It was only his great will to win that enabled Tilden to achieve success in Europe. Covered in boils, he won the "World's Hard Court" title by beating Belgian Jean Washer 6-3, 6-3, 6-3.

At Wimbledon, Tilden rested in a nursing home for a week before defending his title against the challenge of his friend, lively little Brian Norton of South Africa. It was a never-forgotten spectacle. Resilient and confident, Norton had Tilden "rocking on his heels" and led 6-4, 6-2. Then the South African completely withdrew pressure, refused to chase drop shots and gave away two sets, 6-1, 6-0. The crowd, angry and articulate, grew restive. Tilden, given a breather, revived. Norton, too, suddenly sprang to life and at 5-4 reached match point twice. Tilden drove deep, and thinking his shot was over the line, ran up to congratulate Norton. The American's return had hit the line and Norton, possibly imagining the match was over, attempted an impossible angle and lost the rally. Tilden salvaged another match point with a cannon-ball and went on to save the set, 7-5.

It was said, that Norton, who possessed Tilden's own hero-worship complex, did not care to defeat a sick friend. Asked if this were true, he gave a typical boyish "Norton" grin but admitted nothing. Reacting and ready to drop, Tilden fainted in the dressing-room after the match.

Bill Johnston was one of Tilden's greatest friends—and although a huge section of the American press and public would have welcomed a battle of the "Bills" nothing shook the namesakes' mutual regard.

By 1921, Tilden—who retained his U.S. title after crushing Wallace Johnson 6-1, 6-3, 6-1—was thoroughly unpopular at home. His various protégés and his insistence on partnering them in international championships irritated the authorities who also declared Tilden frequently infringed the always tricky borders of amateurism by tennis articles. But the Philadelphian, who commanded attention, if seldom affection, swept these complaints aside contemptuously.

Johnston started the 1922 season brilliantly and was firm favourite when he met Tilden at Forest Hills. As both men had registered two previous victories, this year's winner retained the famous trophy. Tension was, accordingly, tremendous.

Raising hopes amongst his countless followers, Johnston's all-out net offensive captured two sets. Never robust, he forfeited the third set, but came back to lead 3-0, 40-30 on Tilden's service in the fourth. Chasing Tilden across court he came in confidently for still another kill. A pair of long legs streaked desperately over to the backhand corner and an elongated arm raised an incredible diagonal lob that just escaped Johnston's racket.

Pandemonium set in and a male spectator developed hysterics. The shock and the shot shattered Johnston's morale. His opponent seemed at that moment superhuman. Johnston lost six successive games and could not contain Tilden's augmented pace at the finish. (4-6, 3-6, 6-2, 6-3, 6-4.)

"If I can't have the cup myself, I would prefer you of all men to have it," the loser wearily and gallantly admitted to his victor.

Tilden was now pairing up with 19-year-old Vincent Richards. They won at Forest Hills in 1918, 1921 and 1922. But Richards, resting on his volleying laurels, refused to consolidate sound ground strokes and infuriated Tilden. "Richards is no longer a boy wonder . . . he is a man. I have pleaded, reasoned and quarrelled with him to learn a flat drive." The friendship ended in bitter disagreement, officialdom taking Richards's part as he was America's great hope. Tilden, as usual, told officialdom to mind its own business.

Johnston's supporters, banking on his increased confidence after a victory at Wimbledon, expected to see him defeat Tilden in 1923. But Tilden, ruthless and relentless, crushed Norton without removing his sweater and then retained his national title by blasting Johnston off court 6-4, 6-1, 6-4 in fifty-three minutes. The holder never left the baseline and even his bitterest enemies now conceded Tilden's world supremacy.

By 1924, the Tilden-Richards hostility was widely acknowledged, so when the younger man's inspired volleying held Tilden to two sets-all in the U.S. semi-final, he received rapturous deafening applause. Heat and tension were terrific when Richards double-faulted to trail 2-4 in the final set after Tilden demanded a let because a ball-boy had disturbed him. Then, aided by douches of iced water over his head, Tilden hurtled down enough cannon-balls for victory (4-6, 6-2, 8-6, 4-6, 6-4). Richards, near collapse, was assisted off court but immediately received Davis Cup colours.

Not even Johnston could win a set in a tense final (6-1, 9-7, 6-2). Tilden crashed through the first set; a series of wonder passes that escaped one of America's best volleyers saved the vital second; and in the third Tilden swept his man off court, losing only three rallies in the last three games. Experts grant this was his finest performance.

Aged thirty-two, Tilden now appeared invincible . . . nevertheless, on his horizon clouds were gathering. France represented by her famous young "Musketeers", Borotra, Brugnon, Cochet and Lacoste, was in deadly earnest about winning the Davis Cup. It was 19-year-old Lacoste who realised the only way to overthrow Tilden was a superhuman stone-walling defence, plus the ability to handle fearsome services. This, with Gallic thoroughness, he patiently trained to achieve.

But no Frenchman could prevent another "all-Bill" final at Forest Hills in 1925. To win meant another permanent trophy for Tilden— and win he did 4-6, 11-9, 6-3, 4-6, 6-3, saving the critical 42-minute second set in which Johnston led 9-8, 40-love. History had witnessed another cup disappear from the tennis scene and the last of a memorable series of magnificent matches.

Lacoste was, however, soon to prove the value of his amazing tennis insight. In the 1925 Davis Cup final he extended Tilden to 3-6, 10-12, 8-6, 7-5, 6-2. In this, their first encounter, the young Frenchman was four times within a stroke of victory, Tilden saving himself once by a net-cord.

Officials and spectators who had cheered every American opponent of Tilden, were now intensely worried by the prospect of their champion succumbing to these dangerous young Frenchmen. And in the Davis Cup final of 1926, after Tilden had crushed Borotra 6-2, 6-3, 6-3, and the cup was safe, the Philadelphian lost his first serious singles match since 1920. He submitted to the inexorable base-lining Lacoste, 4-6, 6-4, 8-6, 8-6.

. Forest Hills provided greater shocks. In the quarter-final Cochet, volleying with matchless skill, defeated the giant American champion 6-8, 6-1, 6-3, 1-6, 8-6. Coached by Lacoste, he had learnt to block Tilden's cannon-balls and, taking an early ball, came in on the return. When Lacoste beat Borotra (victor over Richards and Johnston) in the final, it was the end of American supremacy.

At this time Richards, Suzanne Lenglen, and U.S. doubles star Mary K. Browne, turned professional. Tilden refused 25,000 dollars to join them. Mr. Pyle, a sports promoter, doubled the offer, again meeting refusal. Tilden describes the final interview—Mr. Pyle leapt up and shouted, "Mr. Tilden, I think you are a damned fool." I (Tilden) replied, "Mr. Pyle, I think you are probably right."

Roused by his reverses, Tilden and his friend Frank Hunter invaded Europe in 1927. Tilden outwitted Cochet in the French semi-final (9-7, 6-3, 6-2) and failed by one point only to beat Lacoste in the final.

After three hours excitement with every rally fought desperately and both masters in turn bringing the gallery to its feet, Lacoste won through 6-4, 4-6, 5-7, 6-3, 11-9. Leading 9-8 in the fifth set, Tilden crashed over what appeared to be a winning thunderbolt but Cochet, acting as linesman, declared it was a fault. Another match point was salvaged by the wonderful defence of Lacoste whose stonewalling eventually survived amidst scenes of unprecedented hysteria.

At Wimbledon, where he commanded huge crowds at his first

appearance on the new ground, Tilden, cheerful and confident, was hitting Cochet off court in the semi-final to lead 6-2, 6-4, 5-1. And then! the U.S. player lost seventeen successive rallies. Before an amazed audience Cochet took the third set 7-5—he gained the net position to capture the fourth set 6-4—and was the master (aided by American double-faults) in the final struggle, 6-3.

After this historic, fantastic 75-minute duel, Tilden gallantly declared he lost because Cochet "came on". Nobody has solved the reason for his collapse, but it is probable that his early unopposed supremacy caused Tilden to sub-consciously loosen his grip of an easy situation. Cochet, a born opportunist, was just the man to profit from any such mental lapse.

Tilden had some revenge in the doubles final when he and Hunter saved two match points against Cochet-Brugnon (1-6, 4-6, 8-6, 6-3, 6-4). The American pair also won at Forest Hills that year, but the U.S. Davis Cup selectors wished to exclude Hunter from the team. Tilden refused to partner anyone else so they finally gave way after bitter, protracted wrangling.

America led France 2-1 in the Challenge Round. Tilden beat Cochet 6-4, 2-6, 6-2, 8-6, and Tilden-Hunter defeated Borotra-Brugnon in five sets. But the Philadelphian had not forgiven the Committee over the "Hunter" incident. He wrote resentfully, "I was absolutely through after the doubles win. I was nervous, my reserves were used up in bickering."

Tilden had produced superb tennis in the doubles to justify his choice of a partner. Since Hunter was the obvious man it was somewhat impolitic of the selectors to worry their leading player —particularly as Tilden had to bear the brunt of the French attack.

On the fatal final day even Tilden's stamina failed before Lacoste's heart-breaking efficiency (6-4, 4-6, 6-3, 6-3). A dozen aces in the first set could not shake off the stoic Frenchman. National sorrow was full when an untrained Johnston fell to Cochet. Tilden and Lacoste sat together during the last struggle and the American was the first to congratulate his young friends.

Soon after, Lacoste's supremacy was re-affirmed when in the U.S. final he beat Tilden 11-9, 6-3, 11-9, saving three set points in the first set and again in the third.

Tilden missed out Paris in 1928, but grimly faced the volatile, volleying Borotra in the Wimbledon quarter-final. Tilden hated playing the beret-swapping Basque, declaring that Borotra's fooling was part of a ruse to upset his concentration. The American's length kept his net-rushing opponent on an unfamiliar base-line and Tilden won 8-6, 3-6, 6-3, 6-2.

30

But Lacoste was waiting in the semi-final—and on the 4th July hordes of Americans flocked to support a Tilden comeback. The Philadelphian produced the best tennis of the tournament to achieve a two set to one lead. He was within a stroke of 4-1 in the fourth—but Lacoste held on, saved that difficult situation, and his age told in the final struggle (2-6, 6-4, 2-6, 6-4, 6-3).

The American tennis authorities had threatened to ban Tilden because he had written articles at Wimbledon during the championship. Possibly Tilden did not take them seriously, but ban him they did for the Inter-Zone trial against Italy. This did not matter as America coped with Italy minus Tilden—but what about the Challenge Round?

The "Musketeers" begged for Tilden to be reinstated, but officialdom was adamant. Tilden must be shown he was just an ordinary mortal.

But this was what he proved not to be. The Committee was in America—the Davis Cup was in Paris. Tilden persuaded his captain to turn a deaf ear to trans-Atlantic threats, and celebrated a piquant situation by a dramatic win over Lacoste 1-6, 6-4, 6-4, 2-6, 6-3. Cochet, however, saved France, beating Tilden 9-7, 8-6, 6-4. Later the Committee banned Tilden for six months, but to his immense satisfaction, he had had his own way.

"I have never felt so frustrated." Champing after his enforced rest, Tilden eagerly paid a return visit to Europe where he encountered, for the last time, a determined Lacoste in the French semi-final. Out to avenge his 1928 defeat, Lacost led 6-1, 6-0, 5-3. A desperate Tilden stormed through the next four games, but Lacoste won the fourth set 6-3.

At Wimbledon where ill-health prevented Lacoste from defending, Tilden lost to Cochet in a semi-final that lacked the drama of 1927. The little Frenchman, in glorious touch, was hitting winners off Tilden's devastating services to lead 6-4, 6-1, 5-1. As against Lacoste in Paris, Tilden won the next four games, but yielded the set 7-5.

Unable to drive his fiercest over five long sets, Tilden now introduced cut shots into his attack. This contributed to his defeats by Cochet and Lacoste, both many years his junior. But in American circles Tilden still towered above his colleagues and in two tournaments won fifty-seven successive games. At Forest Hills in 1929, Van Ryn, Shields, Doeg and (in the final) Hunter, fell before his offensive.

Determined not to be worsted by the "Musketeers", Tilden was back in France in 1930. This was his most strenuous year in tennis. He entered all the Riviera Championships, and if rain delayed play, would be fighting out the finals of one meeting whilst getting through the preliminary rounds of the next.

Cochet, out of form after a Far Eastern tour, was forbidden by his authorities to enter singles tournaments lest the "Cochet hoodoo" be broken. It was felt at this time that he had such a complete answer to Tilden that the American considered himself already defeated before appearing on court. Tilden, accordingly, swept the board that spring.

At this time Tilden teamed up with "my best mixed partner", little Fraulein Cilly Aussem. She denied a romance declaring "Bill and I are just great friends." Six years later, Cilly (to quote Tilden) "married a young Italian count whose name I could never remember and went to live in Africa."

They were victorious in Paris defeating Borotra-Miss Ryan, and the holders Cochet-Mrs. Whittingstall. In the singles semi-final Tilden's lobbing, drained Borotra's stamina (2-6, 6-2, 6-4, 4-6, 6-3).

He had a great chance in the final when he led Cochet by a set and 5-3—only to allow the crowd to upset his concentration and to eventually yield the struggle (3-6, 8-6, 6-3, 6-1).

But a greater chance was presented at Wimbledon where Cochet in a quarter-final sensation lost to unseeded Wilmer Allison.

So the semi-final, Borotra against Tilden, became a virtual final. Borotra was determined to sustain France's 6-year run of supremacy, while Tilden was equally eager to recapture the title he held nine years before. This clash of personality provided the most colourful drama ever staged on the Centre Court.

Borotra, six years younger, swamped Tilden in the first seven games. Tilden kept his head, his service power and his clearing lob—and with Borotra unable to keep up his fire, America won the second set 6-4. But again storming the net, the Frenchman's brilliant volleying captured the wonderful third set, 6-4.

The Basque threw the fourth set to love during which Tilden objected to his opponent delaying whilst towelling at the net. Borotra then requested a ball-boy to accompany him to the base-line and there take away the towel. He could usually raise a laugh and this time was no exception. Tilden watched, glowering, infuriated by the comedy. "I fumed," are his own words. He recovered poise as more fiery French volleys carried Borotra to 4-2. With dynamic aces and passing shots. Tilden overtook his gasping, streaming rival to lead 5-4. Borotra broke service for 5-all, but two games later an uproar of congratulation and commiseration announced Tilden's victory.

The Centre Court again rang with applause for Tilden—who was much more popular in England than in America—when he won

William T. " Big Bill " Tilden.   Considered the greatest-ever player, this dynamic American triumphed at Wimbledon in 1920, 1921 and 1930.

William M. " Little Bill " Johnston (U.S.A.).   His fearsome forehand crushed all opposition at Wimbledon in 1923.

Mrs. L. A. Godfree (Kitty McKane). This valiant Englishwoman recovered from a losing position to win Wimbledon in 1924—and again in 1926.

Jean Borotra (France) making a typical picturesque plunge. The "Bounding Basque"

the championship against a plucky Allison 6-3, 9-7, 6-4. For a man of thirty-seven it was amazing, and gave him a laugh over Lacoste who in "Lacoste on Tennis" had stated it would be interesting to compare the champion of 1930 with Tilden!

An injured leg helped to defeat Tilden in the U.S. semi-final against John Doeg (10-8, 6-3, 3-6, 12-10). Losing his title again was, he admitted, one of his greatest blows.

He was expected to turn professional but did not do so until offered the lure of a talking picture about tennis. "I was mad to do a talkie for years." A contract was accordingly signed, and in 1931 he opposed Karel Kozeluh and, later, Vincent Richards. Cochet, not now so keen, and a tired Vines joined Tilden in 1933. Tilden beat the Frenchman easily and fought Vines, eighteen years his junior, on level terms.

One night in Los Angeles after four hours struggling, Vines overcame Tilden 6-0, 5-7, 21-23, 6-3, 6-1. As they dragged themselves off court, a pretendingly indignant voice called out, "What? No doubles tonight?" It was Charlie Chaplin.

Perry joined the Tilden troupe in 1936. Cochet and Tilden visited Egypt in 1937 and the Far East in 1938. During World War II, his enthusiasm still as keen, Tilden joined forces with Budge and Alice Marble and later teamed with Riggs and Kovacs.

Aged fifty-three, he astonished Perry by asking his advice on how he could adopt a "Continental" forehand. Tilden felt this grip would give him a more aggressive service return. In his fifties he could take on anybody over three sets.

It is the opinion of most champions that Tilden, with his fabulous control of force and finesse, must be regarded as the all-time greatest player. He died in 1953, aged sixty, in his Hollywood home—in the midst of tennis. He was just planning to compete in a professional tournament.

Of his personal unhappiness and imprisonment, I have not written. The world of tennis mourned this deeply, Alice Marble writing of "Bill, that strange man whom no one understands". One thing is certain—Tilden made many jealous enemies. A public figure is a good shooting target. The greater the name, the greater the fall.

C

4

"Little Bill"

FEW players have become tennis immortals because of their defeats. Yet William M. "Little Bill" Johnston, although victorious at Wimbledon in 1923 and in the U.S. Championships in 1915 and 1919, found fame chiefly because of the superb skill he displayed in his losing matches against Tilden in America. Experts who were lucky enough to witness these wonderful exhibitions consider such tennis could never be surpassed.

Small and never robust, Johnston, nevertheless, based his tennis on a merciless attack. He fought until he was ready to drop and his rugged determination made this little Californian the most feared player of his day.

Johnston's game centred around a magnificent "Western" forehand which opened the court for his devastating sliced volleys, produced with his own peculiar crouching action. A safe backhand, first-class spinning service and an inflexible will completed his equipment and gained him a ranking second to Tilden only in the world for many years.

Born on 2nd November, 1894, Johnston's appealing quietness soon attracted a vast following. No more gallant loser or generous winner existed in tennis. His "bad luck you were not in form today" was recalled with gratitude by Lacoste after the American "had beaten me in a terrible manner" several times.

The least dynamic member of a Davis Cup team brimful of magnetism (Tilden, Dick Williams and Vincent Richards, were his colleagues), Johnston was, nevertheless, the most popular of them all. A stockbroker by profession, he was not as "tennis-mad" as his friend Tilden, but shared with him a passion for bridge.

Johnston's supporters fervently claimed that he was, in fact, a better player than Tilden. But the namesakes never let these warring factions upset their own feelings. Johnston certainly defeated the French and Australian Davis Cup men more easily than Tilden did. His strokes, although less varied, were better executed. But the best Johnston produced an even better Tilden and the latter's physical superiority and longer arms and legs were decisive factors over five-set matches.

Tilden always admitted his finest tennis had been played against Johnston, but confessed so often did they meet that it would be impossible to pick out any particular encounter as the most exemplary. In his opinion, Johnston would have had even more championships to his credit had he restrained his fondness for fiery tennis in the early rounds of a meeting. If he had taken these less difficult opponents more easily, the little Californian would not have reached so many finals somewhat battle-weary although still strong enough to beat anyone—except Tilden.

He frequently wore a white cap on court—and Tilden declared he could judge Johnston's reactions by the angle of that cap! If ever he were in need of tactical advice Johnston sought the guidance of a woman champion—his loyal friend, Hazel Wightman, donor of the famous trophy.

Pacific Coast champion in 1913 and 1914, Johnston startled the U.S. authorities by defeating three Davis Cup nominees to win the American title in 1915. Up to this time not much notice had been taken of this frail small young man.

His victims were C. J. Griffin, Dick Williams (holder) 5-7, 6-4, 5-7, 6-2, 6-2, and in the final Maurice McLoughlin 1-6, 6-0, 7-5, 10-8. "Mac" at 25 was America's idol, having as much attraction for the galleries as Borotra or Suzanne Lenglen. He led 6-5 and 8-7 in the fourth set and Johnston, with the crowd yelling for his opponent, must have felt he was tackling Forest Hills single-handed. But when he had at last overcome this great personality, the new 20-year-old champion was so restrained in victory that he was acclaimed an immediate favourite. He retained universal affection and admiration for the rest of his career.

Dick Williams wrested Johnston's title from him in the 1916 U.S. final. It was a game of constant attack won by Williams 4-6, 6-4, 0-6, 6-2, 6-4. Johnston volleyed his man off court to crash through the third set—but his own ferocity drained his stamina. He let the next set go, but springing again to the offensive, established a 3-0 lead in the fifth set. Here his stamina faded again and Williams, who was always variable, now struck a run of brilliance, winning six of the last seven games. In this bitter battle Johnston actually scored four more aces than his victor.

The U.S. Championships of 1919 contained a choice selection of stars. Johnston beat Gerald Patterson (Wimbledon champion) 6-2, 3-6, 6-4, 4-6, 7-5 and he then defeated the holder, R. L. Murray 5-7, 6-1, 6-2, 6-4. Wallace Johnson, America's leading "chop-shot" expert next fell to Johnston's offence 2-6, 6-1, 6-3, 6-3—and in the final Tilden, his backhand beset by a brilliant volleying attack, failed to win a set from his friend (6-4, 6-4, 6-3).

"Rave" notices attended the Californian's triumphant progress— he was now more popular than ever. This victory made him firm favourite for Wimbledon in 1920—an opinion that was strengthened when he beat Tilden 4-6, 6-2, 6-4 at Queen's Club just before the championship started.

The American holder's second-round upset at the hands of England's Rugger-playing Davis Cup star, J. C. Parke, was, therefore, the biggest surprise of the tournament. Parke, probably the fittest man in tennis, ran miles retrieving his opponent's widely placed returns, and by hitting constantly down mid-court he frequently robbed Johnston of speed and angle. It was stated afterwards that a piece of bad news had disturbed Johnston's concentration and had contributed to his four-set defeat (7-5, 6-2, 2-6, 8-6).

Tilden won at Wimbledon and before a wildly excited crowd he and Johnston fought out the U.S. final a few months later. Under a glowering, stormy sky was seen one of the greatest dramas in American tennis.

Armed with a re-modelled backhand, Tilden swept through the first set 6-1 in ten minutes. Johnston, in no way dismayed, retaliated to capture the second set 6-1 in twelve minutes. In a stirring third set Tilden's aces and wonder passing shots finally gained the upper hand, 7-5.

Tilden continued to hold the advantage and at 5-4 in the fourth set his superb defence brought him to match point three times. But Johnston, never faltering in his remorseless, relentless volleying offensive, saved this critical situation bringing spectators to their feet by his magnificent tennis. 5-all was called and then came a remarkable incident. Rain had started and Tilden, thinking the umpire had motioned him to stop play, did not attempt to return a service of Johnston's. The umpire declared the service a winner and a furious Tilden lost the set 7-5.

Nerves were not improved when an aeroplane crashed behind the stadium stands. Johnston held his own until 3-all in the final set when his stamina deserted him. He could not win another game and, after congratulating Tilden, was assisted off court. Pandemonium and partisanship marked the closing stages of this historic final.

At Forest Hills in 1921, the draw was not seeded. Johnston (after coming within two points of losing in four sets to Vincent Richards) was beaten 4-6, 7-5, 6-3, 6-3 by Tilden in a surprisingly quiet fourth-round match. He won the Seabright tournament in devastating style, however. In the last two rounds he overwhelmed Richards 6-2, 6-2, 6-1 and then Dick Williams 6-0, 6-4, 6-2.

1922 was possibly "Little Bill's" greatest year. He swept through a star-studded entry at Seabright defeating Anderson, Kinsey and Williams (6-0, 6-2, 6-3), And in the Davis Cup Challenge Round he set up a record losing only eleven games in two matches. His hapless victims were Anderson 6-1, 6-2, 6-3, and cannon-balling Gerald Patterson (then Wimbledon champion) 6-2, 6-2, 6-1.

To reach another final at Forest Hills, Johnston scattered H. Kinsey 6-4, 6-2, 6-2; Spaniard Manoel Alonso 6-0, 6-2, 7-5 and Richards 8-6, 6-2, 6-1. This year's final against Tilden filled the stadium to capacity. As both men had registered two previous wins, the player who emerged victorious retained the cup.

Brilliant net-play gained the first two sets for "Little Bill". But Tilden had heard his opponent offer up a prayer of gratitude at the shot that had secured the second set. Realising how tired Johnston must be, Tilden felt he still had a chance. Moreover, he was determined to win because a Committee man (whom he hated) had said cheerily to Tilden while he was towelling himself after the second set, "Well, Bill it *has* been a great match". To which the livid Philadelphian had snapped angrily, "And still is!"

Johnston, anticipating the ten-minute interval, threw the third set—and not even Tilden's long legs could prevent his storming to within a stroke of 4-0 in the fourth. After a desperate rally, the Californian worked Tilden out of position and advanced confidently to put away a kill—only to be foiled by a delicate diagonal backhand lob—a shot that only a genius could have produced "in extremis".

At this stage an over-wrought spectator (presumably a Johnston supporter!) sprang up shouting, "He (Tilden) is a liar—he didn't hit it". This sudden disturbance and his disappointment demoralised Johnston. He lost the next six games and never quite got into the battle again. Tilden then put on pressure and retained his cherished prize 4-6, 3-6, 6-2, 6-3, 6-4.

Like all Americans, it was Bill Johnston's greatest ambition to win Wimbledon. In 1923, he won the "World's Hard Court" singles in France where, to quote Lacoste "No American was more applauded". In this meeting he numbered Lacoste and Jean Washer among his victims.

A month later, at Wimbledon, Johnston won the title not defended by Gerald Patterson. In three close sets (6-4, 6-3, 7-5) he accounted for Vincent Richards in the fifth round. The Americans brought so many rackets on court that a ball boy was detailed to carry them. Both men produced brilliant tennis but the shot of the match was a sensational backhand half-volley passing shot from "Little Bill" that won him the opening set.

The Californian then lost his only set—against Cecil Campbell (6-1, 5-7, 6-2, 6-2). Brian Norton was dismissed 6-4, 6-2, 6-4 and in a one-sided 40-minute final he beat Hunter 6-0, 6-3, 6-1.

The huge crowd saluted Johnston warmly; several critics declared they had never seen such great tennis. Johnston himself was supposed to have said that he did not now mind if he never touched a racket again!

37

This state of mind, doubtless, affected his play in America, for although he retained the Seabright trophy, Johnston lost his first Davis Cup single since 1920. He went down before the base-line driving of Australian Joe Anderson, 4-6, 6-2, 2-6, 7-5, 6-2. So surprised was any overseas competitor at defeating the dreaded "Little Bill" that Anderson "could not contain his transports of joy".

Johnston made amends by his handling of J. B. Hawkes (6-0, 6-2, 6-1), but in the U.S. final he lost to Tilden 6-4, 6-1, 6-4. Several critics now declared that Johnston was finished—much to Tilden's annoyance who insisted that his little friend was merely over-played after his European successes.

Perhaps, Tilden, eighteen months older, did not care to think Johnston was passing into the discard at twenty-nine. But in 1924 Tilden was proved correct. In the U.S. semi-final Johnston levelled Patterson 6-2, 6-0, 6-0 in forty minutes. In winning the last sixteen games, Johnston revealed his amazing quick reflexes which enabled him to crash winner after winner off one of the greatest-ever services. His net work, too, was devastating and he admitted making volleys "I never attempted before".

After this annihilation, experts considered that the odds on Tilden retaining his title in the final were very slight. But the Philadelphian knowing the danger of Johnston in such savage mood, played superlatively to win the first set 6-1. A thrilling second set with Johnston volleying brilliantly and Tilden achieving breathtaking recoveries turned in the latter's favour (9-7). The holder never eased his pressure and scoring several faultless backhand passes won the third set 6-2.

This was Tilden's greatest tennis. Fought under a cloud-laden sky the atmosphere was one of almost unbearable drama. As though the heavens could stand it no longer a violent thunderstorm accompanied the players as they left the court.

In the 1925 Davis Cup Challenge Round, Borotra and Lacoste (who had contested the Wimbledon final) both carried Tilden to five long sets. Johnston, however, toppled Lacoste 6-1, 6-1, 6-8, 6-3 and crushed Borotra 6-1, 6-4, 6-0. So sure was he of defeating the Basque that Johnston bet a friend that Borotra, yielding to pressure, would serve more double faults in their match than he had done against Tilden (in five sets). Borotra obliged—although they played only twenty-three games—and Johnston won match and money!

Again it was only Tilden who stopped him. They met for the last time at Forest Hills in 1925 and provided another epic. Johnston, a set up, led 9-8, 40-love in the second. Tilden's resource saved this 42-minute set and won the third set in twelve minutes. Johnston came back in the fourth but had to bow to Tilden's physical superiority, 4-6, 11-9, 6-3, 4-6, 6-3.

America was horrified when Tilden lost to Lacoste in the 1926 Davis Cup. Johnston restored his country's confidence by defeating Lacoste 6-0, 6-4 0-6, 6-0 and accounting for Borotra 8-6, 6-4, 9-7. He was in terrific form. Tilden provided another shock by losing his title to Cochet in the U.S. quarter-final leaving his little friend as the last American in the semi-final (along with Borotra, Cochet and Lacoste).

The way seemed clear for Johnston who had never yet lost to the Frenchmen. And in his "semi" with Borotra, his confident hitting won the first two sets. Borotra appeared on the verge of exhaustion and Johnston eased his aggression. After the 10-minute rest, a revived Borotra sprang to the attack and by wonderful sustained volleying carried the next two sets to win 3-6, 4-6, 6-3, 6-4, 8-6.

These tactics and their effect on Johnston's concentration caused much comment. Tilden was particularly acid. "Borotra apparently dying on his feet—staggering—gasping—sitting on the sand box by the umpire's chair . . . then launched a net attack that swept Johnston out of the tournament."

Johnston's departure was a great disappointment. A lung complaint aggravated by his years of strenuous tennis influenced his desire to retire from the Davis Cup team in 1927. But Richards was now professional so the Californian responded to his country's call.

He was in no physical shape to train and, accordingly, lost for the first time to the methodical Lacoste 6-3, 6-2, 6-2. In the final deciding rubber Cochet had several match points against Johnston in the fourth set. "Little Bill" brought delirious cheers of applause as he had done so often before by winning his service in four aces while pulling up to 4-5. He also led 30-love on Cochet's service, but could not keep it up, the Frenchman eventually winning 6-4, 4-6, 6-2, 6-4.

So the little Californian made his exit from the world of tennis where he was so loved.

In 1930 he recovered from a serious lung illness. Tilden turned professional that year and whenever he appeared in exhibitions at San Francisco his most ardent follower was—Bill Johnston! The giants of the 'twenties always sat together, Tilden recalling what joy these meetings were to them both.

Still vastly interested in tennis, the Californian presented the Bill Johnston trophy in 1946—given yearly to America's best sportsman. Soon after, the world of tennis was saddened by his premature death at the age of fifty-two.

Tilden was overwhelmed by grief declaring something very dear had gone out of life. He dedicated his last book to "Bill"—his very great rival, his friend for thirty years.

5

Under the Shadow of Suzanne

THERE is nothing the Centre Court values more than valour, and no woman possessed more of this quality than Kitty McKane. Although she played her tennis under the shadow of Suzanne, this stout-hearted Englishwoman snatched two singles championships in each case overhauling a redoubtable overseas opponent from what seemed certain victory.

There was a clean-cut, almost masculine, directness about her tennis. Very fast about the court, Miss McKane had a disconcerting habit of suddenly appearing at the net where her volleys possessing the extra value of surprise were, perhaps, the most decisive of their day. Her prowess at badminton—she was All-England champion—helped her to put to death the deepest lob.

Renowned for her remarkable generalship and fighting spirit, Miss McKane rivalled Borotra in her timing of a counter-attack against a tiring or over-confident opponent. Sound as to temperament and tennis equipment, she was even sounder as a match-player. Self-controlled and quiet, she had a large following, and in America she was much respected.

Her early Wimbledons passed uneventfully. In 1919, she lost the quarter-final to Suzanne 6-0, 6-1, and in 1920 she was beaten in the third round by Mrs. McNair. The following year she was eliminated in the second round, failing before the chops and volleys of Elizabeth Ryan, 6-3, 6-2.

The winter of 1921/22 saw her consolidate her game. Neglecting badminton, she concentrated on continual tennis practice with leading men players. Six months hard work and Miss McKane was established as a potential Lenglen successor.

The semi-final of the "World's Hard Court" title at Brussels in 1922 revealed her amazing progress. Down 0-3 to Suzanne, Miss McKane attacked to such purpose that she won three games in a row. In those days it was a feat to win three points in a row from Suzanne. The French champion wavered and her opponent reached 5-4, 40-15. Supreme steadiness saved Suzanne who won 10-8, 6-2.

Just before Wimbledon, Miss McKane beat Miss Ryan 6-3, 6-3 at Beckenham. And on the new Centre Court it was her future husband, Leslie Godfree, who served the first ball.

40

The largest tennis crowd to date gathered for the second round clash of McKane and Lenglen. When the English girl pulled up to 5-all in the second set it was reported "Mlle. Lenglen seemed to be contemplating a heart attack". Harassed, Suzanne summoned enough strength for victory 6-1, 7-5.

In those days, women's international tennis was somewhat limited. In 1923, however, Miss McKane had her hands full. She lost the "World's Hard Court" singles final to Suzanne but three "World's Covered Court" titles (held at Barcelona) came her way, while at Mentone she forced Lenglen to 6-2, 7-5.

Miss McKane was never more resolute than in her Wimbledon semi-final against Elizabeth Ryan. The American commanded the first set playing some of her finest attacking tennis—she lost the second to her opponent's steadiness—but was ahead at 4-3 in the third. Here Miss McKane surged back and hit through her opponent to win 1-6, 6-2, 6-4.

She gathered more games from Lenglen in a 37-minute final than any other player (6-2, 6-2). But if she could volley the first French return, the second found an unguarded corner.

In the first Wightman Cup match in August, 1923, the novel conditions were too much for the British team who lost 7-0. Miss McKane fell before Mrs. Mallory 6-2, 6-3, and Helen Wills 6-2, 7-5. She had settled down by the time the American championship started and in the quarter-final she gave Helen Wills (the ultimate winner) her hardest fight 2-6, 6-2, 7-5.

She excelled in doubles winning the U.S. title with Mrs. Covell. In the mixed final with J. B. Hawkes, she was twice within a stroke of victory—to be foiled by Tilden and Mrs. Mallory, 6-3, 2-6, 10-8.

Throughout 1923 there had been, however, a slight weakening of her game. Her service power seemed less certain, her backhand was, at times, erratic. In 1924, however, she proved the slump was a temporary one. Before her own supporters, Miss McKane excelled against the American Wightman Cup players. Helen Wills lost 6-2, 6-2, and Mrs. Mallory fared little better 6-3, 6-3.

Her 1924 Wimbledon will remain in memory. After crushing Mrs. Mallory in an early round, Miss McKane defeated American Mrs. Jessup 6-1, 6-3 to reach the semi-final. Here two formidable obstacles were removed together when Suzanne beat Miss Ryan and then retired from the championship.

The final seemed virtually over when Helen Wills, leading Miss McKane by a set, was four times within a point of 5-1 in the second. No one in tennis was more fitted to answer such a challenge. Miss McKane's forehand, denying the possibility of defeat, saved that sixth game with withering placements. Revitalised, she found new vigour, and amidst rising excitement, scored a run of five games to draw level.

Helen Wills did not deteriorate—indeed, she played better in the third set—but the initiative slipped to her opponent. The American continued her automatic artillery, but was countered by crisp, clever volleys. It was now that the value of the Englishwoman's fluent, faster footwork was revealed—and after another thirty minutes suspense, an uproar from the Centre Court greeted "Biddy" McKane as Suzanne's successor and welcomed her 4-6, 6-4, 6-4, triumph.

Suzanne, however, was in no mood to let Britain or America usurp her position for long. She beat Miss McKane 6-1, 6-2 in the French final of 1925. A month later in the Wimbledon semi-final Suzanne's passing shots were perfection. Miss McKane could get to game point but never to game and was overwhelmed 6-0, 6-0 by an opponent who refused to release her relentless pressure.

In 1925, Miss McKane took little time to settle down in America. In the Wightman Cup she beat Mrs. Mallory (for the first time on U.S. soil) 6-4, 5-7, 6-0 and lost a terrific battle to Helen Wills 6-1, 1-6, 9-7. In the American championship, despite overpowering heat, she won two bitter matches defeating Miss Ryan 3-6, 7-5, 6-2 and then Mrs. Mallory 4-6, 7-5, 8-6, in what was considered the toughest test at Forest Hills that year. Miss McKane won the first set of the final against Helen Wills but then submitted to a devastating attack 3-6, 6-0, 6-2.

With Hawkes, she went one better this time and captured the mixed. They had their revenge on Tilden-Mrs. Mallory 6-1, 6-1 and won the final from Richards-Miss E. Harvey, 6-2, 6-4.

Early in 1926, while touring in South Africa, Kitty McKane married her team captain, Leslie Godfree, at Kimberley. They had been partners at Wimbledon in 1921 and in the 1924 mixed final Miss McKane-J. B. Gilbert had beaten Godfree-Mrs. Shepherd-Barron.

Meanwhile Helen Wills had thoroughly extended a nervy Suzanne at Cannes and seemed certain to challenge the Frenchwoman again at Wimbledon in 1926. And at this very upset Jubilee championship the Godfrees were the only married couple to receive commemoration medals before—one might well say!—hostilities began.

The women's singles was a stormy affair. Helen Wills withdrew with appendicitis, while Suzanne soon swept out of the tournament in a tantrum. She left Didi Vlasto, France's No. 2, to play Mrs. Godfree in the semi-final.

A one-stroke player with a tremendous forehand, Didi hit through her opponent to lead 4-1. Racing and retrieving, Mrs. Godfree planned to extend the rallies hoping to break down her opponent's attack. Didi liked to win her points quickly—she reacted and fell in with her rival's plans. Losing her touch and eleven successive games, the French girl was beaten 6-4, 6-0.

At the same time, a Spanish newcomer, lovely Lili d'Alvarez, was electrifying Wimbledon. When she beat Mrs. Mallory 6-2, 6-2, critics expected her to swamp Mrs. Godfree in the final. But it was the Englishwoman who, settling down quietly, won the first set 6-2. Then the Senorita sprang to the attack. Wonderful backhands and forehands hit on the rise and often taken as half-volleys, gave her the second set 6-4.

Spain was now in full cry. In the opening game of the final set Lili sent over five sparkling winners. Continuing in this vein, she was soon within a stroke of 4-1.

Mrs. Godfree, profiting from her matches with Suzanne, now adopted Lenglen tactics. Letting the fury of the volleyer burn itself out, she contented herself with good length retrieving.

The Senorita, never a robust woman, found her best shots coming back. Tiring, she lost accuracy. Mrs. Godfree, still attempting nothing spectacular, gradually drew level—and in a sound display of smooth confident tennis captured the last five games and her second championship to the score of 6-2, 4-6, 6-3.

"Biddy" and Lili were cheered to the echo when they left court. The re-crowned champion's joy was complete when she and her husband captured the mixed, toppling the best American pairs, Vincent Richards-Miss Ryan 7-5, 6-4, and Howard Kinsey-Mary K. Browne 6-3, 6-4.

She never played such perfect tennis again. Her 3-6, 6-4, 6-4 quarter-final defeat at Wimbledon in 1927 by Miss Ryan was the sensation of that round. Beaten by Mrs. Mallory and Helen Wills in the Wightman Cup she was, according to the latter, a "shadow of her former self". Illness kept her out of singles at Forest Hills, but she won the doubles with Miss Harvey.

Illness also prevented her playing at Wimbledon in 1928. Next year a son was born to the Godfrees and his mother did not play serious tennis for a year. In 1930, she partnered Mrs. Holcroft-Watson in the Wightman Cup scoring a vital victory over Helen Wills Moody and Helen Jacobs.

She re-entered singles in 1931 but found the space of years too many to bridge. In 1934, she again played Wightman Cup tennis partnering Betty Nuthall.

Sport came naturally to her. She won the All-England Badminton singles several times. An expert rider, she played lacrosse and won prizes at skating. But tennis was her greatest love—the game she taught herself.

6

Peter Pan of Tennis

IN 1922, the new Wimbledon was opened auspiciously by King George V—at the same time the heavens opened, deluging courts, competitors and crowds. But damp spirits were uplifted and interest sustained by the arrival of an intriguing, entertaining newcomer.

He was a 23-year-old Frenchman, a native of the Basque country. Athletic and attractive, he wore a beret to keep his hair in place. Endowed with instinctive charm, he represented the renaissance of France, rising heroically after the devastation of a ruinous war.

Soon the crowds were flocking to see this new personality. "Full up" notices were displayed for his matches—and nobody left court before he did.

He caught the imagination of the Centre Court and established a bond of affection and admiration never surpassed by anyone. His "Good shot" to an opponent and his "À toi" to his partner have been heard in the great arena a hundred times. Nobody can forget his leaps over the barrier into the crowd during a hard-fought rally— and nobody has kissed so many pretty hands on departure!

"Mesdames et Messieurs, Jean Borotra est arrivé!"

He was named the "Bounding Basque" and appeared to be made of elastic. In his early days, the drive was just a means of getting to the net. His service produced many foot-faults due to swinging over the line in a dash up to the net.

Opponents and spectators were spellbound by his amazing, devastating volleys. He came up on every service—the return of service, too, was followed by a dash forward. Anticipation, a telescopic reach and fantastic, dynamic bounds caught the fiercest passing shot.

Wood and grass were his favourite surfaces. Here his daring, his zest for action and his rapidity of thought—encouraged by his early love for Pelota—made him one of the most formidable opponents in tennis.

Borotra's greatest rivals were Tilden, Lacoste and Cochet. He was on a par with the last-named, but could be overcome by Tilden and Lacoste if they maintained a lobbing campaign. His overhead was wonderfully spectacular and even running backwards, Borotra could outpace most colleagues moving forwards. But over a protracted battle, Borotra's fondness for crashing down these high tosses expended his energy and students of tennis like Lacoste and Tilden fed his smashing assiduously.

Tennis by no means filled his life. Indeed, he has always insisted that it be relegated in favour of his business interests.

He lives life to the full. Brilliant, sophisticated, tactful, he holds degrees in engineering and law. Borotra, at twenty-five, was a director of an industrial business which operated in twenty-five countries. It was nothing unusual for Borotra to fly from Paris for a match at Wimbledon and to change into tennis clothes on the journey. He played in tournaments and carried on business activities at the same time.

After one of his most exacting victories over Lacoste—in the Wimbledon semi-final of 1927—Borotra immediately went into conference with two trans-Atlantic executives interviewing them from his bath! And soon after, just before the final against Cochet, Borotra forgot tennis and settled down to a hard-headed business luncheon appointment.

Borotra, and Borotra's beret, were bounding with success across the courts of Europe before the Basque invaded Wimbledon in 1922. He had won the International Championship of Portugal in 1921 and was successful in the "World Hard Court" doubles with Cochet in 1922.

His first bid to win Wimbledon was cut very short in the third round by Gerald Patterson 6-0, 6-1, 6-3. Swamped and even struck— the Frenchman suffered two direct blows on his body—Borotra surrendered to a stream of annihilating drives and services. "I am lucky to be alive" he smiled, little knowing how prophetic those words would be when opposing Patterson in three years time.

Borotra got as far as the fifth round at Wimbledon in 1923 where he was beaten by Brian Norton 6-3, 7-5, 6-3. His popularity was greater than ever, his habit of swapping berets never failing to delight his followers. Nobody valued more the support of the Wimbledon spectators yet, ironically, in his own country Borotra, although well-liked, never fired the crowd's enthusiasm as did Cochet, Lacoste or Brugnon.

1924 proved the turning point in the career of the man America once wrote off as a "Russian ballet dancer" and a "volleying acrobat".

He shook off the tenacious Lacoste to become French Champion 7-5, 6-4, 0-6, 5-7, 6-2. The most formidable American at Wimbledon was Vincent Richards, but this wonder volleyer found the net position wrested from him by Borotra who conducted four of the fastest sets seen on the Centre Court to win 6-4, 4-6, 6-0, 6-3.

45

Borotra then beat Louis Raymond 6-2, 6-4, 7-5 to reach the final.

One of the quickest five-set matches ever seen—few rallies contained more than four strokes—gave him the championship at the expense of Lacoste 6-1, 3-6, 6-1, 3-6, 6-4. The perfect smash had defeated the perfect lob. As they walked off court happily arm-in-arm Borotra said, "I know he will forgive me, for next year he will win."

In America, always happy under cover, Borotra cantered through the U.S. Covered Court singles in 1925 losing one set only in the final to F. Anderson (3-6, 6-3, 6-4, 6-0). He was the first European to win the event. But his prediction that Lacoste was soon to be France's No. 1 was fulfilled when he failed to win a set from his rival in the French final. Lacoste's lobbing was superb and his ability to take a rising ball offset Borotra's net assault.

This final and its result were duplicated at Wimbledon. Guilty of numerous foot-faults, Borotra lost the first two sets, but recovered to produce wonder tennis in the third. He also reached 4-1 in the fourth. Lacoste rallied to reach 5-4, Borotra just missing some vital volleys. Back came Borotra to lead 6-5 with his service in hand. But double faults indicated his fatigue and finally Lacoste's iron control was vindicated 6-3, 6-3, 4-6, 8-6.

After this match which took longer to finish than the five-set final of 1924, victor and vanquished "behaved as though one of the nicest things in the world had happened to them".

The "Musketeers" had set their hearts on winning the Davis Cup. Borotra struck marvellous form against Australia in the Inter-Zone final. He beat Joe Anderson 6-4, 6-3, 8-6 and Patterson 4-6, 6-4, 6-1, 6-3, and carried Lacoste (surprisingly erratic) to victory against Patterson-Hawkes 6-4, 3-6, 6-4, 1-6, 10-8. During the doubles, he was nearly killed by a devastating volley from Patterson which hit him on the temple leaving the Basque a crumpled, unconscious figure on court. Ignoring his injury, he went on playing and pulled his side through to win.

He was crushed by Johnston in the Challenge Round but took Tilden to 4-6, 6-0, 2-6, 9-7, 6-4. At Forest Hills, Borotra was unlucky in meeting Dick Williams on one of his super days and lost 6-2, 6-2, 6-2.

To the delight of the Centre Court, Borotra reached his third final in 1926 and against American Howard Kinsey, he was in his element. Kinsey's un-American game of drops and lobs could not contain the Basque who bounding about in "India-rubber fashion" did not lose a set (8-6, 6-1, 6-3). In one rally Borotra (at the net) slipped, fell flat on his face, leapt up and chased the ball back to the baseline. There he retrieved it, and eventually hit a spectacular winner leaving Kinsey to join in the crowd's applause.

The Basque never generated much gallery appeal in trans-Atlantic tennis. He brought down Richards and Johnston at Forest Hills—but also brought down a storm of protest. The American press declared he feigned fatigue in these five-set matches, lulling his opponents into a false security. In the final, he led Lacoste 4-2, but his own exertions and Lacoste's lobbing put him out of the match 6-4, 6-0, 6-4.

The Wimbledon semi-final line-up in 1927 was Tilden against Cochet, Borotra against Lacoste. Had Tilden beaten Cochet, it is certain Borotra would not have exerted himself to win, knowing that he could not defeat the great American whereas Lacoste now was Tilden's master. But Cochet defeated Tilden, France was safe, so Borotra tackled his team-mate in different spirit.

He went all out to win the first two sets. Noticing that Lacoste's backhand was, for once, uncertain, Borotra avoided it for the next two sets during which he rested, as in America. Refreshed, he then attacked it with fury to win 6-4, 6-3, 1-6, 1-6, 6-2. He may have fooled most people, but certainly not Lacoste. "I was filled with admiration for his intelligence."

But Borotra could not get past "Five-set Cochet" in a fabulous final. He won the first two sets—again took things easy—and reached 5-2 with a flourish in the final set. Six times was he within a stroke of success—and six times the wonder man of tennis produced a super shot, one of which, however, appeared to be a double-hit. Both players appealed to the umpire who gave Cochet the verdict. Losing the sixth match ball was too much even for Borotra's morale. Cochet was champion at 4-6, 4-6, 6-3, 6-4, 7-5.

Tilden beat Borotra 6-1, 3-6, 10-8, 6-1 in the U.S. quarter-final saving three set points in the third set. When France, however, won the Davis Cup Borotra justified his title of the "Bounding Basque".

A visit to Australia in 1928 resulted in Borotra winning three national titles. He was vastly popular there except with cartoonists who complained that he was never still.

But in the other major events of 1928, Borotra did not get further than the semi-finals. This was in France where he lost to Cochet 6-3, 2-6, 7-5, 6-4. In the Wimbledon quarter-final Tilden, raising chalk with his drives, forced the Basque to play—and lose—a base-line battle (8-6, 3-6, 6-3, 6-2).

In the third round at Forest Hills, Borotra's endurance failed against Hunter and he was overhauled 0-6, 5-7, 6-0, 6-4, 6-2. Borotra was now thirty. He could not net-rush for five sets eternally, and concentrated on strengthening his ground strokes. They showed a marked improvement in his hectic 1929 semi-final in France against Cochet. Borotra could not resist some tomfoolery. Cochet lost his concentration and championship 6-3, 5-7, 7-5, 5-7, 6-4.

The final seemed over when Lacoste taking eight successive games led by two sets to one and 2-0 in the fourth. Borotra, achieving difficult passing shots on the run, captured the next six games and forced Lacoste to a desperate finish (6-3, 2-6, 6-0, 2-6, 8-6).

The Wimbledon final gave Cochet revenge. Borotra who had not been foot-faulted until this round was constantly penalised. Cochet, determined not to be shaken, produced perfect tennis to win 6-4, 6-3, 6-4.

Borotra was now recognised as the best covered court player of all time. He could beat Tilden only on wood and did so in the Coupe de Noel final in 1930, 6-4, 6-2, 4-6, 6-1. Tilden reversed this decision in the French semi-final, his lobs exhausting Borotra (2-6, 6-2, 6-4, 4-6, 6-3).

Soon after they met in their greatest match in the Wimbledon semi-final. Borotra, the last Frenchman in the tournament, led by two sets to one after a sparkling display by both men. He then decided to rest in the fourth set. Tilden angrily remonstrated when Borotra hesitated over towelling at the net—and when the Basque commandeered a ball-boy to follow him and catch the towel, the crowd's merriment added to his rage.

Borotra led 4-2 in the fifth set, but Tilden made a wonderful recovery to win this famous drama, 0-6, 6-4, 4-6, 6-0, 7-5.

Soon after, Borotra beat Lott (8-6 in the fifth set) to retain the Davis Cup and defeated Cochet (also 8-6 in the fifth set) to become Belgian champion.

He then announced his retirement from Davis Cup singles. "After playing Lott I could not sleep for nights, my shoulders ached too much." Critics declared the Cup was in danger as Lacoste was unfit and no young man could replace Borotra. The Basque strengthened these arguments by winning the French singles in 1931. Despite seventeen double faults he overcame Satoh, and again hampered by his service, beat Boussus in the final 2-6, 6-4, 7-5, 6-4.

He was No. 1 seed at Wimbledon and in the semi-final met Frank Shields. Borotra handled Shields' cannon balls easily but served fourteen double-faults. Shields led two sets to one and at 4-3 in the fourth sprained his ankle. Borotra was the first to reach him insisting "Frank must rest". After a 12-minute break the American hobbled through to victory 7-5, 3-6, 6-4, 6-4. The loser had restrained his own counter-offensive against an injured rival.

After losing a protracted five-set match to Perry in the Davis Cup, Borotra collapsed in Lacoste's arms. He failed, too, against Austin, and again declared he was finished with Davis Cup singles.

He did not accordingly defend in Paris in 1932. And at Wimbledon his defeat by Enrique Maier 6-3, 6-3, 2-6, 6-2, was the sensation

48

Fifteen-year-old American Sydney B. Wood congratulates René Lacoste (France) at Wimbledon in 1927. Wood became the youngest-ever champion in 1931. Lacoste won the title twice (in 1925 and 1928).

Mrs. Helen Wills Moody (now Mrs. Roark). This beautiful Californian won Wimbledon eight times, a record unlikely to be beaten. Her triumphs were from 1927 to 1930 and again in 1932, 1933, 1935 and 1938.

Frenchman Henri Cochet, Wimbledon Champion in 1927 and 1929. The most effortless player seen on the Centre Court, his volleying rendered him well-nigh invincible for many years.

Comtesse De La Valdène (Lili D'Alvarez).   A sparkling Senorita who reached the Wimbledon final in 1926, 1927 and 1928.

and sorrow of the fourth round. As they left court their arms
entwined (Maier was one of Borotra's closest friends) Queen Mary
smiled and King George V raised his bowler hat in recognition of a
great warrior.

Again the problem of the Davis Cup presented itself. Again
Borotra agreed to play "for France"—but it had to be the last time.

Checking his usual buoyancy, Borotra led the all-conquering
Vines two sets to one. Feeling his stamina failing, the Basque risked
everything on a net attack and before a delirious crowd volleyed
Vines off court 6-4, 6-2, 3-6, 6-4. Pandemonium mounted to hysteria
when Borotra and Vines were presented to the French President.

Borotra finished his Davis Cup singles career in glory when he
retained the trophy by beating Allison after the American had been
four times within a stroke of victory 1-6, 3-6, 6-4, 6-2, 7-5.

He continued to dominate the game under cover. And in 1935
re-entered the Wimbledon singles to "get practice for the doubles".
At the age of thirty-six he played the most brilliant tennis of the
meeting before losing to Menzel 5-7, 6-4, 6-2, 2-6, 11-9 in the
second round—and was immediately denounced by a French critic
for refusing to play Davis Cup singles.

Borotra, d'Artagnan to the finger tips, issued a challenge—they
would fight a duel. Lacoste was appointed his second, but the
quarrel simmered down and was forgotten.

In 1940, he was appointed High Commissioner of Sport by the
Vichy government. His headquarters became a secret centre of
resistance. In 1943, when General Giraud fled to North Africa,
Borotra tried to escape, but was captured and imprisoned.

Feelings were high against Vichy and Borotra's entry for Wimbledon was refused in 1946. In 1947, twenty-five years after his first
Davis Cup match, Borotra and Petra lost to Drobny and Cernik
10-8, 14-12, 6-3.

Peace was restored in 1948 and Borotra received a rapturous welcome at Wimbledon. The beret—"I have lost it"—was missing but
everything else that the Centre Court had grown to love and to
laugh at was still there.

These Wimbledon appearances are for old times sake only. Not
so at Queen's where he regained the championship in 1948 and
1,000 spectators rose to acclaim the feat of this remarkable 50-year-
old Frenchman. He retained the title in 1949.

The Basque has played more Davis Cup tennis than any other
Frenchman, and has appeared in partnership with Brugnon alone
more than a hundred times.

The hero of the ball-boys, Borotra has added to tennis a chronicle
of courtesy and charm.

7

Monsieur Le Crocodile

It was on an August morning in 1923 that the French Davis Cup captain saw his youngest player gazing into a New York shop window.

This pale dark youth of medium height was absorbed by a magnificent toy crocodile. Asked if he would like it, Jean René Lacoste joyfully agreed—it became his emblem and he wore a crocodile badge on his shirt. Paris affectionately named him "Monsieur le Crocodile".

Referring to France's Davis Cup win in 1927, Lacoste spoke of Pierre Gillou's leadership, and the spirit of the "Musketeers". Modest and self-effacing, he always omitted his tactical genius that learned how to overthrow Tilden, backbone of American tennis.

Lacoste might be called the Captain of Industry in Tennis. Practice anywhere, anyhow, even against a cushion if no wall were available, perfected a tennis machine. Sometimes he could only be "heard" at practice—it was too dark to see the player.

Delicate in health, his will was iron, his self-discipline immense. And his tragedy came when, after he achieved his heart's desire and won the Davis Cup for France, Lacoste's health collapsed under the strain, compelling him to retire at twenty-four.

One of the shyest champions, Lacoste's inability to speak English fluently added to his reserve. Nevertheless, his personality was as effective as his more dynamic contemporaries, Borotra and Cochet. Lacoste took his tennis seriously, but his big white cap and solemn expression concealed his enjoyment of the game. He was happiest when engaged in a life and death struggle—and his bitterest enemies were his greatest friends.

Methodical to the last degree, Lacoste was often ragged by his team-mates about his famous notebooks (a dossier of all opponents) but he considered them invaluable, even refusing to sell them for 1,000 dollars.

His concentration was uncanny. Playing Lycett at Wimbledon in 1925, he did not notice the arrival of the Royal Family which caused 15,000 spectators to rise. Only when he started to serve did Lacoste see Lycett standing motionless on court.

Heartbreaking in his base-line accuracy, Lacoste often subdued

far more versatile opponents. He possessed an impregnable backhand and wonderful management of the lob. The Frenchman seldom
had an "off" day—sometimes a super Tilden or an extra brilliant
Cochet would produce enough winners to overcome Lacoste, but it
needed tremendous sustained aggression.

Born on 2nd July, 1905, Lacoste took up tennis to improve his
health, but the fascination of its chess-board possibilities soon
impressed his un-Latin, unexcitable mind. "Tennis is only a game
but it is a game worth playing," sums up his attitude.

He had no natural talent, but he took a long view of tennis. He
was no prolific winner of junior tournaments, but every defeat
taught a lesson and was a stepping stone to ultimate greatness.

Beaten 6-1, 6-0 by Antoine Gentien (later his best friend) Lacoste
became his equal in three months. He lost again to Gentien in the
French junior final 6-4, 7-5, but soon afterwards was French junior
covered court champion.

In 1922, this 17-year-old revealed his tactical skill when playing
that master of sagacity Roper Barrett at Brussels. Lacoste sacrificed
the fourth set to love by ceaseless drops and lobs. His reward was
the fifth set surrendered by an exhausted rival—also to love.

His first appearance at Wimbledon in 1922 was cut short by
Pat O'Hara Wood (6-1, 6-2, 6-2). In 1923, however, he was French
covered court champion beating in the first round "a somewhat
sleepy Borotra at 10 o'clock in the morning after a very short night"
—and at Wimbledon that summer he reached the fifth round.

Here he yielded to Cecil Campbell—the only man to take a set
from Johnston, the ultimate winner. Lacoste led by two sets and
3-1, but was gradually overhauled, 1-6, 3-6, 6-3, 6-2, 6-3.

Lacoste's first visit to America in 1923 where he lost in the second
round to F. T. Hunter (in five sets) drew the comment from Mrs.
Wightman, famous for her insight, that France had a world-beater.

Borotra beat Lacoste 7-5, 6-4, 0-6, 5-7, 6-2 in the French final of
1924. The Basque produced a sustained volleying attack in the last
set. Borotra's nearest rival in brilliance at this time was Spanish
Manoel Alonso, who met Lacoste in the second round at Wimbledon where his scintillating attack, matched by the Frenchman's
economy of stroke, provided an intriguing spectacle. Alonso led two
sets to one, and the third set, won by him at 15-13, produced the best
tennis of the championship. But Alonso's fire failed before his young
opponent's dour steadiness and Lacoste won 2-6, 6-2, 13-15, 6-3, 6-2.

In the quarter-final Lacoste dropped a set to Jean Washer and
repeated this performance in the semi-final against Dick Williams.
The final against Borotra was short and sharp, although five sets
were contested. Most rallies finished at the third or fourth shot. The

51

first set was won by Borotra in twelve minutes and the match was over in an hour and a quarter.

Borotra triumphed 6-1, 3-6, 6-1, 3-6, 6-4, his volleying and possibly his stronger personality turning the tables. Lacoste was a model of concentration and coolness—unlike his mother who watched with great excitement. Victor and vanquished walked off arm-in-arm—France had won!

Only lack of confidence had held Lacoste back, and Borotra forecast his young friend would be next champion. And in 1925 after a stream of perfect lobs over Borotra's racket had given Lacoste his first French championship in three sets (7-5, 6-1, 6-4) these rivals again met in the Wimbledon final.

Down two sets, Borotra tightened up his errors, and some brilliant volleying gave him the third set. Moreover, he led 4-1 in the fourth, but Borotra's foot-faults and his own resourcefulness then saved Lacoste, who proved his humanity by joyfully flinging off his cap and rushing to the net to receive Borotra's congratulations. The score was 6-3, 6-3, 4-6, 8-6.

Although thrilled by Paris and Wimbledon, Lacoste was still unsatisfied—the Davis Cup lay securely behind the shadow of the American giant, Tilden. Lacoste realised that Tilden (twelve years his senior) needed enormous elbow room for his crushing drives.

He planned therefore to run Tilden up and down court, and provoke errors by medium-placed hitting. These tactics entailed the ability to return a barrage of withering drives and cannon-ball services—a task requiring utmost patience.

In 1925, France reached the Davis Cup final. Lacoste, meeting Tilden for the first time, staggered America by almost succeeding in his campaign. Four times within a point of defeat in the fourth set. Tilden only saved himself by his great courage (3-6, 10-12, 8-6, 7-5, 6-2).

At Forest Hills, Vincent Richards eased U.S. minds, when by a brilliant net attack, he beat Lacoste 6-4, 6-3, 6-3 in the quarter-final. But early in 1926 the Frenchmen invaded America again determined to accustom themselves to trans-Atlantic methods. The "Musketeers" made a significant clean sweep in the U.S. covered court singles. Borotra beat Tilden, Brugnon beat Hunter, and Lacoste beat Richards and Van Ryn. Much to American surprise an all-French final was staged, Lacoste defeating Borotra 15-13, 6-3, 2-6, 6-3. But Lacoste's exertions had exhausted him. Soon after, he developed congestion of the lung and in the French championships he failed to win a set from Cochet (6-2, 6-4, 6-3).

Lacoste now realised that if he were to make any impression on Tilden, he would have to miss Wimbledon. This sacrifice paid a

52

dividend, for although America retained the Davis Cup, Lacoste beat Tilden 4-6, 6-4, 8-6, 8-6. This was Tilden's first Davis Cup defeat for six years. To increase Gallic joy, Cochet defeated Tilden in the U.S. singles quarter-final.

Tilden took a line in the Cochet-Lacoste semi-final won by the latter 3-6, 6-4, 4-6, 8-6, 6-2. Lacoste then established himself as the world's No. 1, when he became the first Frenchman to win in America. He played superbly to beat Borotra (conqueror of Richards and Johnston) 6-4, 6-0, 6-4. Borotra led 4-2, but a cascade of lobs then escaped the best smash in tennis and Lacoste won the next ten games.

His defeats nettled Tilden and drew him out of America in 1927. Paris seethed with excitement when he and Lacoste met in the greatest-ever French final. In the third set Lacoste was attacked by cramp. Rain and free fights, all of which bothered Tilden, but never Lacoste, marked the final set. At 8-7, Tilden reached match point twice, but Lacoste hung on, and finally battled through to a desperate finish 6-4, 4-6, 5-7, 6-3, 11-9.

Seeded No. 1 and No. 2, they were expected to decorate the Wimbledon final—yet neither survived the semi-final. Cochet beat Tilden and Borotra, his enthusiasm fired because a French victory was now assured, scored a strategic win over Lacoste, 6-4, 6-3, 1-6, 1-6, 6-2.

But in September a five year dream came true. "A thousand photographs . . . seems like a phantasy . . . l'Elysee"; thus Lacoste describes France's Davis Cup win. He took the lion's share of honour, beating Johnston in three sets and Tilden in four. To cement French supremacy, Lacoste retained the U.S. title defeating Tilden 11-9, 6-3, 11-9.

Resting in the winter of 1927-28, the Frenchman completed "Lacoste on Tennis," a masterpiece of information; and on the 22nd March, 1928, he demonstrated at the Asnieres Club his tennis machine, which, resembling an anti-aircraft gun, could shoot balls across court and could lob to a height of fifteen feet.

At Wimbledon, Cochet and Lacoste were seeded to meet in the final. Lacoste lost a set to J. B. Hawkes in the second round and was then extended by George Lott to 6-1, 9-7, 6-8, 6-2. He had to fight five sets before he got the better of H. W. Austin 6-4, 6-4, 6-8, 1-6, 6-2. Lacoste had a chance to win in straight sets but Austin saved the third set with some enterprising volleying.

After handling Hubert de Morpurgo's difficult service with ease—the Frenchman won 6-2, 6-3, 6-4—Lacoste survived a thrilling semi-final against Tilden. Huge throngs of trans-Atlantic visitors swarmed to Wimbledon for the first meeting of these famous rivals on the Centre Court. Tilden, resourceful and masterful, led by two sets to one and was within a stroke of 4-1 in the fourth. Lacoste held on and saved that all-important fifth game and eventually drew level. In the final set, his generalship against a tiring Tilden helped him to win the best match of the championship 2-6, 6-4, 2-6, 6-4, 6-3.

But he won the final against Cochet much more easily 6-1, 4-6, 6-4, 6-2. Lacoste played wonderful tennis, and was a model of concentration. He once fell head over heels, and despite roars of laughter, did not bat an eyelid. He had practised his forehand passing shot for two hours before the match to combat Cochet's net attack.

The third set decided the match. Ahead at 3-1, Lacoste's lead dissolved and Cochet pulled up to 4-all. Cochet led 40-30 in the next game but Lacoste's wonderful ball control checked the rush of the volleyer. With the third set in his pocket, Lacoste led 4-0, 40-love. The rallies were enterprising and entertaining. Cochet saved the fifth game but soon after, a racket hurled into the sky announced that Lacoste had regained his title—and had given his self-control a break.

Tired after Wimbledon, Lacoste's Davis Cup defeat by Tilden (1-6, 6-4, 6-4, 2-6, 6-3) shocked France. Another complete rest restored his confidence, and in the French Championship of 1929, Lacoste avenged himself on Tilden in the semi-final (6-1, 6-0, 5-7, 6-3) and then won a thrilling final from Borotra, 6-3, 2-6, 6-0, 2-6, 8-6.

It was Lacoste's lobbing that turned the scale in the final. Borotra was in wonderful form, having accounted for Hunter and Cochet. Lacoste seemed to have the key to victory when an 8-game break took him to 2-0 in the fourth set. But Borotra pulled himself together and with his rival coming in unexpectedly to finish the struggle, he produced several difficult passes to win six games in a row. The fifth set was a desperately fought battle, Borotra leading 3-1, but eventually surrendering to the stoic stonewalling of his opponent. Together they won the doubles with victories over Tilden-Hunter 6-3, 6-2, 3-6, 6-3, and Cochet-Brugnon 6-3, 3-6 6-3, 3-6, 8-6.

These battles finished Lacoste for 1929. He could not defend his Wimbledon title or the Davis Cup. A year went by and he married France's golfing star, attractive Simonne de la Thaume. He was Davis Cup captain in 1931, but when Borotra collapsed in his arms after playing Perry—and Vines arrived on the scene—something had to be done to assist Cochet to retain the trophy.

Lacoste accordingly risked his stamina and re-entered tennis in 1932. He sent the crowd mad with delight when he put out Sydney Wood, reigning Wimbledon champion, in the most sensational match of the French Championships, 6-1, 6-0, 3-6, 6-8, 7-5.

But the strain was too great, and Lacoste's concentration was not now so powerful. He lost his next match in four sets to H. G. N. Lee, and could never again play serious tennis.

France now realised with a sigh that her youngest "Musketeer" could offer her his wonderful brain, but no longer his body. Lacoste remained Davis Cup captain for many years, and was recognised for the kindness he showed to young players.

Today his tennis is a fragrant reminder of the 'twenties. Lacoste played in wonderful company. He partnered Suzanne at her zenith, he engineered the fall of Tilden. But his greatest love was for France. Glory for Lacoste meant nothing compared to glory for France—and to this end he directed all his skill and stamina.

8

Where there's a Wills...

A LOVELY Californian, appropriately named Helen, can claim the greatest number of singles championships. Faultlessly featured and physically perfect, Miss Wills, daughter of a San Francisco doctor, developed a game of simplicity and strength. Her tactics were straightforward and consisted of probing and then pounding any weakness with a barrage of bewildering beautifully placed shots.

She drove with great pace on both wings often neglecting an efficient volley for greater security on the base line. There was no weakness in her game which was rounded off by a severe service and smash.

Perhaps her greatest asset was her single-minded determination and the ability—denied even to Suzanne and Bill Tilden—to concentrate entirely on her tennis. Helen did not believe in chatting or smiling at opponents—her one idea was to win, and as quickly as possible. Applause and antagonism alike meant nothing to the American.

Human drama was absent from her tennis and the U.S. public likes human drama. At first they doted on "Little Poker Face" hoping to see her wrest the Wimbledon crown from Suzanne. Then at the height of her fame Miss Wills became "Two-Set Helen"— and finally when America had had enough of her inevitable, uninteresting successes, she degenerated into the sardonic "Queen Helen".

Her clothes were workmanlike and, indicating her approach to tennis, were the most suitable for quick cool victories. Inventor of the utilitarian white "Wills" eye-shade, Helen was not interested in the attractively coloured bandeaux or expensive jewellery produced by Suzanne.

The American never created the aura of suspense that surrounded Suzanne. Her victories were always too certain to allow for any sensational result. She did not possess the sunny cheerfulness of Betty Nuthall nor the colourful radiance of her other contemporary Lili d'Alvarez.

Nevertheless, this beautiful, aloof Californian drew immense crowds. She seemed destined to lead a unique, solitary, yet not lonely, life. Although artistic by nature—Helen exhibited a series of paintings successfully in America in 1928—she was never excitable and certainly possessed no fiery gestures.

Helen had the advantage of parents who were anxious for her sporting supremacy. Her training was supervised by her father—her matches were witnessed by her mother. Even when she married, Helen never played so well unless this quiet grey-haired lady was at the side of the court. Mrs. Wills attended all her daughter's games, even in rain.

Hours of Californian sunshine helped to develop her stamina—hours of play against men helped to strengthen her tennis. She lacked the genius and footwork of Suzanne but surpassed her in speed and temperament.

In 1922, Molla Mallory was American champion and was considered virtually unbeatable at Forest Hills where she had a victory over Suzanne to her credit. Her opponent in that year's final was plaited 16-year-old schoolgirl Helen Wills who, trying to provoke errors by soft-balling, was swept summarily out of the picture, 6-3, 6-1.

But Helen was to win the Pacific Coast championship soon after, not conceding more than two games in any set. Coached by Mrs. Wightman, she attacked the mighty Molla in the 1923 U.S. final and to the stupefaction of the spectators hit winners off her opponent's savage returns.

Wills beat Mallory 6-2, 6-1. From 1-2 in the first set she reached 5-2 losing one point—and in both sets she scored 31 winners to her famous opponent's 17.

Unlike Suzanne who kissed nearly everyone in sight after beating Mrs. Chambers at Wimbledon, Helen took her victory with the calmness of a veteran. She was quite annoyed when embraced by the enthusiastic umpire.

Helen went back to her studies and in 1924 accompanied the Wightman Cup team to England. She lost both singles matches (to Mrs. Covell and Miss McKane) and was a great disappointment. Her simple clothes, too, were compared unfavourably to the elegant outfits of the leading Europeans.

Settling down in the championships, however, she soon proved the quality of her mettle. She improved with every match, power-charging her way to the final with wins over Mrs. J. L. Colegate 6-1, 6-0, and Mrs. Satterthwaite 6-2, 6-1.

Suzanne had given Miss McKane a walker-over to the final. Starting with great confidence Helen, a set up, was four times within a stroke of 5-1. But "Biddy" McKane, one of the bravest women in tennis, fought her way back into the game. She launched a net attack and aided by her remarkable anticipation, scored enough low volleys to win the second set to waves of cheering.

Helen did not falter—it was Miss McKane who had successfully gained the net position. They struggled for every point, until Miss McKane, aided by one critical net-cord, nosed out a plucky winner 4-6, 6-4, 6-4.

The loser admitted tears when changing after the match. So intent had she been on the play that she was actually unaware the battle was finished and indeed asked the score. At one stage, Helen accidentally served twice in succession—unnoticed.

With Mrs. Wightman, Helen won the doubles title when they defeated Miss McKane-Mrs. Covell 6-4, 6-4. As a team they were unbeaten and they also captured the Olympic title held that year at Colombe in Paris. Helen, finding conditions to her liking, was in dominating form in the singles, beating Mrs. Satterthwaite, Mrs. Mallory, Mme. Golding, and in the final Mlle. Vlasto (victor over Miss McKane) 6-2, 6-2.

Her studies at the University of California prevented Helen visiting Europe for two years. Meanwhile her stock rose steadily in the Western Hemisphere.

Back home in 1924 she became triple champion of America. Next year she inflicted revenge on Kitty McKane in the U.S. final. Despite torrid heat, Helen's stamina was unaffected. After losing the first set to her opponent's shrewd volleying, Helen unleashed a brand of aggressive tennis never seen before in America. She won 3-6, 6-0, 6-2, storming through the last four games in a display that drew from one critic "Here was the Tilden of women's tennis".

It was to test herself against the great Suzanne that Helen, accompanied by her mother, arrived on the Riviera early in 1926. The rivalry between Suzanne and Molla Mallory had been "news value" for years. Now rumours of antagonism between Helen and Suzanne were quickly circulated—despite the fact they were on good terms.

America declared Suzanne feared meeting Helen, while the latter also came under fire because she withdrew from a tournament. Eventually they clashed in a mixed final at Nice, Lenglen-Hubert de Morpurgo beating Wills-Charles Aeschliman in the "bitterest battle seen on the Riviera".

When at last they did meet in singles in the Cannes final, proceedings resembled a bull fight. It was even reported erroneously that they had quarrelled and were no longer on speaking terms.

Suzanne's greater genius, her vaster experience and her ability to slow up the game gave her the first set 6-3. In the second set, with Helen unafraid to hit those softer shots, the score went to 3-all. The American eventually advanced to 5-4 amidst rising excitement—

only to lose the tenth game to love. Then Suzanne advanced to 6-5, 40-15. Helen's winning shot in the next rally landed on the line—somebody apparently shouted "Out"—and they shook hands at the net.

The umpire, however, re-started the match and a harassed Suzanne lost the twelfth game. Helen was within a stroke of 7-6, but the Frenchwoman steeled her nerves, placed superbly—and after a double fault at match point—saved the set and match, 8-6.

This was probably her greatest ordeal—and after receiving congratulations, embraces and flowers, Suzanne gave the crowd even more money's worth by having hysterics.

The least excited person present was the prime cause of the uproar. Helen stood fascinated by the pantomime; here was something that justified a journey to Europe!

Her reverie was broken when a young American whom she had just met came on to court and said, "You played awfully well." His name was Freddy Moody. The doubles final had to be postponed while Suzanne recovered. In two tense sets, Suzanne (for once a passenger) and Didi Vlasto defeated Helene Contostavlos (Didi's cousin) and Helen Wills.

Tennis was anticipating a return match as it was obvious the difference between the finalists was very slight. Suzanne, so dependent on her nerves, might certainly have gone down in a third set.

Appendicitis then interrupted Helen's career. While convalescent she received some wonderful flowers from the woman the press repeatedly named "her deadly rival"—Suzanne Lenglen!

After visiting Wimbledon as a spectator Helen re-started tournaments. She won at Easthampton, but lost the Seabright final to Miss Ryan and was advised by her doctor not to defend at Forest Hills.

After her stormy session at Wimbledon in 1926, Suzanne turned professional. Helen was accordingly seeded No. 1 in 1927. She beat Miss Sterry 6-3, 3-6, 6-3 (this was the last set she was to lose for six years) and then overcame Miss Lumley Ellis, Eileen Bennett, Elsie Goldsack, Mrs. Peacock and Joan Fry to reach the final.

Her last opponent was Lili d'Alvarez, the Spanish beauty. Lili was twenty-two, Helen five months younger, and they provided an epic encounter.

In this backhand-to-backhand duel, "Lili took the ball on the rise," Helen hitting a much later stroke. American steadiness won the first set 6-2. Then producing a series of wonder shots, Lili led 4-3 in the second set having captured the seventh game with a peerless backhand down the line.

The turning point in the eighth game was a 40-stroke rally played at top speed and packed with exuberant full-blooded strokes. It ended with the Senorita just failing to reach a beautiful arching Californian lob. Alverez who had made the pace throughout was exhausted, and even Wills had to lean on her racket as the Centre Court acclaimed their skill in generous applause.

Helen recovered breath and control, but not Lili, who won only one more rally. Her stamina spent, the Senorita could only walk to the net to congratulate her opponent.

This 6-2, 6-4 victory proved that California and not Spain now ruled women's tennis, a fact further stressed in the American season. Helen crushed Joan Fry 6-2, 6-0 and Mrs. Godfree 6-1, 6-1 in the Wightman Cup—and regained her Forest Hills title beating Mlle Kea Bouman (the French title-holder), Helen Jacobs and, in the final, Betty Nuthall 6-1, 6-4.

In 1928 Helen, champion of France, Wimbledon and America— a feat that had so far escaped any woman player—assumed a Lenglen-like control over the game. At her first appearance in Paris she won the final from Eileen Bennett 6-1, 6-2. In the Wimbledon quarter-final she crushed Mrs. Holcroft Watson 6-3, 6-0—next accounted for Miss Ryan 6-1, 6-1—and then encountered another Alvarez assault in the final.

This time Helen again had to prove she could run—the Senorita's backhand, often hit almost contemptuously on the half-volley, saw to that. In the first set, however, from 2-all the next four games went to the unruffled driving of the Californian.

Then the Centre Court saw Lili rise to the occasion. With a stream of daring, devastating drives mixed with volleys and smashes, she attacked her opponent. Even Helen could not hold the Senorita who, to riotous applause, broke service twice to lead 3-0.

Reaction and the regularity of Helen's returns cost Lili the next four games. Tiring rapidly, she made her final onslaught, three wonder shots taking her to within a stroke of 4-all—then with an easy winner at hand, she hit the ball into the net! Utterly weary, the Senorita could make no further effort. Helen won the next six rallies for victory and retained her title in forty-five minutes. At Forest Hills she was successful in three championships defeating Helen Jacobs in the final of the singles 6-2, 6-1.

Handsome little Helen Jacobs (Helen II) had now become a force in American tennis and was the hope of anti-Wills' spectators. Both were members of the Berkeley Tennis Club and a feud, denied by the namesakes and fostered by their supporters, arose in trans-Atlantic circles. Popular Helen Jacobs keenly felt the icy reserve of Helen Wills who, commenting on the much-discussed antagonism declared, "Miss Jacobs was scarcely an enemy."

In April, 1929, was announced the engagement of Helen Wills, described as a "tennis player, fair to middling painter" to Frederick S. Moody, Junior, "stockbroker, fair to middling tennis player". The champion said she would continue playing as long as she could hold a racket.

1929 revealed little change in her position as leader of tennis. She won in Paris, beating Eileen Bennett 6-2, 7-5 and Mme. Mathieu 6-3, 6-4.

At Wimbledon, Helen opened with four love sets and lost only sixteen games in six matches. Lili d'Alvarez fell unexpectedly to Mrs. McIlquham, and it was Helen Jacobs who this year contested the final. But she was no match for her namesake and was hit off court 6-1, 6-2.

The schoolgirl of 1924 was now a beautiful sophisticated woman. Presented at court, Helen had a circle of friends ranging from Bernard Shaw to the Bishop of London. Her interest in art brought her in contact with Augustus John who painted her portrait. The shadowy Mrs. Wills remained in the background. Her daughter was much more popular in England than in America where her detachment did not provoke such resentment.

18-year-old Betty Nuthall, driving like Jehu, extended Helen to 8-6, 8-6 in the Wightman Cup at Forest Hills in 1929. Spectator Bunny Austin was so embarrassed by the U.S. public's marked affection for Betty and obvious antipathy to Helen that he started to applaud all the latter's shots!

This attitude caused Helen—who came of Nordic stock—to withdraw and to appear even less emotional on court. She did explain, however, that it was impossible for her to try to gain sympathy (she had none of Borotra's technique).

In the U.S. championships the storm broke . . . Mrs. Mallory, attempting a come-back, defeated Betty Nuthall only to lose 6-0, 6-0 to Helen in record time in the semi-final.

A reporter, incensed at the treatment handed out to America's much-loved and respected veteran star, denounced Helen as the "Killer of the Court", a merciless tennis machine. He declared that this crushing defeat was witnessed by a hushed, uncheering crowd feverishly applauding the few points won by the smiling loser. Helen, unmoved, went on to win the final against Mrs. Watson 6-4, 6-2. She knew that to triumph, her concentration was essential.

In December, 1929, she married Freddy Moody. They had planned a quiet wedding but the press saw they received all the publicity they did not want.

By beating Helen Jacobs 6-2, 6-1, Mrs. Moody retained her French title in 1930. At Wimbledon she lost five games to Mme.

Mathieu (6-3, 6-2) in the semi-final. No other competitor was able to do so well against the holder who in the final dismissed the evergreen Elizabeth Ryan 6-2, 6-2.

Helen then forsook tournaments for a year. Meanwhile, however, she engaged in strenuous practice with Howard Kinsey. In the autumn of 1931 she was in marvellous form and overwhelmed Helen Jacobs at Seabright 6-0, 6-0. At Forest Hills, too, her tremendous hitting swept the board. In the final Mrs. Eileen (Bennett) Whittingstall (conqueror of Helen Jacobs and Betty Nuthall) secured five games (6-4, 6-1).

Blistered feet hampered Helen in the 1932 French championships. The Swiss champion, Mlle. Payot, held her to 6-2, 7-5, and in the semi-final she was several times within a stroke of losing an arduous second set to Fraulein Krahwinkel (Fru Sperling) 6-3, 10-8.

In the final, Simonne Mathieu, coached by Suzanne Lenglen, led Helen 4-1. Then the Californian, forgetting her feet, started her deep pounding to the base-line, neutralising Mathieu's clever placing. Helen led 5-4, France pulled up to 5-all, but this was virtually the end, Helen winning 7-5, 6-1.

The Californian found the turf of Wimbledon more restful and soon asserted that she was still in a class of her own. Thirteen games were all that six opponents could win from her. In the quarter-final Dorothy Round was overwhelmed 6-0, 6-1; Mary Heeley did little better in the "semi" 6-2, 6-0, and in the final, although Helen Jacobs did keep her rival on court for a 46-minute match, Mrs. Moody won comfortably 6-3 6-1.

When she defended her Wimbledon title in 1933 Helen, again the victim of blistered feet, was noticeably slower. Dorothy Round had, meanwhile, taken a meteoric rise in tennis. Deadly drop shots and a fluent net attack had helped her to beat Jacobs and Mathieu at Bournemouth—and after again defeating Helen II in the semi-final, she challenged Mrs. Moody at Wimbledon.

A close first set went to the Californian—but Dorothy Round was finding open spaces with drop shots, while at the same time her much quicker foot work was coping with Helen's widely-hit, choice returns. Her volleys, too, were firm and well-placed.

Raising England's hopes as only Kitty McKane had done, Dorothy, after having been close to defeat in the tenth game of the second set, broke service to lead 7-6. But the great American, determined to avert a third set, reached 40-30 and when her opponent drove out during the next rally it appeared that Helen's remarkable consistency of return had equalised the score.

The linesman, however, declared the Englishwoman's stroke had landed on the line. The crowd grew agitated and articulate. Helen, for once, lost her poise—and two rallies later lost her first set for six years.

But it was Dorothy Round who succumbed to the strain. In the third set Helen was again in full control of her nerves whereas her opponent, her concentration shattered, tried the drop shot too frequently. She lost accuracy and her mistimed shots brought relief to the tired American. Helen won her sixth championship 6-4, 6-8, 6-3.

A strained back kept Mrs. Moody out of the Wightman Cup in 1933. Against her husband's advice she competed at Forest Hills. Here in the semi-final she lost another set before defeating Betty Nuthall (2-6, 6-3, 6-2).

Helen Jacobs, whose game had profited from Suzanne's coaching, was defending champion. She had beaten Dorothy Round in the semi-final and was playing remarkably well.

Helen II won the first set against her namesake, 8-6. Mrs. Moody using all her reserves of stamina, took the second 6-3. The third set, after the players returned from the 10-minute interval, was started amidst tremendous excitement, for it was recognised that Miss Jacobs was going to strain every sinew to achieve her greatest ambition. And with a brilliant mixture of aces, volleys and passing shots, the little holder overwhelmed Mrs. Moody to lead 3-0.

At this stage, Helen Moody retired, declaring her leg was hurting too much. Amidst uproar, Helen Jacobs, all sympathy, helped her opponent to don her jacket, and Mrs. Moody made her exit never to play at Forest Hills again.

The Helen "feud" was revived with a vengeance. Whilst she lay convalescent, Mrs. Moody had little to say on her defeat. Helen Jacobs, to general disgust, was equally silent.

Next year, Helen Moody reported on Wimbledon and in 1935 she re-entered tennis. She lost 6-0, 6-4 to Kay Stammers at Beckenham but, by Wimbledon, had regained her confidence. Here she met in the final the "other Helen" and these trans-Atlantic rivals provided another thrilling epic.

With no quarter asked or accepted, Helen II, volleying magnificently, reached 5-2 in the third set. At 5-3 she was within an ace of victory. A desperate lob saved Mrs. Moody and eventually her sounder base line game triumphed 6-3, 3-6, 7-5.

Delighted with her come-back, Helen restricted her tennis in 1936 and 1937 to mixed doubles. In August, 1937, her marriage was dissolved and she re-entered tennis next year.

She lost at Queen's Club to Fru Sperling, but gradually worked back to form. At Wimbledon she had her revenge, defeating Fru Sperling 12-10, 6-4, to enter the final against Helen Jacobs!

Helen Moody led 4-2, but was caught at 4-all by her volleying opponent. In a desperate ninth game, Miss Jacobs racing across to the net twisted her ankle. She was in great pain and could hardly move. Undeterred, Helen Moody hit twenty-eight winners in the last thirty-one rallies. She showed no reaction to her opponent's plight. Her 6-4, 6-0 victory was greeted with hostility and perfunctory applause. It was a sad ending to a great career.

On 28th October, 1939, Helen Moody married polo-playing Adrian Roark, an Englishman, who had become an American citizen. Some years later her tennis playing and painting (right) hand, severely bitten by a dog, necessitated an operation. Like Tilden, she successfully changed her grips. Her interest had in no way lessened, although she had relinquished tournaments.

The Californian combined the precision of the old school with the power of the new.

Beautiful and baffling, Helen Moody became one of the great enigmas of tennis.

Contessa Della Corte Brae (Cilly Aussèm).   Despite recurrent ill health, this attractive little German won Wimbledon in 1931.

H. Ellsworth Vines. On his first visit to Wimbledon, this volcanic young Californian routed a formidable array of rivals to become the Champion of 1932.

Australian Jack Crawford, whose superb strokes won a spectacular victory over Vines in the Wimbledon Final of 1933.

Mrs. L. Little (Dorothy Round). Her beautiful backhand and brilliant volleying won the Championship twice for Britain (1934 and 1937).

9

Sportsman of Destiny.

TILDEN had trouble with officials . . . Borotra had an array of berets . . . Suzanne had hysterics. Most champions could claim some characteristic—so Cochet made a cult of nonchalance. The word became his copyright and has been always used to describe his easy ambling attitude on court.

The greatest genius of the "Musketeers"—some say of all time— Henri Cochet was unorthodox, not so much in his strokes, as in his methods of play and position on court. Aided by amazing anticipation, he excelled in converting defence into attack and several of his most successful coups started from an (apparently) losing position.

Born in 1901, Cochet's tennis commenced on his father's court at Lyons, and immediately "the game became a passion with me". His effortless, improvised wizardry has been called "errand-boy tennis" implying a swift retort by a quick-thinking brain to any unsuspected stroke or strategy.

Unlike Borotra, a volleyer, and Lacoste, a staunch base-liner, Cochet was a master of the all-court game. He replaced Lacoste's industry by indolence. Where Borotra galloped with energy, Cochet glided with ease—and his trick of seemingly invisible movement has never been duplicated.

A mild service was offset by the cleanest, deadliest smash executed by a small man. When roused, Cochet produced wonder backhands, but it was his magnificent forehand taken casually on the rise that prepared his net attack.

The Frenchman was a great believer in the value of half-court play. By this method, plus the ability to handle cannon ball services from a position within the base-line, Cochet broke up the driving attacks of many big-hitting Americans.

Due to his inclination not to take all opponents seriously—because his keenness, an essential part of his tennis equipment, had not been stimulated—spectators often believed that Cochet was not really trying. Wandering casually into "no man's land", Cochet would produce volleys and half-volleys off his very toes. Placed down the line or almost parallel to the net, these shots were executed with easy abandon.

Sport came easily to him. He played rugger and hockey and took up ski-ing and flying. He ran and he skipped—but nothing got Cochet into better mental condition than a complete break from tennis and a holiday in the country. This was the way he usually prepared for an important championship or a Davis Cup final. Then, inspired by excitement, he was transformed. His self-contained attitude was unchanged, but a stream of wonder shots flowed from his racket with effortless ease.

Naturally lazy, no other champion has recovered so often from a losing score. Against a lesser opponent, Cochet never produced his best tennis and frequently lost the first two sets. Then alive to the danger he would spring to the attack. Few players have fought out more five-set matches—and as an outcome of his several lengthy battles, tennis named him "Five-set Cochet".

Military champion of France in 1921, Cochet also won the Regional championship at Lyons that year. Next year he hit the headlines. He won the French national championship, beating the holder, J. Samazeuilh 8-6, 6-3, 7-5, and captured three titles in the "World's Hard Court" championship at Brussels. In the singles final Cochet beat Count de Gomar (Spain) 6-0, 2-6, 4-6, 6-1, 6-2, and won the doubles titles with Borotra and with Suzanne Lenglen. Still another triumph was the "World's Covered Court" singles at St. Moritz, where he defeated Borotra 4-6, 2-6, 6-3, 6-3, 6-0.

At his first Wimbledon, however, Cochet did not survive the third round, going out 6-3, 6-0, 6-4 to hard-hitting Australian Joe Anderson.

His Continental record, too, suffered eclipse in 1923. He lost his French title in the semi-final to F. Blanchy, and was also beaten in the "World's Hard Court" championship by Jean Washer. He did, however, retain the "World's Covered Court" title at Barcelona.

1924 saw an improvement, Cochet beating Indian Mohammed Sleem, the greatest-ever stone-waller, 6-4, 0-6, 6-4, 2-6, 6-0, in the Davis Cup. The Frenchman again produced some wonder tennis in the Olympic games, beating American Dick Williams and Borotra before losing the final to Vincent Richards 6-4, 6-4, 5-7, 4-6, 6-2. This colourful match raised uproars of applause as both volleyers sought the net in turn and Vincent Richards, victor over Tilden in many battles, has since declared that it was the best performance of his career.

At his second Wimbledon in 1925, Cochet started his series of Centre Court battles with Borotra. They met in the semi-final which Cochet reached at the expense of American star John Hennessey 7-9, 4-6, 6-1, 6-3, 6-0. He won the first set against his countryman and had a point for the next. He then started to foot-fault (an unusual occurrence for Cochet) and Borotra tightened his own errors, eventually coming through 5-7, 8-6, 6-4, 6-1.

The value of meeting the aggressive game of the Americans was never more evident than in French tennis circles in 1926. Vincent Richards, ranked No. 3 in tennis, was hoping to emulate Tilden and Johnston and carry all before him in a European tour that year. In the French championships, however, his serve-volley attack was routed by Cochet who, taking every ball on the rise, produced passing shots from all corners of the court. Cochet toppled his opponent 6-1, 6-4, 6-4, and regained his title.

At Wimbledon, Cochet scored another victory (in the third round) over Richards. Tuned up to great form, he and Borotra decorated the semi-final in a match that drew from Bunny Austin, "A poor shot would have been welcomed." These meetings between the two French volleyers could be guaranteed to produce exhilarating tennis, and though lacking international flavour, caused great excitement. Borotra won 2-6, 7-5, 2-6, 6-3, 7-5, and went on to regain his championship.

In America that year Cochet, meeting Tilden for the first time, scored his greatest win to date when he dramatically de-throned the famous American (title-holder since 1920), 6-8, 6-1, 6-3, 1-6, 8-6. A succession of scintillating shots won Cochet the last two games. He generated speed from Tilden's hitting and the loser admitted "crying out" as Cochet's last victorious volley eluded his reach.

Tilden acted as linesman in the Lacoste-Cochet semi-final that followed. Lacoste, realising the uselessness of trying to combat Cochet in such volleying form, assumed the unusual rôle of aggressor. "It was better for me to play badly at the net to oblige Cochet to play worse at the back of the court." These tactics paid a dividend, Lacoste defeating his team-mate 3-6, 6-4, 4-6, 8-6, 6-2.

All fashionable Paris turned out for the Tilden-Cochet semi-final in 1927. The American, knowing his opponent was anticipating an attack on his backhand, switched his driving power on to Cochet's stronger wing. Cochet for once appeared non-plussed and before he could adapt himself to this novel form of attack was out-witted in three sets (9-7, 6-3, 6-2).

1927 is considered the most remarkable Wimbledon ever—thanks to Cochet. Down two sets to Frank Hunter, the Frenchman started that easy paralysing glide from the base-line to the net. There a wonder volley or a devastating kill settled the point. Hunter sent for Tilden whose presence was always an inspiration to him. Together they won seven more games (3-6, 3-6, 6-2, 6-2, 6-3).

Another upheaval occurred in the semi-final when Tilden, aided by cannon-ball services and cyclonic hitting, led Cochet by two sets and 5-1. Suddenly Cochet stiffened—those terrific drives and services flew back—and the bewildered Centre Court saw him pocket seventeen successive points and the set 7-5.

Moreover Cochet went to 4-2 in the fourth set, was pulled back after a desperate effort by Tilden to 4-all, but gaining confidence and mastery with every shot, proceeded to equalise at two sets all. Tilden had spent his stamina in that set. The initiative now lay with the nimble little Frenchman, who nonchalantly volleyed his way through an amazing match 2-6, 4-6, 7-5, 6-4, 6-3.

In his final encounter, Cochet trailed his opponent by two sets. Borotra, having achieved this advantage, had also spent a good deal of stamina. He had made Cochet's backhand the subject of a virile volleying campaign, but in the third and fourth sets, Cochet started to pull out several amazing backhand passes that left the Basque stranded.

Borotra, however, returned to a ferocious assault in the fifth set and even Cochet could not prevent him reaching 5-2. But perilous though his plight was Cochet, gaily confident, pulled up to 5-all after being six times within a stroke of defeat.

One of Cochet's volleys that salvaged a match point was considered by many spectators to be a double-hit. Borotra thought so too—he appealed to the umpire who decided in Cochet's favour. The last time the Basque was in sight of victory he saw his opponent produce a backhand down the line that raised a cloud of chalk. He lost heart and the last two games, and Destiny awarded Cochet the title 4-6, 4-6, 6-3, 6-4, 7-5.

The "Musketeers" achieved their ambition after Wimbledon when they won the Davis Cup from America. Tilden defeated Cochet in a tense four-set affair, but it was Cochet who made the rubber safe for France when he overcame Johnston in the last single. Overjoyed by his success, Cochet sent a ball into the sky—and his wife fainted in the midst of the French Davis Cup team.

At Forest Hills in the American championships, Cochet lost unexpectedly to John Hennessey 6-4, 6-4, 3-6, 4-6, 6-1. His consolation came in the mixed final when with Eileen Bennett he beat Lacoste and Mrs. Wightman 1-6, 6-0, 6-2.

Cochet always partnered the prettiest girl in tennis. His tandem with Eileen Bennett always drew huge crowds, but although they were considered the strongest pair in tennis for some years, they never got further than the semi-final at Wimbledon. However, they scored several good wins on the Continent and captured the French title in 1928 and 1929 (defeating on both occasions Frank Hunter and Helen Wills).

Paris 1928 revealed a superhuman Cochet. His opportunism, his boundless confidence, and his touch on the volley rendered him—to quote Helen Wills—"invincible". His victims included Sydney Wood, Hunter, Borotra and Lacoste (5-7, 6-3, 6-1, 6-3).

At Wimbledon he had an easy passage to the final. He had his revenge on Hennessey and then beat his young countryman, Boussus. Lacoste, victor over Tilden, was his opponent in the final—and in their only encounter at Wimbledon Lacoste was a somewhat comfortable winner 6-1, 4-6, 6-4, 6-2. The new champion gave a display of mechanical accuracy, his beautifully produced passing shots escaping Cochet time and again.

By beating Hennessey (5-7, 9-7, 6-3, 6-0) and Tilden (9-7, 8-6, 6-4) in the Davis Cup, and by winning the U.S. title, Cochet was ranked No. 1 for 1928—a position he held for four years. At Forest Hills—where Tilden banned for six months was only a spectator—the Frenchman beat in succession F. Mercer, Gregory Mangin, Wilbur Coen, Frank Shields, and in the final Hunter 4-6, 6-4, 3-6, 7-5, 6-3. The last match was a brilliant affair and Hunter, coached by Tilden to withstand the French attack, had defeated Borotra and nearly emerged victorious against Cochet.

Cochet was displeased with the American courts and the running of the tournament and, indeed, conditions were far from perfect. It was generally realised he would be unlikely to defend his title. When he did return four years later, the Committee did their utmost to accommodate him—with disastrous results. It was unfortunate as Cochet was by no means a difficult man to please.

Pantomime helped to put him out of the French semi-final. Despite the terrific tempo, Borotra, falling, decided to roll over on his face. Rising, he ejected a pebble—and then, another. Repeated bursts of laughter startled Cochet who twice missed his return, forfeiting a valuable lead. Enraged, he lost touch and title to the tune of 6-3, 5-7, 7-5, 5-7, 6-4.

Wimbledon provided an opportunity for revenge, "Never did I feel so sure of myself." This was apparent in the semi-final when taking Tilden's services with incredible ease and even hitting winners off them, Cochet led 6-4, 6-1, 5-1. The desperate American fought frantically to avert defeat and pulled up to 5-all, but had to yield the next two games to a stream of wonder volleys.

In the final Cochet, deadly from the back of the court, and overwhelming at the net, outplayed and outpaced even the scurrying Borotra.

Lacoste was not defending his title but had flown from Paris to see the final. He expected another epic, as in 1927. But this time, Borotra, constantly foot-faulting, could not get a grip of the game. He tried swapping berets to change his luck, but Cochet, refusing to let Borotra shake his concentration, produced perfect tennis to win 6-4, 6-3, 6-4.

Cochet's superiority was again in evidence when in the Davis Cup he gained his easiest-ever win over Tilden 6-3, 6-1, 6-2. Against George Lott, Cochet conceded a set, but stormed through the other three 6-1, 3-6, 6-0, 6-3.

Cochet was popularly supposed to "mesmerize" Tilden. About this so-called "hoodoo" Cochet declared, "I had a feeling that the result was being influenced by forces mysterious yet real which were operating in my favour. I invoked these feelings while Tilden feared them." Cochet then explained this sensation by the fact that he was at the top of his game, whereas Tilden's power was diminishing and that the American had come to expect defeat when they met.

Tilden played brilliantly when opposing his rival in the French final in 1930. He led by a set and 5-3, and then allowed himself to get distracted by the crowd, who were objecting to the umpire's decisions. Cochet, ever an opportunist, then put on pressure and Tilden could capture only five more games (3-6, 8-6, 6-3, 6-1).

It seemed as though nothing could stop Cochet at Wimbledon as Lacoste was now out of tennis. His quarter-final defeat (6-4, 6-4, 6-3) by unseeded American Wilmer Allison was a world surprise. Allison played a brilliant attacking game. The Frenchman set a standard that was definitely "sub-Cochet" and was guilty of a large number of driving errors.

Shaking his head sadly and slapping his thigh to stir himself, Cochet could not summon back his genius this time. He took his defeat with a cheerful smile and declared, "No bad luck. Allison won by marvellous tennis."

French fears for the future of the Davis Cup were allayed when Cochet, back in form, defeated Lott 6-4, 6-2, 6-2. With Brugnon he beat the Wimbledon champions, Allison-Van Ryn, the toughest tandem in tennis; and on the final day his ability to turn defence into attack once again overcame Tilden 4-6, 6-3, 6-1, 7-5. This was their last meeting as amateurs.

Borotra, at this time, was considered a closer rival to Cochet than Tilden was. In the Belgian final he produced a brilliant attack and beat Cochet 4-6, 6-3, 4-6, 6-4, 8-6. It was a glorious match and both players were completely exhausted at the finish. It was, too, a sign that both "Musketeers" were not as young as ever and Borotra, indeed, was already suggesting that Boussus should be included in the Davis Cup team to replace Lacoste.

Influenza and malaria prevented Cochet from playing in the French championship in 1931. Convalescent at Wimbledon, the first round proved fatal. The Frenchman was unlucky to meet baseliner Nigel Sharpe, an opponent of considerable tenacity. Sharpe won 6-1, 6-3, 6-2 and Wimbledon mourned the early exit of her leading "wonder man".

But the excitement of the Challenge Round re-created the master touch. In his opening rubber, Cochet trailed Austin by a set and 1-4. Then came three games to the Frenchman, roused by the elegant defence of his opponent. Austin, however, had a set point at 5-4 and another at 8-7. But Cochet was now thoroughly alert, and cheered by his supporters, gave a dazzling display to win 3-6, 11-9, 6-2, 6-4. In the final match with the score 2-all, Cochet beat Perry 6-4, 1-6, 9-7, 6-3. The crisis came in the third set in which Perry's well-placed forehands often left Cochet standing. But the little Frenchman produced such a stunning mixture of drives, volleys and half-volleys that he left no doubt of his world superiority. A backhand half-volley passing shot, hit with almost insolent indifference, frequently left Perry shaking his head in amazement—and brought rapturous acknowledgment from a delirious crowd. When the match was over, thousands of cushions were flung on court and the spectators leapt the barrier carrying "Henri" around the Stade Roland Garros.

Cochet received a wonderful professional offer from Tilden after this display of genius. As France's mainstay, however, he refused the temptation.

Despite American boosting of a new Tilden (Ellsworth Vines) all seemed well in that spring of 1932 when Cochet swept the board at Paris beating Del Bono, Pat Hughes, Gregory Mangin, Marcel Bernard and de Stefani, the ambidextrous Italian. At Wimbledon, he was confidently expected to win. In an article written just before the championship, Austin had stated, "There is one man who stands out from the rest of us (tennis players)—Henri Cochet".

Cochet was seeded No. 1. Something, however, went wrong in the second round when he made a sensational departure at the hands of Ian Collins 6-2, 8-6, 0-6, 6-3. Although not then realised, this was the first sign of a declining Cochet. He timed the alarm as usual for the third set and played six fluent, forceful games, but its warning failed to rouse him again in the fourth. Cochet's stamina, too, now lacked its former resilience and the assault he made in the third set left him too weary to raise the attack again in the fourth.

He was embraced by his wife as he came off court. Mme. Cochet was unable to hide her tears of disappointment. But he accepted defeat as gaily as he accepted victory and immediately entered for the Plate. He became the first player to win this consolation event after winning the championship.

The Davis Cup Challenge Round started in intense excitement.

71

It was felt that France was making her last stand against the upsurging might of young America.

To everyone's amazement Borotra beat Vines. Cochet followed and had a revenge on Allison beating him 5-7, 7-5, 7-5, 6-2. He played to instructions which were to keep Allison on court as long as possible to tire him for his subsequent matches. Leading 5-3, Cochet allowed Allison to overtake him. The crisis came in the third set, Cochet trailing 3-5. Here he produced a comeback and keeping his weary opponent on the run, only lost two more games.

Borotra had settled the issue in France's favour when Cochet and Vines came on court. Cochet bewildered his young opponent by his amazing anticipation and gained a two-set lead. Here he seemed to dally with the idea of extending the match. Vines threw off his caution and leapt into his Wimbledon form. Two wonderful hard-fought sets went to America and in the final set Vines' deep power-ful drives denied Cochet the net position. In a great personal triumph Vines came out victorious 4-6, 0-6, 7-5, 8-6, 6-2, after scoring 170 winners to Cochet's 168.

Cochet had intended to tour Australia that autumn. Now to avenge his first Davis Cup defeat since 1927, he decided to tackle Vines at Forest Hills. They were placed at opposite ends of the draw—and the U.S. authorities, mindful of Cochet's dissatisfaction in 1928, arranged all his matches with scrupulous care. Confident and cheerful, Cochet conquered Alonso, Van Ryn and Shields to meet Allison in the semi-final.

On the afternoon of the semi-final it was decided that Vines should first play Clifford Sutter (presumably a three-set win for the former) followed by the Cochet-Allison match, calculated to be a longer tougher affair. To the Committee's dismay, Sutter won the first two very long sets and it took Vines seventy-five games to win.

Cochet's match came on in the late afternoon. Allison played wonderful tennis and after four bitter sets the umpire decided to postpone the match until next day owing to bad light. Cochet pro-tested—he was sailing for France the following night—if he were to beat Allison it might mean playing twice in one day. He was, however, over-ruled and next morning defeated Allison in the last set, winning 6-1, 10-12, 4-6, 6-3, 7-5.

Although Vines only aced Cochet six times his deep, devastating drives, foiling the Frenchman's net attack, really won their final (6-4, 6-4, 6-4). Interviewed after the match Cochet admitted he was tired and anxious before play started—due to completing his battle with Allison in the morning.

Early in 1933 Cochet, toying with the idea of joining Tilden, was forbidden to make a film combining romance and tennis. In the

72

French final after losing a superb first set, Cochet's stimulus vanished and he was beaten by Jack Crawford 8-6, 6-1, 6-3.

About this reverse Vines wrote, "Cochet knows—as he has a right to know—he is a super player. Competition has lost its flavour". A record Wimbledon crowd gathered for the Vines-Cochet semi-final. Cochet was considered to have a great chance, for in beating Lester Stoeffen in the quarter-final 3-6, 6-4, 6-3, 6-1, he had displayed his old wizardry, his backhand passing shots being particularly brilliant.

But against Vines, Cochet disappointed his countless supporters. He lost the second set after leading 5-2—and although he captured the third to great applause, it was obvious that he was fighting a losing match. Vines stormed through the fourth set to win 6-2, 8-6, 3-6, 6-1.

In the best Davis Cup match of 1933, however, Cochet returned to rarified heights when beating Austin (recent victor over Vines and Allison) 5-7, 6-4, 4-6, 6-4, 6-4. After his heart had been pronounced fit during the interval for an all-out offensive, Cochet's breath-taking volleys saved the last set from 2-4 down. Joyfully sending a ball sky-high Cochet wrung Austin's hand—and collapsed. Cheers changed to consternation as France's "Henri" left court on a stretcher.

Soon after, occurred the "Cochet" week. After ceaseless rumours that kept Paris guessing for six days, Cochet signed up with Tilden. He did an enormous amount of travelling visiting Russia in 1936, Egypt in 1937 and the Far East in 1938. He did legion work visiting prisoners-of-war and was the guiding spirit of the Suzanne Lenglen Tennis School in Paris. In 1942 Cochet was reinstated as amateur, and in 1943 after defeating Petra eight times, the 43-year-old ex-champion was again ranked France's No. 1. He still plays with effortless ease and has preserved that marvellous mobility.

To Tilden, Cochet was "the greatest player the world has ever seen". Certainly no champion has given his supporters more thrills or his opponents more shocks than this gallant, gay-minded little man from Lyons.

73

10

Lady of Spain

SUZANNE LENGLEN brought a new era to women's tennis ... Helen Wills brought beauty and a mysterious detachment . . . Dorothy Round brought her own tennis balls to her first tournament. But there was a spirited Senorita who brought such colour and charm to the Centre Court that she startled Suzanne and contributed considerably to the Frenchwoman's farewell to Wimbledon.

Here was glamour and gaiety and amazing gallery appeal. Here was—Lili d'Alvarez! Her glittering game and her "Je ne sais quoi" proclaimed the Jean Borotra of women's tennis. Here, too, was a novel attack—a wonder half-volley hit with speed and assurance from losing positions on court.

Lili was born in Rome and her father taught her to play tennis at the age of eight. Three years later she was beating him. Swiss covered court champion at thirteen, Lili's Riviera successes attracted considerable attention. When she came to Wimbledon in 1926, she was twenty-one. How would the Senorita react to grass?

Lili had an answer. She thrived on the faster surface, and according to Helen Wills "hit harder than anyone I played". Against most players, the Californian kept an emergency "reserve" speed. Against Lili "there was no reserve possible".

Lili might have achieved more success had she played safe—this would have suited her physique, but not her temperament. She valued a sensational shot more than a prize, thus sacrificing many winners. But had she been restrained herself, tennis would have been duller and the Centre Court the poorer for missing the riot and the rhapsody of the Spaniard in full cry.

She took Wimbledon by storm and was named the Norma Talmadge of Tennis. Lili threatened Suzanne in the realm of grace —to Helen Wills' calm beauty she added animation—she reproduced the daring genius and the mistakes, too, of Cochet. Like the Frenchman, her career consisted of unexpected victories and unexplained defeats.

Dependent on her touch, if this were disturbed, the structure of her game fell down. Lili did not mind. An eloquent shrug of an elegant shoulder and the Senorita prepared to slam the next shot.

When Suzanne discarded the mantle of tennis fashion, Lili accepted

74

it gladly. Dressed by Paris, she frequently favoured the Spanish colours of red and gold, a compliment to her great admirer, King Alfonso. Tennis was only a part of her life. Rich, versatile, she spoke five languages fluently. An expert at ski-ing and riding, Lili also excelled at billiards and golf.

Beneath the glitter, Lili was a wonderful sport and had a sympathetic human understanding. She detested pretentiousness, never failing to de-bunk it in others. Strangely juvenile, she loved practical jokes and had a schoolgirl's hatred of hats.

The Jubilee Championship of 1926 seemed to be collapsing. Suzanne withdrew, Helen Wills developed appendicitis, Elizabeth Ryan had a terrible cold. Lili restored excitement by an astounding semi-final defeat of Mrs. Mallory. The American might have had the hardest forehand in tennis—against the Alvarez attack she garnered only four games (6-2, 6-2).

In the final, Mrs. Godfree, lacking Lili's brilliance, possessed sounder stamina, greater generalship. A volleyer herself, she decided on base line brickwall tactics. A set down, Lili then attacked at her splendid best, winning the second set and coming within a point of 4-1 in the third. Tiring, she started missing shots, and Mrs. Godfree's sagacity was rewarded with a run of five games and an exciting victory 6-2, 4-6, 6-3.

In 1927, Lili again graced the Wimbledon final—this time against Helen Wills. Both players attacked the rival backhand, producing shots never seen before. America won the first set before Spain settled down. Then came the Alvarez avalanche. Helen Wills proved she could run but could not prevent a 4-3 lead for her opponent. In the eighth game a scintillating rally of forty strokes ended when a lob just escaped Lili's smash. Two exhausted women leant on their rackets amidst a crescendo of cheers. Helen revived, but not Lili, who accepted defeat at 6-2, 6-4. "I did not know women could play such tennis," commented an American Davis Cup star.

1928 . . . and another Wills-Alvarez final to thrill the Centre Court. Compelled to spend a day in bed after beating Australian Daphne Akhurst, Lili nevertheless, gave an exhilarating 40-minute exhibition. Cheers rose when, rushing Helen Wills off her feet, Lili hit the lines to lead 3-0 in the second set. Then came four games to the stoic Californian. Tiring, Lili made a last stand. Two peerless backhands and a priceless drop and she was within a stroke of 4-all —when she mishit an easy volley! Completely spent, Lili surrendered her third final 6-2, 6-3.

The Senorita never played so wonderfully again. In 1929, she provided the sensation of Wimbledon by losing the fourth round to unseeded Mrs. McIlquham 6-4, 4-6, 6-2. In no way depressed,

Lili drew cameras and comment next day looking magnificent in scarlet from top to toe.

Owing to ill-health, Lili frequently withdrew from tournaments while her other interests also made wide demands. In 1930, she beat Simonne Mathieu in Paris, but was exhausted and fell easy prey to Helen Jacobs in the semi-final. Seeded at Wimbledon, she had to retire. Next year, Lili lost the French semi-final to Cilly Aussem. She surprised Wimbledon by wearing fantastic trousers, wrap-over skirt and one red sock, but was beaten in the third round by Dorothy Round. At St. Moritz, in February, 1936, she announced that she had secretly married Comte Jean de la Valdène. Playing No. 2 for France she lost in the fourth round at Wimbledon in 1936 and 1937 —in each case to the ultimate champion (Miss Jacobs and Miss Round).

Lili d'Alvarez never won a major singles championship but she emblazoned her name and fame in the story of tennis. Never robust, she was, nevertheless, radiant. There was about her a zest, a challenge to life. No one has fired the imagination of the Centre Court more brightly than this dynamic daughter of the Toreadors.

11

The Youngest-Ever Champion

WHAT champion would admit he only "half won" at Wimbledon? Yet this is what Sydney B. Wood generously said of his victory in 1931. The youngest-ever title-holder was referring to the walk-over given him in the final by his injured friend and team-mate, Frank Shields.

Possessor of a cannon-ball service, a wonderful deep backhand, and a beautiful touch on the volley, Wood was a genius at handing out what his opponents disliked. His forehand was at times a comfort to his adversaries, but Wood atoned for this by his supreme intelligence.

Although Wood looked amazingly confident often strolling up to the net behind his forcing shots, his lack of stamina denied him nervous repose. This, coupled with his fondness for sacrificing winners for more sensational shots, produced some inexplicable defeats.

Tilden was his unstinted admirer. Admitting that "sometimes he (Wood) is beaten by being a little too clever rather than a little more straightforward". Tilden, nevertheless, declared that Wood played "tennis as I understand tennis, the game that combines grace, beauty, intelligence and courage".

Wood was born on 1st November, 1911. Handicapped throughout his career by bad health and a poor physique, Wood was compelled to let his stamina dictate his strategy. There were occasions when, after delighting the galleries by a display of beauty and power, Wood, overwhelmed by fatigue, was compelled to play out the match at his opponent's dictation.

Temperamentally he was not as sound as he might have been, although he had plenty of determination and will to win. Highly strung, Wood concealed emotion by a baffling air of serenity. His tennis was instinctive—few young players have displayed such natural cleverness on court.

In 1927, the Centre Court was astonished by one of the first round matches in the men's singles. It was Lacoste against an unknown 15-year-old American boy, Sydney Wood—who marched into the vast arena clad in white plus-fours and golfing stockings. He seemed in no way perturbed by the fact that his opponent was ranked No. 1 in tennis and had just beaten the great Tilden in Paris. Even in that first appearance Wood showed signs of genius in his backhand and volleying—and he won five games entirely on merit, 6-1, 6-3, 6-1.

In 1928, Wood lost in the third round of the French championship 6-1, 6-0, 7-5 to Cochet. He then returned to Wimbledon to defeat Nigel Sharpe, one of the most difficult stone-wallers, 10-8, 6-1, 12-10, before losing to the hard-hitting of Frenchman Pierre Landry 4-6, 6-1, 6-1, 8-6.

Wood's best performances in 1929 were to extend John Doeg to 6-2, 4-6, 6-3, 11-9 in the third round at Forest Hills—and to defeat H. W. Austin 9-7, 6-3 at Los Angeles. Austin was a Wimbledon semi-finalist that year.

1930 secured Wood a No. 4 ranking in America—and a place in his country's Davis Cup team. At Seabright, Ellsworth Vines had reached the final hitting his way through Hunter and Frank Shields. He was expected to knock Wood off court. The latter, however, showed his early knowledge of tactics in reducing his opponent's terrific power by keeping a good length and hitting at half-pace. Vines, forced to make his own speed and demoralised by the way Wood handled his services, lost 6-2, 6-2, 6-0.

At Southampton, Lott, Shields and Allison fell before Wood's inspired volleying. This augured well for Forest Hills where he defeated Wilbur Coen 6-2, 1-6, 6-1, 6-4, in an early round. But in the semi-final he met Shields on one of the latter's good days. Shields crashed over a series of service aces and Wood had to admit defeat 6-2, 6-3, 4-6, 6-3.

With the passing of Tilden from amateur tennis, Wood and Shields were nominated for Wimbledon in 1931.

On his return to the Centre Court after an absence of three years, no one would now have recognised the little boy in plus-fours who was such a delight to the cartoonists. In his place was a 19-year-old sandy, scheming—but smiling—college student. Cochet's unexpected first-round defeat by Nigel Sharpe made things easier for Wood, who was expecting to contest the quarter-final against the Frenchman.

It looked as though another seed would fall when Wood was confronted by the enterprising volleying of New Zealander Cam Malfroy. Wood survived an extended battle 6-3, 10-12, 10-8, 6-4. In the semi-final Wood led Perry 4-0 and then lost the next six games. He proceeded to dislocate his opponent's hard-hitting tennis by a judicious mixture of pace—and with his own volleying improving—Wood took the next three sets 6-2, 6-4, 6-2.

This was his last match, for in the Shields-Borotra semi-final, Shields emerged triumphant but with a sprained ankle. In view of Davis Cup commitments, Shields gave Wood a walk-over in the final —a disappointment to both players and to the Centre Court.

The victorious Americans, however, bowed to Britain in the Inter-

Zone final of the Davis Cup. Wood, superior in smash and service to Austin, lacked the Englishman's deep steady forehand. He lost 2-6, 6-0, 8-6, 7-5, after pulling up from 1-5 in the fourth set. Perry, too, reversed the Wimbledon result beating Wood 6-3, 8-10, 6-3, 6-3. He gave the American some of his own "slow-balling" tactics. Both men were guilty of many errors, but Perry, physically stronger, was prepared to run miles retrieving Wood's deep shots.

Wood was very unhappy over the whole rubber. His victory over Perry had been confidently expected to settle the issue. He complained that his captain, Sam Hardy, had criticised him after his defeat by Austin and had unnerved him for his next match against Perry.

These losses continued in America. At Newport, Wood beat Doeg 6-1, 6-1, 8-6, but retired in the semi-final to Perry with the Englishman leading 6-1, 5-7, 2-6, 6-1, 6-5, 40-30. Wood was a victim of cramp at this stage. At Forest Hills he lost the third round to F. Bowden 2-6, 6-0, 6-8, 6-3, 6-3, and reporters complained that Wood's overconfidence caused his downfall.

Although he was Wimbledon champion, Wood was not selected for the Davis Cup in 1932. Instead, he came to Europe on a private tour. At Paris in "the most memorable match of my career" Wood lost to Lacoste. The Frenchman captured twelve of the first thirteen games to lead 6-0, 6-1. The third set went to Wood 6-3. After the interval (to quote Wood) "the ball crossed the net 10,000 times". The American was hoping to out-last and out-steady Lacoste and a feast of beautiful driving gave him the desperate fourth set 8-6. Lacoste was tiring, but he was firmer, if far less venturesome, and amidst pandemonium he struggled through the last set 7-5.

The beauty and variety of Wood's tennis was displayed in every match that brought him to the Wimbledon quarter-final where Cochet should have opposed him. Again the Frenchman had disappeared and it was Japanese Jiroh Satoh who confronted the holder.

This contest between American aggression and Japanese guile thrilled a packed Centre Court. Wood's service was much stronger, but Satoh placed his deliveries so cunningly that control of the ensuing rally was his entirely, and he won several service games to love.

Satoh won the first set 7-5 with a love game. Three love games helped him to lead 4-2 in the second set. Wood took three games brilliantly to lead 5-4, but the stoic Satoh pocketed the set, 7-5. He rested in the third set losing it 6-2. The Japanese then led 4-1 in the fourth set—lost three games to Wood's net-rushing—but again broke service for 5-4 and then took the last game to love.

This fascinating encounter produced one of the best matches in the championship, and one cartoonist added the remark, "Mr. Wood proved he was a great loser. His smile in defeat was as wide as anything seen at Wimbledon this year."

At Forest Hills, too, the "Last Eight" proved fatal to the ex-champion. Wood lost to Allison 5-7, 6-3, 6-2, 6-4. The Texan's straightforward hard-hitting usually overcame Wood's manœuvres.

In 1933, Wood confined his tennis to America. At Forest Hills he made Crawford (newly crowned at Wimbledon) fight for his life in the fourth round. A two-hour spectacle—a feature of which was the beautiful backhand of both contestants—resulted in a victory for Australia 6-4, 6-4, 2-6, 8-6.

Wood defeated a somewhat battle-weary Vines at Dixie. At Rye he struck his greatest form of the season. He defeated Lester Stoeffen and then gave a polished display to crush Clifford Sutter in the final 6-1, 6-4, 6-4.

With Vines out of tennis, Wood and Shields re-formed the Davis Cup team in 1934. Under the captaincy of Dick Williams—whom he partnered at Wimbledon—Wood was much happier.

Twenty-two Davis Cup players competed at Queen's Club in 1934. Wood gave such a peerless exhibition at this tournament that several critics backed him for Wimbledon. He beat Stoeffen in a terrific match 3-6, 18-16, 6-3, and then, aided by raking drives and "Cochet-like" volleys, defeated Shields 11-9, 6-0 in the final.

At Wimbledon, Wood disposed of South African Vernon Kirby comfortably to enter the semi-final. His next match was a thrill-laden five-setter against Perry that provided the greatest excitement of the championship. The Englishman was in better physical condition and showed, possibly, greater fighting spirit, but Wood produced some magical tennis. His plan to upset Perry by varied pace nearly succeeded. In the final set with Perry leading 4-3, Wood succumbed to nerves and lost the eighth game by a double-fault. Another tragedy for America—a net-cord—gave Perry victory 6-3, 3-6, 7-5, 5-7, 6-3.

In the Davis Cup Inter-Zone final Wood lost to Vivian McGrath 7-5, 6-4, 1-6, 9-7. He had beaten McGrath set-less at Wimbledon, but was plagued by foot-faults and double-faults. He recovered his form for his match against Crawford winning 6-3, 9-7, 4-6, 4-6, 6-2. In the last set the American produced tennis that made the critics gasp. There was nothing Crawford liked better than chess-board manœuvres but he was frequently outwitted by Wood's plotting. Rally after rally terminated with Wood's glorious backhand down the line.

Wood lost another tremendous match in the Challenge Round against Perry 6-1, 4-6, 5-7, 6-0, 6-3. They were expected to contest the U.S. final, but the "semi" saw Wood beaten by Wilmer Allison 6-3, 6-2, 6-3.

H. W. " Bunny " Austin, the Englishman who introduced shorts to the Centre Court.   A great stylist and a wonderful Davis Cup player, he reached the Wimbledon Final in 1932 and 1938.

Frederick J. Perry whose overwhelming attack gained great glory for Britain. Wimbledon Champion in 1934, 1935 and 1936. Now an American and a professional.

Two famous Californians, Miss Helen Jacobs (Champion in 1936) and Miss Alice Marble (Champion in 1939) enter the Centre Court for the Semi-Final in 1938. Miss Jacobs won 6–4, 6–4.

The last meeting . . . the battle of the " Helens " terminates in an unfortunate Final at Wimbledon in 1938.

In 1935, at his own request, Wood was omitted from the Davis Cup team, but he came over to Wimbledon. He met Crawford in the quarter-final, and lost the first two sets through volleying mistakes against a man determined not to forsake his base line. Then Wood improved and squared the match, but had little energy left with which to fight the deciding set. Crawford won 6-4, 6-3, 6-8, 5-7, 6-1.

In the American championships, Wood defeated Gregory Mangin and B. M. Grant to reach the final. Here he encountered Allison in top form and was defeated 6-2, 6-2, 6-3. At the end of the year Wood underwent an operation. By 1936 he had not recovered his old form and lost to H. M. Culley at Forest Hills 6-4, 5-7, 6-3, 6-3. Culley was No. 14 in America, ranked nine places lower than Wood.

America hoped Wood's health might allow him to join the Davis Cup team in 1937. At Southampton, however, he collapsed through exhaustion in a three-set match against Riggs. At Forest Hills his form was watched anxiously. In the fourth round against Frank Parker (the only player to take a set off Budge at Wimbledon that summer) Wood gave a dazzling display. Winner after winner escaped the steadiest player in America to give Wood the first two sets. He threw the third to re-charge his batteries—and then attacking again was within a stroke of 4-0 in the fourth. Here his stamina failed and he played out the rest of the match to give Parker a complete victory, 3-6, 4-6, 6-1, 6-3, 6-0.

But in 1938 he did come back, and although he limited his appearance in tournaments he achieved a No. 5 world ranking. In the U.S. quarter-final, his low volleying and killing against Grant was the best seen that year. Wood won 6-2, 6-3, 6-2, but went down in the next round to Budge 6-3, 6-3, 6-3.

1939 proved Wood's last year in serious tennis. He made his exit in the third round at Forest Hills beaten by Grant 6-3, 16-14, 6-4. Nevertheless, he was often ranked highly in America during the war years. In 1942 Wood-Ted Schroeder lost the U.S. doubles final to Mulloy-Talbert, and as late as 1948 Wood lost the third round at Forest Hills to Mulloy 8-6, 6-4, 10-8. After this defeat Wood asked, "Can anyone lend me a pair of legs to walk to the club-house?"

One of his greatest blows was the loss of a scrap-book depicting Wood's career which he had kept for his tennis-mad son.

Later, Wood experimented with his famous backhand and produced a two-handed stroke declaring it extended his tennis "life" by five years.

Sydney Wood was one of the most interesting players of his day. On form he was dazzling, and on those occasions he was second to Cochet only as the wonder shot-maker of the 'thirties.

F

12

Five-Foot Fraulein

A MAN and a girl are having an after-dinner drink in their Riviera hotel. The man is tall, tanned, a typical 37-year-old American. His five-foot companion is a German brunette, the picture of dainty prettiness.

The drinks are surprisingly soft. The man is in training, the girl even more so. She takes life seriously, this pocket Venus. Too dam' seriously, thinks the man. People passing whisper, "Look, they're together again. I hear they are engaged".

The background is exotic, the setting romantic, yet conversation waxes warm, even hostile. The man's sardonic smile is, however, a mask. He has not acted on Broadway for nothing.

The season is spring, the year is 1930. Bill Tilden and Cilly Aussem are discussing a subject dear to both their hearts—Cilly's tennis.

All Tilden's male protégés had been disappointments. Here he felt sure was a world-beater. Helen Wills was now Mrs. Moody, her tennis playing years were accordingly numbered. Lili d'Alvarez was on the decline. Cilly, with her flashing forehand and Lenglen-like accuracy, was their natural successor. She could overcome lack of stature and stamina—if only she overcame her delusion that defeat was a disgrace.

To this end Tilden admitted, "risking a row". In response to Cilly's agitation over losing to her friend, Elizabeth Ryan, he replied indifferently, "Nobody cares, anyhow". "Won't you mind if we lose?" demanded Cilly hotly. They had just teamed up together. Tilden grinned and shook his head. The Fraulein stared dumbfounded at the great man of tennis. The shock shattered her, but assured her of a place in the history of the game.

It was a marathon win 6-2, 4-6, 6-0 over Simonne Mathieu in the 1927 French championships that brought Cilly to notice. Several rallies contained over fifty strokes. But at her first Wimbledon, where her vivacious looks registered tremendous photo appeal, Cilly lost the second round 6-3, 6-2 to 16-year-old Betty Nuthall.

1928 . . . and Cilly proved her courage in an amazing second round match in Paris. Down 2-6, 2-5 to the fierce forehand of Mrs. Holcroft-Watson, Cilly, in desperation, retaliated with aggressive backhand cross-courts—and did not lose another game!

She failed to win more than three games against Helen Wills in her next match, but was seeded at Wimbledon soon after. Here, provoking errors by a well-timed defence, she led Lili d'Alvarez 5-1 in the quarter-final. The Spaniard then produced an attack that swamped Cilly (7-5, 6-2).

Depressed—and, to her mind, disgraced—Cilly was also insulted. She never liked d'Alvarez and the winner had not removed her cardigan!

Cilly suffered from eye inflammation throughout 1929. Her best effort was to beat Bobby Heine in Paris 5-7, 6-3, 6-4 before losing the semi-final to Simonne Mathieu 8-6, 2-6, 6-2. At Wimbledon she fell before the looped returns of Joan Ridley 8-6, 6-1 in the fourth round.

Cilly still often served under-arm. Her backhand was sound, but she frequently ran around it, little scampering feet lessening the dangerous opening of the forehand court. Delicate health and defeatism were her greatest enemies.

It was here that Tilden entered her life. Cajoled, coaxed and counselled, Cilly realised that difficult matches were stepping stones to greatness. The thrill of a hard encounter was to her a new experience.

Her game assumed new power. Cilly attacked with her backhand, her forehand raked the lines. She served over-arm and smashed with confidence. The spirit of Tilden was also manifest in her new enjoyment of tennis.

They won in Paris in 1930, defeating Cochet-Mrs. Whittingstall (holders) 6-4, 6-4. In singles, Cilly lost the semi-final 6-2, 6-1 to Helen Wills. "Never mind, you beat Ryan"—4-6, 6-1, 6-0 in the quarter-final.

At Wimbledon, Cilly "exhibiting control worthy of Suzanne" overwhelmed Helen Jacobs 6-2, 6-1. But in a thrilling semi-final against Elizabeth Ryan the Fraulein sprained her ankle at 4-all in the third set. She fainted and St. John Ambulance men carried her away in the most dramatic exit seen on the Centre Court.

Tilden left amateur tennis in 1930 and the rumoured romance never materialised, but his hopes were justified in 1931.

In Paris, Cilly beat d'Alvarez 6-0, 7-5, and her angled shots defeated hard-hitting Betty Nuthall 8-6, 6-1 in the final. At Wimbledon, nobody could out-place her. Resembling perpetual motion, her delightful footwork enabled Cilly to retrieve any shot.

In the semi-final a terrific drive from Simonne Mathieu knocked Cilly over. She bounded up, flashed across court and delivered a spectacular winner—to Simonne's dismay and the spectators' delight. Cilly triumphed 6-0, 2-6, 6-3.

To her consternation, her doctor advised her to withdraw on finals day against Hilde Krahwinkel (Sperling). Cilly refused and, relying on defence, out-steadied the great stonewaller, 6-2, 7-5. It was tedious tennis, Cilly volleying only once.

This match almost finished her career. After undergoing a delayed appendicitis operation Cilly resumed playing too soon. She retired at set-all to Betty Nuthall in Paris in 1932 and could not defend at Wimbledon. Asked about her plans Cilly burst into tears declaring her tennis was finished. According to Tilden the old defeatist element had revived.

But she did come back in 1934 saving six match points in the toughest battle of the French championship against Jadwiga Jedrze-jowska 3-6, 6-4, 8-6. She then beat Kay Stammers 6-4, 6-2, before losing the semi-final to the ultimate champion, Peggy Scriven (7-5, 6-3).

At Wimbledon, Cilly won four rounds, losing five games, but in the quarter-final, on her last Centre Court appearance, she was out-played by Helen Jacobs 6-0, 6-2. She regained prestige by three wins over Peggy Scriven after Wimbledon.

Tennis dresses were on the wane. Not for Cilly, who could be terse when roused. "They should see their back views" was her comment.

A secret wedding to Italian Count Della Corte Brae took place in Munich in March, 1936. Cilly accompanied her husband to Libya where a jungle fever seriously affected her eyesight. They returned to Europe but Cilly never re-entered tennis.

In her day increasing stress was being laid on shorts and stamina. This charming Contessa proved, however, she could become world champion without forsaking any femininity.

13

A Volcano Arrives at Wimbledon

IT is not a rarity to see a cannon-ball service on the Centre Court . . . sometimes a smash has almost bounded up into the Royal Box . . . many a devastating drive has been dispatched by an unexpected deadly volley. But no champion has generated such continuous withering speed as H. Ellsworth Vines, the 20-year-old Californian who hit Wimbledon in such cyclonic fashion in 1932.

On court this likeable young man was no Borotra. He looked grim, almost forbidding until a sudden smile acknowledging an opponent's winning shot would transform his expression. The possessor of a gangling, Gary Cooper outline, Vines walked with very slow deliberate movements.

Vines often wore a white peaked cap. Shorts came into fashion during his tournament days, but he never adopted them.

The Californian built his tennis on terrific, but controlled, speed. His 128 miles per hour service involving slight lift and spin was a terror to his opponents. It was his greatest weapon—and even at the end of his tennis career Vines averaged two aces per game in his exhibition matches against Donald Budge.

His smash was equally lethal and was beautifully placed. If he had to jump for the lob, Vines seemed to be able to stretch his already long body twice its normal length. Cochet had such respect for Vines's overhead, that he only offered the American two lobs in their semifinal meeting at Wimbledon in 1933.

The ideal position for the waist-high drive, Vines had a murderous forehand and a very good backhand. His flat-hit volleys terminated many rallies. Added to all this fire, was a phlegmatic yet determined temperament that played a great part in his amazing success story.

Vines made tennis appear very easy and there was much savage beauty in his game. In 1930 he won the Pacific South West singles in the presence of Dick Williams, famous team-mate of Tilden and Johnston. Williams drew the authorities' attention on to Vines declaring the young man was the best thing in U.S. tennis for a decade.

Williams proved no mean prophet. Sydney Wood and Frank Shields, America's Davis Cup pair, had mopped up Wimbledon between them in 1931. But in the American season Vines superseded them whilst his national ranking soared from No. 10 to No. 1. Not even Tilden could claim such a glorious run of trans-Atlantic tournament triumphs.

Only one fellow countryman—George Lott—succeeded in toppling Vines in 1931. This was in the New Orleans semi-final won by Lott (8-6 in the fifth set). Vines captured the U.S. Clay Court championship with a 6-3, 6-3, 6-3 defeat of Keith Gledhill, his doubles partner and closest friend. Then came Seabright in the final of which Vines clashed with John Doeg, the U.S. national champion. After a tremendous five-set struggle in which both players capitalized on their terrific overhead strength, Vines overhauled Doeg, who had led by two sets and 3-1 (10-12, 6-8, 6-3, 8-6, 6-1).

Doeg had won two victories in the Longwood Bowl—one more triumph and he could retire the famous trophy. But in a desperately fought final he had to yield again to Vines whose backhand passing shots saved the day (4-6, 6-3, 6-3, 3-6, 6-3). Still another triumph was recorded at Newport where Shields, Van Ryn and Perry fell before the young Californian, now recognised in America as Tilden's successor.

It was Vines's ability to keep on hitting throughout an extended duel that made him so formidable. And the depth and pace of his great forehand broke up the net attack or the base-line steadiness of players of top class calibre. Although Doeg was champion, the seeding committee had no option but to award Vines the top honour at Forest Hills in 1931.

A win over Berkeley Bell brought Vines to the U.S. semi-final. Down two sets to the steady driving of Fred Perry, Vines, whose own control was singularly lacking, scorned caution. He hit even harder, and with Perry losing his concentration over a disputed decision in the fourth set, Vines drew level. He got well into the fight and Perry was forced to admit defeat from this calm cannon-balling Californian (4-6, 3-6, 6-4, 6-4, 6-3).

10,000 spectators gathered to watch Lott try to shake Vines in the final. By lobs, and by a judicious mixture of loops and cut shots, Lott attempted to upset the rhythm of his opponent's ruthless control. He led 5-2 in the fourth set but went down before a barrage of drives and volleys that frequently outpaced him by half the court (7-9, 6-3, 9-7, 7-5).

A remarkable season was completed when Vines beat Van Ryn, Mangin and Perry at Los Angeles—and followed by a win at San Francisco again claiming Perry as a victim (6-3, 21-19, 6-0). In this match Vines served twenty-three aces in the second set.

France was now champion country. But their Davis Cup committee, which had breathed a sigh of relief over Tilden's departure from tennis in 1930, were now perturbed over Vines's exploits. Ill-health had forced Lacoste out of the game and the committee looked anxiously at Cochet, now over thirty and even less inclined to train as in the days when Tilden was his greatest menace.

When an uncertain Vines lost to Hopman at Queen's Club in 1932, French hopes rose. Vines failed to impress the critics at the start of his European trip. His fine service was neutralised by double-faults and Cochet, seeded No. 1, was firm favourite at Wimbledon.

Usually the holder opens proceedings on the Centre Court. This year although Sydney Wood was defending his championship the honour was presented to Vines. And as it happened he hit the last ball there.

The leading Frenchmen made early departures. Cochet taking things too casually failed against Ian Collins, whereas Borotra fell before the power game of Spaniard Enrique Maier. It was against Maier in the quarter-final that Vines gave the Centre Court a taste of his devastating attack. So far in the championship he had played somewhat subdued tennis.

Stimulated, perhaps, by Maier's big-hitting game, Vines unleashed his fury. His cannonball service made the Spaniard's ginger-laden delivery look innocuous, and in annihilating his man 6-2, 6-3, 6-2, Vines scored the quickest victory of the last eight.

Even more devastating was Vines's 40-minute defeat of Crawford. The Australian's beautifully balanced game had overcome Perry, but Vines out-hit Crawford, 6-2, 6-1, 6-3. Vines produced winners off Crawford's powerful services, while he captured four of his own service games to love and won three more to fifteen. One service game yielded four aces.

This one-sided massacre on a damp court drew from Cochet "Pretty good—wonderful—never seen anything like it".

Austin's classic tennis had beaten Shields and Satoh, but from 3-all in the final, he was powerless against Vines. The American started to drive Austin's services to the corners of the court and to hurl down a stream of aces. He won the first set 6-4—murdered Austin's beautifully produced strokes to win the second set 6-2—and finished with an incredible display of power tennis to capture the last set to love.

Austin, no doubt demoralised, made little effort to stem the 45-minute avalanche which, to one Davis Cup player was "terrifying". Vines, who became champion with a service ace, was a friend of his opponent and photographs showed him offering anxious sympathy rather than receiving congratulations!

Excitement mounted in Paris over the impending Cochet-Vines clash in the Davis Cup Challenge Round. But on the opening day, in the first match, 33-year-old Borotra handled Vines's service with a master touch. Deserting his usual volleying Borotra, parcelling out

87

his physical reserves, captured the first two sets to the frenzied delight of the crowd.

Then with Vines improving—the American had started nervously—the Frenchman yielded the third set. At 3-all in the fourth it seemed that youth would triumph—but Borotra, throwing his last reserve of stamina into a net attack, now gave Vines a demonstration of what was meant by the "Bounding Basque".

He caught the widest passing shot, he buried the deepest lob. Vines bowed to the French storm—and when he netted Borotra's first match point the crowd rose in uproar. After this 6-4, 6-2, 3-6, 6-4 victory Borotra and Vines were presented to the French President.

Although the Cochet-Vines match had no bearing on the result—Borotra had already won the trophy by beating Allison—there was much personal prestige at stake. Cochet had achieved a reputation for pulling matches out of the fire—this time it was his opponent who extricated himself from an apparently hopeless position.

Down two sets to Cochet's wizardry, Vines, after a consultation with his captain then abandoned caution. As at Wimbledon, he hit out fearlessly. A feast of beautiful tennis followed, Vines's deep drives preventing even Cochet from ambling up to the net. The fourth set produced a magnificent spectacle, but when Cochet lost that at 8-6, he could not avert defeat. To the amazement of the crowd—Cochet had not lost a Davis Cup match since 1927—Vines won 4-6, 0-6, 7-5, 8-6, 6-2.

Had the fate of the Cup been at stake it was claimed that Cochet would have never let the match continue for so long—he would have clinched victory in the third set. To restore his superiority in tennis the little Frenchman accordingly entered the U.S. championships that autumn.

Vines was seeded No. 1 amongst the home players, Cochet was placed first amongst the overseas contingent.

Both duly reached the finals. Vines, after defeating Gledhill and Lester Stoeffen set-less, all but when down in the semi-final to Clifford Sutter (conqueror of Austin). Heart-breaking in his steadiness, Sutter only acknowledged a reverse because Vines was able to produce a a cannon-ball service when facing defeat. In one of the longest semi-finals ever played at Forest Hills, Vines was victorious (4-6, 8-10, 12-10, 10-8, 6-1).

In the final Vines beat Cochet 6-4, 6-4, 6-4 and established himself as the leading player in tennis. Cochet was unlucky in having to complete his semi-final against Allison that morning and he handled Vines's services superbly. But although the Californian could only produce six aces, it was Vines's ability to keep Cochet from the net that was the deciding factor. Time and again a terrific drive would hit the line neutralising Cochet's clever mixture of defence and attack.

His win made Vines the idol of American sport. On 1st October, two days after his twenty-first birthday, Vines was married.

The young Californian now seemed poised for a Tilden-like career. He would, however, have done well to have taken a leaf out of Cochet's book and rested from tennis—instead, he accompanied an American team on an ill-fated Australian tour. Vines's only victory was at Sydney where he accounted for Van Ryn, and in the final Allison, 4-6, 6-1, 2-6, 6-4, 7-5. In the Victorian final, Crawford giving a beautiful polished display beat Vines 1-6, 6-4, 6-4, 2-6, 6-4.

Crawford stood well into Vines's thunderbolts. He seemed undisturbed by the torrid heat whereas the American, stale after three years continuous tennis, was playing a mechanical tired game. In January, 1933, occurred the biggest shock of the tour. This was in the Australian quarter-final when 17-year-old Vivian McGrath hitting a (then) novel two-handed backhand defeated Vines 6-2, 2-6, 8-6, 7-5. Reports from Australia described the Wimbledon champion as "weary and overplayed".

It was not an encouraging tour, particularly as experts were now tipping Crawford as the next Wimbledon winner. Back in America, Tilden made Vines a tempting professional offer which according to Tilden, Vines found "deeply interesting". Furthermore, Tilden assured Vines that if he lost to Crawford or Cochet at Wimbledon the offer still stood.

These negotiations reached the ears of the U.S. authorities. When Tilden wrote Vines wishing him luck in Europe in 1933, Vines's captain insisted on reading the contents even declaring he would bar Vines from the Davis Cup unless he acquiesced.

This bickering did not help Vines at Wimbledon. Nevertheless, although he was by no means the conquering hero of 1932, the Californian's speed was greater than that of any other competitor. His accuracy, however, was not so much in evidence as in the previous year.

His dynamic service took him to the semi-final after a victory over Czech Roderic Menzel 6-2, 6-4, 3-6, 6-3. Here before a record crowd he beat Cochet 6-2, 8-6, 3-6, 6-1. The second set saved by Vines, who scrambled back volleys from all over the court, settled the issue. Cochet did wonders at the net but his backhand (on that day very erratic) was a source of profit to Vines. In the fourth set Vines's cyclonic attack left Cochet standing.

Vines, so violent, and Crawford, so classic, provided one hundred minutes of thrills in the final. Crawford yielded first blood to Vines's service aces but the Australian, refusing to leave his trustworthy baseline, won the long vital second set. Even Vines's strong serving arm was now feeling the strain—fewer cannon-balls were scoring and the pressure on Crawford accordingly lessened.

Both men then threw a set apiece—to resume a desperate fight in the fifth. Play had been brilliant and resourceful and at 5-4, Crawford suddenly adopted an unexpected net attack. This ruse caught Vines unprepared. He netted twice in surprise to give the Australian a magnificent victory 4-6, 11-9, 6-2, 2-6, 6-4.

In the Davis Cup Inter-Zone final in Paris a few weeks later, Vines's game touched bottom. He was routed by a super-steady Austin 6-1, 6-1, 6-4. The Englishman handled Vines's deliveries much more easily than he had done on the fast turf of Wimbledon in 1932.

In his last Davis Cup match Vines sprained his ankle in the fourth set against Perry. He gallantly continued only to faint in a sprawling heap on court when Perry reached match point. The score in Perry's favour was 1-6, 6-0, 4-6, 7-5, 7-6, (40-15).

Back home Vines lost 6-2, 6-4, 6-4 to Shields at Newport. He was completely out of favour with officialdom and to aggravate his depressed frame of mind a committee was formed to question his amateur status.

Vines, fully vindicated, declared he was overjoyed. Tension released, the Californian reacted. Now only a shadow of his former glory, he lost in the fourth round at Forest Hills succumbing to the phenomenal retrieving skill of Bitsy Grant 6-3, 6-3, 6-3.

In October 1933, Vines followed Cochet into the professional ranks. His decision shook the U.S. authorities, many of whom believed (as was later proved) that Vines was still their greatest player. Moreover, no champion had renounced amateur status so soon in his career and it was feared that Vines's decision might have far-reaching effects.

Vines beat Tilden over a series and never lost to Cochet. In 1934 he played wonderful tennis at Wembley beating Martin Plaa, Hans Nusslein and Tilden (9-7, 7-5, 6-2).

The Californian completely regained his form in 1935—and according to Tilden, Vines's forehand was the hardest and steadiest he had ever encountered. Vines won the French professional title beating Plaa and Nusslein. At Southport he overcame Ramillon and then Tilden (6-1, 6-8, 4-6, 6-2, 6-2). The man who had slumped so disastrously in 1933 finished a wonderful season at Wembley with victories over Stoeffen (4-6, 6-2, 6-8, 6-1, 9-7) and Tilden (6-1, 6-3, 5-7, 3-6, 6-3).

In 1935, Tilden and Vines could have beaten any American Davis Cup team. The authorities still looked on them with suspicion. When Vines and Tilden offered to train any prospective champion that year they were turned down—as being old-fashioned!

After touring China and Japan with Tilden in 1936, Vines defeated Stoeffen on an American tour. He drew level with Perry 37-all in 1937. Although forty pounds heavier and devoting much time to golf, Vines defeated Perry 49-35 in 1938 and lost to Budge by the narrow margin of 17-22 in the following year.

With animosity forgotten, Vines was asked to coach 18-year-old Jack Kramer in 1939. His skill helped to produce another champion.

The Californian has become one of America's great professional golfers. Mrs. Vines had said that her feet preferred watching his tennis matches!

His achievements at tennis, the game that first made him famous, remain outstanding. A shooting star, Vines rocketed across the amateur sky in 1932 in never forgotten fashion.

14

One of the Classics

THE young unknown man had just taken the World No. 4 to 4-6, 6-3, 1-6, 7-5, 6-4 in the semi-final. The star, recognised as a renowned and redoubtable volleyer, had encountered a stream of elegant passing shots and a succession of dislocating lobs that forced him back to an unwelcome baseline.

The youth was 19-year-old Jack Crawford—his famous opponent was Jean Borotra—the match was in the Australian championships in 1928. After having been compelled to summon all his reserves of stamina and nervous energy Borotra gasped "Nowhere have I seen a young player of such promise".

Crawford was instantly acclaimed by local sports writers as the best thing in Australian tennis since the heyday of Norman Brookes.

The man who had given Borotra such a thrilling run for his money developed a game of elegance and ease without crushing power anywhere. There was an atmosphere of majesty and magnificence in his approach to tennis, and as an artist, Tilden considered him second only to Cochet.

When on form, Crawford's timing was perfect. But he was dependent on the fineness of his touch and if this were disturbed, he would present a series of double-faults and netted forehands. But even when he played badly—and few champions have performed so indifferently when off colour—he put a sweeping graceful action into all his strokes as though it were a matter of supreme indifference to him where they landed. The most spectacular shot of his artistic répertoire was a graceful sliced backhand possibly the most photographed backhand in tennis.

Tall and heavily built, Crawford looked older than his years. A long-sleeved cricket shirt—the Australian sometimes even neglected to roll up the sleeve of his right arm—long trousers and his famous square-headed racket, lent a background to this mature appearance. His dress, his quiet demeanour and his delightful style of tennis bore a distinct resemblance to R. F. Doherty.

Patterson, Hawkes and Anderson had been dominating Australian tennis for a decade. In 1928, Crawford showed his mettle by overcoming them all in inter-state matches. In the Victorian singles final he fought Patterson for three hours before admitting defeat (7-5, 6-1,

92

5-7, 1-6, 7-5) and as a result of his brilliance was given a place in the Davis Cup team.

On his first European trip, Crawford won the Roman championship. He lost to Lacoste 6-0, 6-1, 7-5 in the quarter-final of the French championships but responded much better to the faster surface of Wimbledon. It was the first of eight visits to the Centre Court where the grace of his game guaranteed an immediate following. No Australian had been more popular—no sportsman has done his country better service.

In the third round he beat Dr. J. C. Gregory, one of England's best players 9-7, 6-4, 6-3. Gregory, on his day, could be devastating overhead, but he sacrificed a 5-2 lead in the first set and with that his chance of victory.

This win brought Crawford against Borotra (seed No. 5). The Australian played a lovely match. He could hold his own in the baseline rallies often scoring with a disguised cross-court backhand. But a baseline duel was not Borotra's idea—and he volleyed his way to victory, 3-6, 6-4, 6-2, 7-9, 6-4.

Some critics now declared that Crawford's position inside the baseline was a weakness for a man who did not frequently rush the net. But the Australian, aided by wonderful anticipation, was seldom found out of position. Delicately poised, he possessed a Lacoste-like ability to "block" the fiercest shots—and to direct his returns into unexpected corners.

In 1930, Crawford returned to Europe as Davis Cup captain. It was, however, a disappointing tour, the Australian failing to reproduce his best tennis anywhere. He lost to Gregory easily in Paris 6-3, 6-2, 6-3, while at Wimbledon he did not survive the third round, going down to H. F. David 6-2, 6-3, 3-6, 6-4. Crawford redeemed himself by winning the mixed doubles with Miss Ryan beating the favourites Cochet-Mrs. Whittingstall in the semi-final, and in the final, Prenn-Fraulein Krahwinkel 6-1, 6-3.

On his return home Crawford, whose business was connected with sportswear, wanted to stage a sartorial exhibition. Officialdom refused but showed its appreciation of his tennis acumen by leaving the selection of Australia's next Davis Cup team to Crawford.

By 1931, he dominated the field at home. 2,000 turned out to see him defeat his great friend Hopman to become national champion for the first time. Other singles successes were recorded at Sydney and Melbourne.

A third appearance at Wimbledon in 1932 saw Crawford seeded for the first time (No. 8). He beat Gregory, Boussus and Olliff, and then displayed much all-court brilliance to defeat Fred Perry, seed No. 4, after two hours very good tennis 7-5, 8-6, 2-6, 8-6.

It did not do him much good, however. After forty minutes in the semi-final Crawford was hit out of the championship by a devastating Vines (6-2, 6-1, 6-3). The court was slippery but this did not affect the American who gave one of his most overpowering, fiery exhibitions. Vines served aces galore and treated Crawford's heavy deliveries with contempt.

America did Crawford great service by sending a team to Australia in the winter of 1932-1933. It gave him a chance to come to grips with the big-hitting game of the Americans. And of all the titles he held in Australia Crawford surrendered only one—at Sydney—where handicapped by a strained back which restricted running, he lost to Allison in the semi-final 7-5, 4-6, 6-2, 4-6, 6-3.

At Melbourne, Crawford achieved a great ambition—a revenge for his Wimbledon rout. Encouraged by his home supporters, indifferent to torrid heat, Crawford returned enough cannon-balls to overcome Vines in the final 1-6, 6-4, 6-4, 2-6, 6-4. His unflurried mobility, his angled passing shots (worthy of Cochet at his greatest) and his amazing steadiness broke up the American's "storm tactics".

A further U.S. setback took place in the Australian quarter-final where Vines lost to Vivian McGrath. The title was eventually retained by Crawford who beat Allison and Keith Gledhill (victor over McGrath).

Apart from his close friendship with Hopman—whose tennis-playing wife was a friend of tennis-playing Mrs. Crawford—the Australian champion had a great regard for young McGrath. This 17-year-old admired Crawford so much that he felt his captain's defeats as severely as the latter did himself. McGrath, Crawford, Adrian Quist and Don Turnbull made up the Davis Cup team in 1933.

That year Mrs. Crawford, whose presence was always a help to her husband, gave up tennis so that they could both concentrate on his matches. Crawford was favourite for the French title because of his successful winter against the American tourists. Cochet, the holder, was still a great player but not now in the form that had subdued Tilden and all comers for years.

In the quarter-final Crawford defeated Boussus 6-3, 6-3, 6-4. Jiro Satoh, the wily Japanese, had overcome Perry but his guile was powerless against Crawford who drove majestically to win 6-0, 6-2, 6-2. In the final Cochet produced brilliant tennis in the first set. Losing that, he was repeatedly trapped and wrong-footed by Crawford who defeated the Frenchman's net sorties by frequently coming in himself. Crawford won 8-6, 6-1, 6-3.

The Wimbledon seeding was Vines first, Crawford second and Cochet third. But on the opening day, Enrique Maier (who had sensationally defeated Borotra at Wimbledon in 1932) nearly disposed of Australian hopes. Crawford seemed to have the measure of his man when he won the first two sets 7-5, 6-4. Then Maier got his cannon-ball working and behind this he launched an offensive that threw Crawford temporarily out of gear. The third and fourth sets were taken by Maier (6-2 and 6-3).

Moreover, he broke service and led 4-2 in the fifth set. Crawford seemed to be weakening under the Spanish artillery. But he pulled himself together and resumed a rock-like regularity of return to sweep to 5-4. Maier reacted, and lost the last game to love.

A four-set win over Satoh 6-3, 6-4, 2-6, 6-4, gained Crawford a place in the final. The crisis came in the ninth game of the fourth set when the inscrutable Satoh was three times within a stroke of 5-4.

The final, before a packed, expectant Centre Court, revealed Crawford at his greatest. Fittingly, it gave him the game's most coveted crown. Vines, aided by dynamic aces, took the first set 6-4. He hit harder and wider, volleyed more frequently, and made his opponent cover much more ground. But Crawford, poised and perfectly balanced, stayed supremely steady. The long vital second set —a rich prize—went to Australia, 11-9.

Vines rested in the third set and lost it 6-2. Crawford followed suit in the fourth—6-2 to California.

Back to the fight came both warriors. Vines still produced magnificent attacking tennis, and was within a stroke of breaking through to lead 3-2. A volley saved Crawford whose resourceful defence took him to 5-4. He then cleverly and courageously altered his tactics, and came in to volley. Vines, in surprise, netted twice—to lose a love game!

Mrs. Crawford fainted and the stands rose to victor and vanquished. "The best tennis I have ever seen," declared Suzanne Lenglen excitedly. Mrs. Crawford, revived with smelling salts, could not wait. She ran to the men's dressing room to embrace her husband through the window.

It was Crawford's great desire to win the four major championships in one year. It seemed as though nothing could stop him when Vines lost to Grant at Forest Hills. Crawford beat Sydney Wood, Clifford Sutter and, in the semi-final, Frank Shields. While defeating Shields 7-5, 6-4, 6-3, Crawford had a heavy fall and said jokingly after rolling over, "Now I suppose Perry (the other finalist) will beat me".

Perry was playing brilliant tennis. He had recently lowered Cochet's colours in the Davis Cup, but no one expected him to do more than give Crawford a good game. That is no one except, possibly, Perry himself.

The final was contested on a hot, windy day. The first set went to Perry 6-3, the next two to Crawford 13-11, 6-4. The Australian

95

had speeded up during the third set and seemed to have the key to victory. During the 10-minute interval Crawford sat in the stand with his wife, while Perry wisely had a shower. Refreshed, Perry then launched an acrobatic net-attack that left Crawford standing. The Englishman was so agile that he was able to guess the direction of his opponent's sliced backhands, a feat no one else at Wimbledon had accomplished. He won the last two sets 6-0, 6-1.

It was a terrible disappointment to Crawford and seemed to affect his future matches with Perry. He admitted he would have to play better than he had done throughout 1933 to beat Perry that day. The Englishman appeared to have the same influence on Crawford's game as Cochet had against Tilden. It was Perry's extra speed of foot that unsettled the classic, deliberate stroking of the Australian.

Greeted with enthusiasm on his return home Crawford, however, stated he was "tennis-tired". A rumour that he had been offered £10,000 to tour professionally with Tilden, Cochet and Vines was refuted.

He defended his Victorian title in November but although he beat Hughes and Lee, he could not combat the sustained volleying offensive of Perry who won 6-4, 2-6, 6-4, 6-3. Crawford was ordered complete rest by his doctor and forgot tennis for a while but when he met Perry in the 1934 Australian final, he lost in straight sets 6-3, 7-5, 6-1.

The Australian could not retain the European titles he had won so brilliantly in 1933. The French championship, however, seemed in his grasp when Perry fell to de Stefani. Crawford dropped a set each to M. Sleem, Hughes and Boussus to reach the final. Here Von Cramm, very fit and mobile, won the first set but was then subjected to a brand of the best chess-like Crawford driving. At 5-4, in the fourth set the Australian was within a stroke of victory. After a wonderful rally, he hoisted a perfect lob to which Von Cramm replied with a spectacular smash.

Crawford was tiring and he lost his service, Von Cramm led 6-5 and two Australian double-faults helped him to win the next game. Don Turnbull brought Crawford a brandy but he could not summon up enough strength to keep back the virile German who converted defeat into victory (6-4, 7-9, 3-6, 7-5, 6-3).

At Wimbledon, Crawford developed "Wimbledon throat". He spent several days in bed between play but recovered to beat Lester Stoeffen 7-5, 2-6, 7-5, 6-0 and then gave an elegant exhibition to win his semi-final against Frank Shields (conqueror of Austin). "I couldn't have played better," was Shield's comment after surrendering 2-6, 4-6, 6-4, 6-3, 6-4.

Crawford led Perry 3-1 in the final. Then in a swift overwhelming

Baron Gottfried Von Cramm. This magnificent but unlucky German player lost the Wimbledon Final in 1935, 1936 and 1937.

Crimson-haired and very popular, Donald Budge (U.S.A.) brooked no opposition at Wimbledon in 1937 and 1938.

Robert L. Riggs, the wily little American who was never beaten at Wimbledon. In his one appearance in 1939, Riggs became triple Champion.

The Tricolour again! Yvon Petra, giant Frenchman, who cannon-balled his way to win Wimbledon in 1946.

rush Perry won twelve games, losing eight rallies. Crawford, run off his feet, was powerless to stem the torrent of volleys and smashes. But in the third set the battle was joined again. Crawford broke service to lead 5-4 but lost the next two games. At match point he served and ran in to volley—was foot-faulted—and then double-faulted! Few players have produced an attack comparable to Perry's onslaught in the middle of the match when he admitted he "went mad".

These reverses were offset by Crawford's magnificent tennis that winter in Australia where he controlled his wayward shots and regained the originality of his offensive tactics. In his best tennis for eighteen months, Crawford defeated Perry, now suffering from an overdose of competition 7-5, 2-6, 6-3, 1-6, 7-5 to win at Sydney. At Melbourne, Perry lost to Quist whom Crawford beat in the final 6-2, 8-6, 6-3.

In the 1935 Australian final, Crawford again overcame Perry (2-6, 6-4, 6-4, 6-4). The latter, not as agile as usual, could not cope with his opponent's length nor was he happy against Crawford's spinning services. The Australian used his "mascot" racket that had won Wimbledon—it was his favourite, having been re-strung dozens of times.

But Perry's slump proved a temporary one. A few months later he was back in marvellous form. At Paris he and Crawford contested the semi-final and the Englishman, ever at the net, triumphed 6-3, 8-6, 6-3.

At Wimbledon, a month later, this semi-final clash was repeated, Crawford having accounted for Sydney Wood, 6-4, 6-3, 6-8, 5-7, 6-1 in the quarter-final. Perry treated his great rival with respect, choosing his advances to the net with caution, but Crawford could not claim more than one set (6-2, 3-6, 6-4, 6-4). At both Wimbledon and Paris, Crawford and Quist carried off the doubles title.

In 1936, Crawford opened his Wimbledon campaign brilliantly. Dovetailing artistry and aggression he won four rounds without losing a set. But in the quarter-final he found Von Cramm too active. The German was kept at full stretch but Crawford, contributing to his own downfall by numerous double-faults, lost 6-1, 7-5, 6-4.

It was felt at this time that Crawford might make this his last Wimbledon. In 1937, however, although not in training, he was again sent abroad with the Davis Cup team.

At Wimbledon he was un-seeded, which excited some criticism. And to justify his supporters, Crawford on the opening day played some of the finest tennis of the meeting. He met and beat Czech Roderic Menzel, seed No. 7, 6-4, 7-9, 4-6, 6-3, 6-4. Both large men, they produced an ornate, magnificent spectacle. Crawford led 5-0 in the last set. Menzel pulled up to 4-5 but in the tenth game a brilliant backhand return of service won the match for Australia.

Crawford then went on to the quarter-final, there to encounter Von Cramm in a lively duel. The German won the first set 6-3 and the second (in which Crawford led 6-5) at 8-6. Then came an Australian revival. The next two sets 6-3, 6-2 were captured by Crawford, the crowd now applauding every winner he made.

At this stage, he had Von Cramm on the run. But at the start of the final set Crawford fell heavily. The German, much fitter, increased his pressure and won the last set 6-2. It was a great ending to Crawford's Wimbledon career. Untrained and unseeded, he had fought the World No. 2 to a standstill.

Still under thirty, Crawford's tennis was drawing to a close. He was an education to a partner, a pleasure to an opponent, a delight to the spectators. Tennis came to him with utmost ease. In a land of freak and ugly shots, his classical interpretation of the game remains outstanding.

15

"Dorothy Rounds up the Tennis"

AT her first tournament she brought her own tennis balls—after her first tournament, she shortened her tennis dress by two inches. Nobody connects a Sunday School mistress with sporting proclivities yet Dorothy Round proved that world champions do not spring entirely from self-possessed, sophisticated types.

A Dudley girl, Dorothy's fluent flat-hit sweeping strokes responded best to a fast grass court. Her beautiful backhand was described by some sports writers as second only to Suzanne's; her drop-shots were deadly, and since she possessed a gifted volleying touch, Dorothy could, on her day, play amazing tennis. But nerves were her enemy and sometimes played havoc with her service and forehand.

She learnt tennis on a home court with her three brothers. Strictly educated, Dorothy caused a minor international sporting crisis by refusing to play on Sundays in French and American tournaments.

Shyness hid a sense of humour. Crowds caused her to withdraw into her shell. Later in her career she was connected with a sportswear firm and then the Dorothy Round of 1928 was scarcely recognisable.

There was a marked physical resemblance between Dorothy and Fred Perry. They were both born in 1909 and both first played at Wimbledon in 1929. Perry became famous by defeating a foreign potentate—Italian de Morpurgo—in 1930. Dorothy followed suit in 1931 by her win over Spanish Lili d'Alvarez. In 1934, the English couple both registered their first Wimbledon singles victories—and it was with Dorothy Round that Perry won his last Wimbledon championship title in 1936.

Few women have practised harder. In junior tennis, however, Dorothy never enjoyed the success of Betty Nuthall—and it was Betty who beat her 6-1, 6-1 at Wimbledon in 1929.

Freda James provided Dorothy's departure from Wimbledon the next season 4-6, 6-3, 6-4. In 1931, however, the quiet Worcestershire player sprang into prominence when she became known as "The girl who beat Senorita d'Alvarez at Wimbledon". This happened in the third round and Dorothy's deep drives dislocated the Senorita's famous and favourite half-volley attack (6-3, 6-3). She survived until the quarter-final where the already ominous defence of Hilde Krahwinkel proved too strong (7-5, 6-3). Dorothy was rewarded by a nomination for the third singles in the Wightman Cup. She lost to the court-craft of Mrs. L. A. Harper, 6-3, 4-6, 9-7.

In 1932, she played second string for England in the international match. She won five games from Mrs. Moody and lost to Helen Jacobs 6-4, 6-3. At Wimbledon, however, she was hit out of the quarter-final—annihilated by the power of Helen Moody 6-0, 6-1.

No player has profited so much from defeat—no player has provided such meteoric advancement. Toiling at her tennis throughout the winter of 1932/33 Dorothy, in one year, developed into a potential Moody-beater.

She exhibited her phenomenal improvement at Bournemouth. Helen Jacobs and Simonne Mathieu (ranked respectively No. 2 and No. 3 in tennis) were competing, Dorothy's drop shots were too much for the fluent Frenchwoman (6-1, 7-5), and in the final she disclosed what a good match player she had become. On a slow court her paceful drives were at a disadvantage against the Jacobs chop. She accordingly took on her opponent at her own game and won 3-6, 6-2, 6-3.

Seeded No. 2 at Wimbledon, Dorothy had several backers for victory because of her disguised drop-shot, the only stroke considered likely to upset Mrs. Moody, always shy to leave her indomitable baseline. But first Helen Jacobs had to be overcome in the semi-final. With lethal serving and smashing, Miss Jacobs won the first set. Then Dorothy abandoned the lob and started getting her polished drives past the volleyer. The American tired in the heat and the third set went to Dorothy comfortably (4-6, 6-4, 6-2).

The final proved a never-forgotten drama. Brilliant tennis with the crowd applauding as the rivals changed court—then a novelty at Wimbledon—gave Mrs. Moody the first set. Then Dorothy swept the corners, volleyed whenever possible and produced those priceless drop-shots. No English girl had made Helen Moody work so hard for a decade.

Hearts thumped as Dorothy broke service for 7-6 in the second set. Helen, unperturbed, forced her opponent to over-hit for 7-all. The umpire announced "7-all"—but the linesman declared the ball hit the line.

Pandemonium mounted as Dorothy's plea that the point be awarded to Helen was refused. A question mark settled on the match. When two rallies later Dorothy won the first set Helen had surrendered for seven years, there was a feeling of uneasiness in the applause.

The stoic Californian regained her poise but, mentally, Dorothy was out of action. Helen won the third set tamely and merely by keeping the ball in play. "The best opponent I have met for a long time," was her comment after her 6-4, 6-8, 6-3 victory.

Back home, Dorothy received a diamond wristlet watch from her townsfolk in recognition of her Wimbledon efforts. But her next two ambitions—to win the Wightman Cup and to cross swords again with Mrs. Moody—were thwarted by Helen Jacobs.

Mrs. Moody was unwell and Helen II led America to victory in the Wightman Cup. The poor condition of the courts at Forest Hills favoured her spin-infested defence which prevailed against Dorothy's pace 6-4, 6-2. In the U.S. semi-final, too, Helen II was impregnable—she was to beat Mrs. Moody in her next match—and she overcame Dorothy 6-4, 5-7, 6-2.

In America, the English team adopted the new fashion of shorts and were criticised for their brevity. The Sunday school teacher, of course, received special attention.

Round and Jacobs had become great rivals—and great friends. Dorothy, at her volleying best, could defeat Helen's defence—any lapse and Helen's steadiness prevailed. This took place just before Wimbledon in the 1934 Wightman Cup, Helen winning 6-4, 6-4.

Few favoured Dorothy when she faced Helen in the Wimbledon final. But the sun-baked court was ideal for attack, and accompanied by cheers, she hit her way through the first set, 6-2. The Californian's great-hearted defence prevailed in an exciting second set, 7-5. And the tide seemed to be flowing in her favour when within a stroke of 3-1 in the third set, she crashed over an apparent winner only for Dorothy, on her knees, to scoop the ball back on the half-volley—as a net-cord!

Four clean hit winning drives and Dorothy led 3-2. Back came Helen and 3-all. Running like a hare, Dorothy again broke through for 4-3. Then came a succession of wonder volleys and the Centre Court rose to greet another girl champion (6-2, 5-7, 6-3).

Tension relaxed, Dorothy submitted to emotion. It was the gallant Californian who gently consoled her and helped to compose her before the inevitable cameras. Later she returned and with R. Miki defeated Austin-Mrs. Shepherd-Barron, 3-6, 6-4, 6-0 to win the mixed doubles causing the caption "Dorothy Rounds up the tennis".

To be Wimbledon champion means to have the world "gunning" for you—it gives opponents an added incentive to win. Dorothy, sensing this, seemed to fear difficult matches throughout 1935. She won the Australian singles but faltered before Kay Stammers' forehand in the Bournemouth semi-final (7-9, 6-2, 6-1). At Wimbledon, double-faults and mistimed drives revealed anxiety when she played Australian Joan Hartigan in the quarter-final. The Australian, hitting a withering forehand, won 4-6, 6-4, 6-3 but her limited equipment

101

would never have overcome the Dorothy Round of 1934. In the Wightman Cup, Dorothy beat Mrs. Arnold, 6-0, 6-3, but was no match for Helen Jacobs (6-3, 6-2).

It was in the Wightman Cup that Dorothy returned to form in 1936. She beat Helen Jacobs 6-3, 6-3 and Sarah Fabyan 6-3, 6-4. But in the Wimbledon quarter-final she countered arch-stonewaller Sperling. The German, provoking errors by her long-armed defence, led 6-3, 5-2. Dorothy, realising the futility of swapping drives, staked everything on a net attack. Brilliant volleys pulled her up to 5-all. Here she broke a shoulder strap. Hampered, she asked the umpire's permission to leave court. Fru Sperling (within her rights) objected declaring she would get cold. Dorothy instantly agreed and lost an uncomfortable second set on a double-fault, 8-6.

Chilean Anita Lizana defeated Dorothy three times at the beginning of 1937. These losses together with other unexpected reverses brought Dorothy's seeding down to No. 7 at Wimbledon.

Almost unnoticed, she tightened her errors and reached the fourth round losing five games. But British hopes rose when she beat Helen Jacobs 6-4, 6-2 in dazzling fashion—and increased when Dorothy's greatest jinxes Lizana and Sperling were eliminated by Simonne Mathieu and Alice Marble respectively.

In the semi-final after a fluent display, Dorothy swept Mathieu off court 6-4, 6-0. She lost only seven points in a 10-minute second set.

This was her last season of big tennis. Her engagement to Dr. Leigh Little had just been announced. Would she withstand the "battering ram" forehand of Polish Jadwiga Jedrzejowska and leave the game in glorious fashion?

"Jed's" thumping onslaught on the backhand was met by "dream" cross-court winners. But Dorothy seemed to weaken as "Jed", attacking with greater insight, captured the second set and raced to 4-2 in the third. Dr. Little shared the Centre Court's anxiety . . . in a temperature of 83°. Excited by her first final, "Jed" defended her lead—to let Dorothy recover with a perfectly-timed counter-attack. A love game against service signalled the end and Dorothy, on the crest of a wave, had won Wimbledon again 6-2, 2-6, 7-5.

The delighted, thunderous applause carried two messages . . . "Well done" and "Farewell". Cheers for the champion . . . and there goes the bride.

16

Bunny - But no Rabbit

IF Austin had a better service . . . if he had greater lasting power . . . he might well have won Wimbledon. He was the most polished driver of his day. His backhand eluded the fastest volley and his forehand, into which he leant delightfully, switched the ball across court or down the line preparing the way for a net assault. His command of the low volley was exemplary while he possessed a shoulder-high volley that was extremely dangerous.

Austin's timing synchronised so beautifully with his sweeping forward action, that anything above the level of his shoulder upset the delicate poise of his tennis.

Service and smash were his weakness. Austin could not hit as hard as most of his contemporaries. Subject to cramp, his lack of stamina proved his greatest handicap and as a match lengthened so his chances of success lessened.

He was, accordingly, a much more formidable proposition in Davis Cup tennis than in a championship. If he won through to the last stages of a tough tournament, his physical and nervous reserves were expended completely.

At the age of sixteen Henry Wilfred ("Bunny") Austin became triple junior champion in 1922. His graceful, effortless style recalled the Dohertys and like "H.L." he had the same instinct for the volley. Six years later in 1928 he hit the headlines at Wimbledon, when he became the only player (apart from Tilden) to take Lacoste to five sets. This was in the fourth round when Austin, facing a straight-set defeat, courageously attacked his man. He ran Lacoste all over the court—and ran himself out of energy. The Frenchman, waiting for the storm to die down, triumphed 6-4, 6-4, 6-8, 1-6, 6-2.

1929 saw Austin go further at Wimbledon than any Englishman had done for six years. He "brought the house down" by toppling seed No. 4, powerful American Frank Hunter, 6-3, 6-2, 4-6, 6-3 in the second round. His volleying then proved too much for Jacques Brugnon, 6-3, 6-4, 6-0. Next, he gallantly saved three successive match points against Charles Kingsley in a titanic battle, 6-2, 4-6, 6-1, 4-6, 11-9.

Not content with all this glory, Austin defeated Bela Von Kehrling seed No. 8, 6-2, 8-6, 6-2 to meet Borotra in the semi-final. Austin won a set (6-1, 10-8, 5-7, 6-1) although he found "the net was full of Borotras".

His physical reaction was soon evident against Prenn in the Davis Cup. Overcome by cramp, Austin was carried off court in the fifth set.

Austin had his revenge on Prenn beating him 6-3, 6-4, 7-5, in the Davis Cup in 1930. But although seeded for the first time (No. 9) at Wimbledon he lost the fourth round to American Gregory Mangin. Austin had a chance to win the first two sets. Losing these, he was out of the fight (9-7, 10-8, 6-0).

He retained his world ranking by some spirited tennis against Borotra. Austin beat the Basque in the London-Paris match and again in the I.C. series, while in the British covered court final, his wonderful steady defence took Borotra to 6-1, 0-6, 2-6, 6-2, 6-4.

In 1931, Austin married actress Phyllis Konstam. In 1931, too, he played some of his best tennis.

He just failed to beat Frank Shields in an exciting Wimbledon quarter-final. Once he had become accustomed to Shields's terrific power on service and drive, Austin, responding with his own beautiful shots reached match point at 5-4, 40-30 in the fourth set. He had been exploiting Shields's backhand weakness, many volleys escaping his opponent's long reach. In desperation, Shields produced a fateful backhand cross court that beat the volleyer. Weary and shaken, Austin lost the next eight games and the match 6-3, 2-6, 5-7, 7-5, 6-1.

The Inter-Zone final gave him a chance to prove his quality and he overcame Wood 2-6, 6-0, 8-6, 7-5. Wood had one of the best brains in tennis but it could not stop an inspired opponent.

In the deciding rubber Shields led Austin 5-2, 30-love on his service. Austin salvaged that set 8-6, and then by faultless drive-volley tennis had his revenge 8-6, 6-3, 7-5.

In the Challenge Round, Austin was twice within a stroke of establishing a two-set lead against Cochet. It was the calibre of his offensive that stirred Cochet to win 3-6, 11-9, 6-2, 6-4.

The Englishman kept the rubber alive by beating Borotra 7-5, 6-3, 3-6, 7-5. Despite rain and a crowd shouting for his rival, Austin's policy of abandoning the net and relying on quick-footed retrieving was justified.

A stockbroker by profession, Austin did not live entirely for tennis. To quote Perry "he (Austin) even goes to the Louvre when there is a Challenge Round close at hand!" The humorous side of tennis always appealed to the latter. He was playing Japanese Ryuki Miki when a stranger asked his wife "Excuse me, which is Austin?".

At Wimbledon in 1932, he again defeated Shields, 6-1, 9-7, 5-7, 6-1, his matchless strokes playing havoc with the American's power tennis. Rain interrupted his next battle—against Jiro Satoh. In this

104

slippery semi-final Austin had several falls. Eventually he put socks over his shoes and from 4-5 produced perfect tennis to win 7-5, 6-2, 6-1.

Austin needed time for his classical touch and this was the last thing Vines allowed him in the final. The American attacked with such fury that after losing the first set Austin was numbed by a succession of aces and devastating drives and volleys. In a 45-minute torrent Vines had won 6-4, 6-2, 6-0. "Return it?—I didn't even see it!" lamented the loser, when asked about Vines's cannon-ball.

In 1933, Austin was again the last Englishman at Wimbledon and met Satoh in the best match of the quarter-final. A heat wave worried Austin and his usual accuracy was missing—his volleys, too, lacked decision. Nevertheless, he fought back to two sets-all—here his stamina waned and he lost 7-5, 6-3, 2-6, 2-6, 6-2.

Austin, the pioneer of shorts, was undisturbed by Margot Oxford remarking she saw fur on his legs. He certainly seemed to benefit from the change-over and his 6-4, 7-5, 6-3 win over McGrath put Britain in the Inter-Zone final.

Austin was very popular in Paris where he was nicknamed "Le Petit". In the Inter-Zone final, he handled Vines's thunderbolts comfortably, several service returns landing on the baseline. Superbly steady, he offered Vines no pace. The fourth game of the third set brought the only crisis. After nine deuces, Austin, hitting winners off the hardest shots, drew up to 2-all. He was ahead at 4-2 and finally a tumult of "Austin" indicated that an exquisite stop volley had eluded Vines and given Britain a sensational victory, 6-1, 6-1, 6-4.

His victory over Allison 6-2, 7-9, 6-3, 6-4, settled the issue. In the Challenge Round, Austin defeated young Merlin 6-3, 6-4, 6-0, but on the last day after two and three-quarter hours wonderful tennis, he fell to Cochet. Superb against the rampant Frenchman, Austin's backhand passing shots were glorious. He led 4-2 in the final set but Cochet in his own swan song "for France" produced a fabulous game to win 5-7, 6-4, 4-6, 6-4, 6-4.

A marked improvement overhead was demonstrated by Austin at Wimbledon in 1934. He won four rounds losing only twenty-four games. He gave the most alluring display of the championship to lead Shields by two sets and 3-1. Tiring, he lost his faultless timing, and Shields, realising he still had a chance, started a robust counter-attack.

At two sets-all, Austin renewed his vigour. At 5-4 he was six times within two points of victory—but he could not finish off the match. Almost unable to stand, Austin accepted defeat 4-6, 2-6, 7-5, 6-3, 7-5.

He was amply revenged in the Davis Cup Challenge Round. Rested and resilient, he passed Shields fourteen times and won 6-4, 6-4, 6-1. He also played rousing tennis to beat Wood, 6-4, 6-0, 6-8, 6-3.

Many critics consider Austin played his greatest tennis at Bournemouth in 1935—but his failure to beat Perry again demonstrated his physical inability to win a championship final.

A versatile, intelligent attack gained a two set to one lead. In the fourth set he needed a point for 3-1 and seemed to have the key to victory. He had been volleying Perry's backhand with assurance but now checked his forward rush. The reason was soon obvious. Austin was beset by cramp and Perry won the last eleven games (0-6, 6-4, 3-6, 6-2, 6-0). Austin was much more upset by the return of this dormant disability than by his defeat. "I was being beaten all end up," declared Perry after the match.

In Paris, too, Austin's stamina failed. After overcoming Menzel in an exhausting five-setter, he stood up magnificently to Von Cramm's aggressive services in the semi-final, but was too weary to resist in the last set (6-2, 5-7, 6-1, 5-7, 6-0).

Budge provided Austin's quarter-final exit at Wimbledon. The Englishman, in superlative touch, led by a set and 5-2, but he had been drawing freely on stamina and now began missing volleys and serving double faults. Budge saved the second set. Austin returned to the attack but after two hours brilliant tennis was beaten 3-6, 10-8, 6-4, 7-5. Utterly exhausted, Austin stretched himself flat out on the ground for a few minutes before collecting his rackets.

In the Davis Cup he defeated Allison and Budge.

Allison could not beat Austin—and Austin could not beat Von Cramm. Thus at Wimbledon in 1936, Austin defeated the American 6-1, 6-4, 7-5 but lost the semi-final to the German 8-6, 6-3, 2-6, 6-3. He and Von Cramm provided delightful tennis but the dynamic service of the winner turned the scale.

Adrian Quist "never playing better" defeated Austin 6-4, 3-6, 7-5, 6-2 in the Davis Cup but the loser had gained the first point for Britain when he beat Crawford 4-6, 6-3, 6-1, 6-1. He had never before overcome Crawford in an important match. He neutralised the Australian's advantage in hitting power by his faster footwork, and conducted a successful volleying campaign.

Without Perry and Von Cramm, it seemed that the French title would at last fall to Austin in 1937. But after ninety minutes in a heat-wave, he surrendered the final to Henkel 6-1, 6-4, 6-3. The German's passing shots were neatly judged, many lobs also advertising Austin's weakness overhead.

Another German—Von Cramm—caused Austin's semi-final defeat at Wimbledon. This time he triumphed 8-6, 6-3, 12-14, 6-1. The loser fought desperately to save the third set but had nothing left for the fourth.

Britain, without Perry, could not keep the Davis Cup. Her only winning rubber was secured when Austin beat Parker 6-3, 6-2, 7-5. In his last Davis Cup match Austin thoroughly tested Budge (8-6, 3-6, 6-4, 6-3).

For the rest of his career, Austin played limited tennis.

In the 1938 championships he gained a considerable revenge on Henkel in the semi-final 6-2, 6-4, 6-0. In the final, however, he could find no weakness in Budge's répertoire and was beaten summarily 6-1, 6-0, 6-3. But although he collected less games than against Vines in 1932, Austin offered sterner resistance.

Austin was top seed at Wimbledon in 1939. He had hardly played any tennis for a year having been invited to lecture in America on Moral Rearmament. Completely out of touch, he lost the quarter-final 6-3, 6-0, 6-1 to Elwood Cooke.

Bunny Austin played in four Inter-Zone finals and six Challenge Rounds. Out of these sixteen Davis Cup matches, he registered twelve triumphs. The man who had never won a Wimbledon championship claimed victories over five Wimbledon champions—Wood, Borotra, Vines, Budge and Crawford.

17

Britain's Black Panther

In 1909, A. W. Gore won the Wimbledon singles. In that year, too, Frederick John Perry was born. And not until Perry was twenty-five, could England again salute a champion.

This was in 1934, and then for three years Perry's brilliance dominated tennis and put his country back on the map.

Tall, slim, strong as an ox, Perry possessed graceful, lithe movements. Alert and aggressive, his attitude was "Let me get at them". Tireless, he won some great matches because, still fresh, he could hustle opponents into defeat even in a fifth set.

Taking a cue from Cochet, Perry hit a rising ball. A magnificent Continental forehand prepared the way for a devastating net attack, which revealed his beautiful volleying touch. With a safe, but unspectacular, backhand Perry says, "Watch Austin do it—and then feel envious".

A former world table tennis champion (in 1929), Perry eventually overcame his temperamental lapses. He learnt to accept ball boys and cameras as a necessary part of big tennis. Never a great trainer, Perry relaxed in golf and bridge and plenty of sleep before his matches.

A teetotaller, he smoked little and the French named him "Monsieur Lemonade".

Losing accuracy when learning to hit an early ball, Perry was dropped from his club team—five years later he was world champion! His father, a Labour M.P., generously released Perry from business for one year to allow him time for tennis. This decision, questioned by many, proved well worth while.

Accepted at Wimbledon in 1929, Perry survived two matches before losing to John Olliff. In 1930, he packed Court 3 when he defeated the seeded Italian, Baron H. L. de Morpurgo 10-8, 4-6, 6-1, 6-2. Facing a 5-1 deficit in the opening set, Perry then handled de Morpurgo's kicking services on the rise, coming in to kill the return.

In his first appearance on the Centre Court, Perry won two sets from Dr. Gregory, England's No. 1.

Awarded Davis Cup colours in 1931, Perry lost the Wimbledon semi-final to S. B. Wood 4-6, 6-2, 6-4, 6-2. The American cleverly slowed down the game causing his opponent to net many backhand returns.

There were certain elements who resented Perry's success and self-confidence. At this Wimbledon they practised such absurdities as ordering clothes on his behalf, removing his own clothes for cleaning, and even buying (but not paying for!) a house in Perry's name.

These same people upset him in his match against Wood. Later, Perry rose above such petty interference.

He turned the tables on Wood in the Inter-Zone final of the Davis Cup 6-3, 8-10, 6-3, 6-3. To general surprise, Britain defeated the Americans and challenged France. In his best tennis to date, Perry beat Borotra 4-6, 10-8, 6-0, 4-6, 6-4.

Controlling his net rushing, Perry stuck to the baseline, his lobs exhausting Borotra. Always afraid of lightning, the Englishman won just before an impending storm, overcoming a partisan crowd and the Basque who, like a wounded tiger, was always most dangerous when almost down.

In the deciding rubber, Perry fought valiantly against Cochet. He forced the French player to produce all his wizardry before succumbing 6-4, 1-6, 9-7, 6-3.

Vines was the only American to beat Perry in the U.S.A. that year. They had some terrific battles, and Vines defeated his rival 4-6, 3-6, 6-4, 6-4, 6-3, in the semi-final at Forest Hills. Perry allowed himself to be upset by a decision in the crisis of the fourth set.

1932 is called by Perry the "crash" year. His best play was in the Wimbledon quarter-final where he lost a two-hour battle, full of good tennis, to Jack Crawford, 7-5, 8-6, 2-6, 8-6.

But in the same round at Paris, Perry, nettled by an adverse decision, threw away a 5-3 lead in the final set against Menzel, and did not win another game. While in the fourth round in America, Perry became irritated because Sydney Wood changed his shoes during their match. He lost twelve games running and could not come back (3-6, 4-6, 6-0, 6-0, 7-5).

Even worse was Britain's fourth round Davis Cup loss to Germany. In the final deciding match, Perry reached match point at 5-2 in the fifth set against Dr. Daniel Prenn, but was foiled by his opponent's doggedness. "Never have I experienced a worse ordeal . . . to cap all, my nerve broke, not another game could I win. . . ."

Austin and Perry were bitterly criticised, one reporter even calling them "cab-horse" players—a name Perry did not easily forget.

1933 did not start auspiciously when at Wimbledon the first seed out was—Perry! His 7-5, 6-1, 3-6, 4-6, 6-4 exit at the hands of

South African, Norman Farquharson, was the sensation of the championships.

It was now that Perry realised that he must lose himself in his matches— or else be resigned to losing the matches themselves! The effect was immediate. In the Davis Cup Inter-Zone final he beat Vines and Allison, and in the Challenge Round he virtually settled the issue by his 8-10, 6-4, 8-6, 3-6, 6-1 win over Cochet.

Although he lasted the course better than Cochet, Perry fainted afterwards in the dressing-room. He was too exhausted to partner Hughes in the doubles, but won the cup for Britain when he beat André Merlin, 4-6, 8-6, 6-2, 7-5.

Feted when he returned home, Perry was soon off to America. But although he beat Quist and Stoffen at Forest Hills, he found few backers for his final against Crawford (Wimbledon champion).

Crawford led two sets to one, but the heat and a very long second set tired him. Perry then launched a devastating net attack and lost only one more game.

"I could not miss a ball." American pressmen enthused over the new champion, calling him "the sleek terror of the courts" and "Britain's Black Panther". To celebrate this 6-3, 11-13, 4-6, 6-0, 6-1 triumph, Austin cabled "Well done, old cab-horse".

Perry found he had the beating of Crawford, when he pressed the attack at close quarters. He defeated his rival setless in the Australian final of 1934, and again at Bournemouth a few months later.

A sprained ankle helped to defeat Perry in his quarter-final match against Georgio de Stefani in the French championship. The double-handed Italian, offering no backhand to attack, always proved a menace to the Englishman.

At Wimbledon, Perry and Stefani were expected to dispute the quarter-final. Stefani, however, fell to George Lott, who in turn lost a tough four-set match (6-4, 2-6, 7-5, 10-8) to Perry.

Wood v. Perry always provided drama, and none was lacking in their meeting at that Wimbledon semi-final. At 3-all in the fifth set, both men were feeling the strain. But Perry, with greater reserves of stamina, showed less signs of nerves. Wood served a fatal double-fault to surrender the eighth game, and then lost the match on a net-cord (6-3, 3-6, 7-5, 5-7, 6-3).

In his first final, Perry dethroned Crawford 6-3, 6-0, 7-5. From 1-3 in the first set, he rushed to 1-0 in the third. In the second set he lost only eight points. Crawford rallied in the third set, but the battle terminated abruptly when he double-faulted at Perry's first match point.

Soon after his triumph, Perry's engagement to actress Mary Lawson was announced. When he went to America, the engagement was ended by mutual consent. This pretty brunette was, unfortunately, killed in an air raid.

Perry retained the Davis Cup for Britain, when, despite a strapped-up back, he beat Frank Shields 6-4, 4-6, 6-2, 15-13 in a thrilling encounter that kept 14,600 spectators at concert pitch. And in the U.S. final he warded off the challenge of fighting Wilmer Allison 6-4, 6-3, 3-6, 1-6, 8-6.

Even Perry was now tennis-tired. He refused a wonderful offer to make films, but was constantly badgered about his plans. In Australia, reporters sometimes telephoned him at midnight, to ask whether he intended turning professional.

His tennis slumped in 1935. He lost to Crawford at Sydney, and to Quist at Melbourne, while in the Australian final Crawford again mastered a listless, base-lining Perry 2-6, 6-4, 6-4, 6-4.

Sailing home on the *Berengaria*, Perry met an old friend—film star Helen Vinson. On this voyage they fell in love. Although he confessed it was hard to concentrate Perry now played, perhaps, his greatest tennis. His volleying put him in a class by himself. So devastating was his attack that he could numb even the most aggressive opponents into submissive defence.

At Paris in 1935, after many failures, Perry swept the board, losing eight games to Maier, nine to Turnbull and five to Boussus. Crawford lost 6-3, 8-6, 6-3 and although Von Cramm (holder) won a set by desperately seeking the net, Perry was not extended (6-3, 3-6, 6-1, 6-3).

At Wimbledon, Perry was the complete master. He beat Crawford 6-2, 3-6, 6-4, 6-4, and shedding his customary buoyant exuberance paid Von Cramm the compliment of continuous pressure in the final. His merciless forehand returns made light of the German's menacing service, while Von Cramm could find no comfort in Perry's backhand. The score was 6-2, 6-4, 6-4.

Confident he could retain his U.S. title, Perry stumbled and drove his racket handle into a kidney while playing Allison in the semi-final. After seeing a doctor he continued, but lost 7-5, 6-3, 6-3. Allison had been so sure of defeat that he had taken an aeroplane ticket to return home to Texas that evening!

A sudden wedding at 11.30 p.m. followed by a party that made even New York think, united Perry and Helen Vinson. Perry then rested from tennis for six months. Cured of his injury, he beat Austin 6-2, 8-6, 6-3 at Bournemouth in 1936. But in the French final he lost to Von Cramm. In a remarkable battle of light and shade the German won the first eight games and lost the next six. At two sets all, Perry lost touch completely, and Von Cramm won as he liked with his well-placed volleys (6-0, 2-6, 6-2, 2-6, 6-0).

111

Perry was not worried by his back or his beating. What puzzled him was his inability to get into the fight again after losing his first service game in the final set.

A sobered Perry played grim tennis in the Wimbledon semi-final against Donald Budge. He led two sets to one, but Budge's crisp volleying took the American to 4-2 in the fourth. Perry then went out in a typical onslaught winning fourteen of the last sixteen points by cleanly-hit aces.

He was out for revenge against Von Cramm in the final. But what promised to be an epic collapsed when Von Cramm pulled a muscle in the second game. Perry won 6-1, 6-1, 6-0.

Despite a lucrative job with a sports firm, Perry intended to turn professional. He refused to commit himself, however, realising how much greater his value would be if he could win again in America.

In the greatest final at Forest Hills since the Tilden-Johnston battles, Budge often eluded the swooping Perry by his glorious backhand passes. The Californian led 5-3 in the fifth set, but Perry, finding that extra punch that he alone possessed at that time, won by his greater steadiness and stamina 2-6, 6-2, 8-6, 1-6, 10-8. This victory gave him the cup outright.

Perry toured professionally with Vines, and later played Tilden and Budge. He won the U.S. professional title in 1938.

The ex-champion is now an American citizen, and served as a sergeant in the U.S. Army in World War II. His first marriage was dissolved in November, 1940. His second wedding to model Sandra Beaux lasted from 1941 to 1945, while his third marriage to Mrs. Lorraine Walsh terminated after six years in 1953. Perry then married Mrs. Barbara Friedman, sister of actress Patricia Roc.

In 1948, Perry easily beat Petra (Wimbledon champion in 1946) 3-6, 6-4, 6-2, 6-1 in the Slazenger professional final at Scarborough.

Fred Perry was one of England's greatest players—certainly the speediest she has produced. He won thirty-five out of thirty-nine Davis Cup singles matches and proved that an Englishman, given stamina, skill and financial security, could scale the same heights as Australians and Americans.

Mrs. Robert Addie (U.S.A.). *As Pauline Betz, she took everything in her stride at Wimbledon in 1946—even the net!*

Jack Kramer, Champion in 1947. This athletic American was so far ahead of his rivals that interest lessened at Wimbledon that year!

Names that have become world-famous. Miss Louise Brough (Champion in 1948, 1949, 1950 and 1955) and her fellow American, Mrs. Margaret Osborne Du Pont (Champion in 1947).

Robert Falkenburg, a fiery American whose amazing victory at Wimbledon in 1948 caused an uproar of comment.

18

Helen II

COURAGE is an essential quality of any champion, and few possessed more than Arizona-born Helen Jacobs. Perhaps her bravest effort was at Forest Hills in 1933, when she appeared in little shorts, complete with elegant black stripe down the sides. Such unheard-of garments had been forbidden in the Wightman Cup. In the championships, however, Helen was a free agent. Her attractive Grecian appearance took the gallery by storm and the seal was put upon public approval when cartoonist Tom Webster declared Helen looked smarter than any footballer he knew.

This popular Californian with the beautiful profile was born on 6th August, 1908. Small but sturdy, her tennis equipment lacked a reliable forehand—instead, Helen cultivated a sliced shot. But this was offset by a wonderful backhand, a lethal smash and, for many years, the hardest first service in women's tennis.

Fluent footwork produced heart-breaking recoveries, while her acumen caused Alice Marble to declare ". . . Helen had the finest tennis brain. . . ."

A serious-minded girl, Helen's tennis was not all-absorbing. Two years resident in England, her Kingston home boasted a wonderful garden. She rode to hounds, and was presented at Court by the wife of the U.S. ambassador.

Helen's kindness was demonstrated when, after signing an autograph for a child in hospital, she also handed over a racket saying "I'm sure she would prefer this".

At her first Wimbledon in 1928, Helen lost in the last sixteen to Australian Daphne Akhurst (6-8, 6-1, 8-6). The two-hour struggle ended in darkness and drama for in hitting her final winner, Daphne Akhurst slipped and sprained her ankle.

Helen was runner-up to Helen Wills (6-2, 6-1) at Forest Hills in 1928. Asked to select a partner for Europe in 1929, Miss Wills surprisingly chose Edith Cross—although Helen Jacobs (Helen II) was America's no. 2.

Now started the famous "Helen" feud that permeated U.S. tennis over a decade. Jacobs was far more popular. Wills kept her—and most people— at a distance.

Helen II could not afford a European trip herself so anonymous

113

H

friends financed her in 1929. She repaid their confidence by reaching the Wimbledon final—to be smothered by Helen I, 6-1, 6-2.

A visit to the French Riviera in 1930 ended in pleurisy. On Tilden's insistence (their close friendship lasted all his life) Helen dropped tennis until the French championships, when she beat Mrs. Holcroft-Watson 5-7, 6-3, 6-1 and Lili d'Alvarez 6-1, 6-0, before losing the final to Helen Wills 6-2, 6-1. As usual, the winner directed her services and drives on to Helen's sliced forehand.

Still tired, Helen could do little against Cilly Aussem's persistence in the Wimbledon quarter-final (6-2, 6-1). Ordered a complete rest from all competitive tennis, she missed Forest Hills and entered a sanatorium. After a few months, her normally strong constitution righted itself.

Beaten 6-3, 6-2, by Betty Nuthall in the French quarter-final of 1931, Helen reversed this decision in the same round at Wimbledon (6-2, 6-3). But she then had her greatest disappointment to date when she sacrificed a first set 5-2 lead to a comparatively unknown German stonewaller, Hilde Krahwinkel, and lost 10-8, 0-6, 6-4.

1932 proved the turning point in Helen's career. Her confidence grew and her lasting powers—improved by drinking small quantities of orange juice instead of glasses of water during play—seemed limitless.

She lost the French quarter-final to Simonne Mathieu 6-4, 6-4. At Wimbledon, however, Helen nursing a "lucky shoulder" had a variety of shot to defeat Continental baseliners. In the semi-final, after seventy-five minutes under a blazing sun, Helen beat Mathieu 7-5, 6-1. She used chops and graded drives to upset Mathieu's rhythm, but it was tedious tennis, one rally going to ninety-eight shots.

After a perfunctory handshake, Simonne marched off court alone. Later she said Helen had upset her concentration by delaying at the net after the first set. They were, however, old friends—peace was soon restored.

In a 46-minute final Helen led Mrs. Moody 3-1, but lost the next seven games and was beaten, 6-3, 6-1. At Forest Hills, however, came the death of what Helen called her "runner-up" complex. In Mrs. Moody's absence, Helen became American champion beating Carolyn Babcock 6-2, 6-2.

Helen's natural elation suffered a set-back when Moody supporters declared her victory was a hollow one. She offered to play Helen I in an exhibition match but her idea was promptly refused.

1933 was also a milestone in Helen's career. In France she met and made friends with Suzanne Lenglen, who taught her a forehand strong enough for a successful net attack.

Helen led Simonne Mathieu 5-1 in the French semi-final. She

114

could never maintain her best form for long at the Stade Roland Garros. Simonne overhauled her, Helen deteriorated, and went down 8-6, 6-3.

As in 1932, the American had her revenge at Wimbledon. Here she toppled Mme. Mathieu 6-1, 1-6, 6-2 in the quarter-final. But Dorothy Round had now become a force in tennis. Displaying remarkable severity overhead, Helen won the first set from the English player. She gained a lead in the second and seemed to be heading for victory when Dorothy stopped lobbing. Beautiful backhand passes saved that set and won the next more easily (4-6, 6-4, 6-2).

By the U.S. season, however, Suzanne's coaching bore sensational results. In the Wightman Cup, Helen was the mistress of Dorothy Round 6-4, 6-2.

Forest Hills . . . and Helen was no longer the girl who always lost to Helen Moody but the first player to beat her for seven years. Helen's claim that shorts improved her game by thirty, seemed justified when in the semi-final she played brilliant tennis and again defeated Dorothy Round, 6-4, 5-7, 6-2.

Mrs. Moody had relinquished the Wightman Cup match because of a strained back. Helen II, too, had been receiving medical attention during the championship. But their meeting in the U.S. final proved a spectacle of never-forgotten drama. Helen Jacobs, attacking brilliantly, took the first set 8-6. She had never before won five games in one set from Mrs. Moody. The latter, then exerting all her reserves of stamina, won the second set 6-3.

A noisy pro-Moody demonstration upset Miss Jacobs at this stage, and she threw her racket on court.

After the 10-minute interval, she recovered and, with volleys worthy of Borotra, reached 3-0, twice breaking Mrs. Moody's service. The latter then retired—her back and leg were troubling her. Helen Jacobs, all sympathy, helped her on with her jacket, and asked her to rest and perhaps continue later. Mrs. Moody refused.

Helen Jacobs then suggested her opponent should leave the court before the photographers arrived, and to this the older player agreed.

Molla Mallory, Helen Jacobs' great friend, broadcast in her inimitable, staccato style, a biting commentary of the final, recalling the occasion when Suzanne defaulted, in similar circumstances, to her.

This drew from one critic the reply that Molla's several defeats at Helen Moody's hands had warped her feelings. Mrs. Moody retired to bed while Helen Jacobs developed a cold, merely declaring she was glad to have retained her title

In the French final of 1934, Helen (victor over Mathieu 6-2, 6-2) fought three long losing sets against Peggy Scriven, who cleverly slowed down the game. Helen's appeal against failing light was dismissed and the match finished with the Californian unable to see anything. Peggy Scriven won 7-5, 4-6, 6-1.

Helen had complete revenge in the Wightman Cup a month later. She beat Peggy Scriven 6-1, 6-1, and also Dorothy Round, 6-4, 6-4. This gave her a No. 1 seeding at Wimbledon, where she defeated Cilly Aussem 6-0, 6-2 in the quarter-final. When Cilly declared "Helen was marvellous—more accurate than any champion I have met", few favoured Dorothy Round's chance in the final.

But Dorothy's blistering drives off a fast court won the first set 6-2. Helen won a touch-and-go second, 7-5, and then her opponent, with a burst of inspired volleying against unrelenting steadiness, won a thrilling final set 6-3. Helen praised Dorothy's tennis but remarked "Wimbledon will soon tire of seeing Helen Jacobs lose the final".

After Wimbledon, Helen refused a professional offer to appear on radio at 1,000 dollars a week. She had consolation when she retained the American singles trophy and became triple champion. Her mixed partner was her friend, comedian George Lott. Lott delighted in shocking spectators. "Damn it, will you get to the net," he once shouted at Helen before a large and startled audience at Forest Hills.

After winning the Egyptian championship in 1935, Helen suffering from a temperature, attended an official lunch. Her hostess ordered her a large brandy. Helen's neighbour was a genial general who was unaware of her plight. Noticing Helen's poor appetite, desultory conversation and the drink, the general decided on a strong line, "Do you always drink brandy during tournaments?" he suddenly barked. Informed of Helen's temperature, the gallant soldier apologised, generously offering his own doctor

Rallies of over fifty strokes were witnessed when Helen lost 7-5, 6-3 in the French semi-final of 1935 to Hilde (Krahwinkel) Sperling. In a return match in the Wimbledon semi-final, Helen gave a faultless display (considered by many critics, her best-ever performance) winning, 6-3, 6-0.

The final against Mrs. Moody, now completely fit again, was the most dramatic match at Wimbledon since the Lambert Chambers-Lenglen final in 1919.

Mrs. Moody won the first set, 6-3. Helen Jacobs, retrieving wonderfully, captured the second set by a similar score, and with some brilliant volleying reached 5-2 in the third set.

A critical "not up" decision robbed her of a vital point, but she fought her way to match point, only to be foiled by a clever lob.

Excitement rose as Mrs. Moody calmly pulled up to 5-all and, with Helen Jacobs never faltering, and still attacking fiercely, Helen I just survived a desperate last set, 7-5.

Mrs. Moody was delighted to prove she was not afraid of defeat,

116

but the fact that she threw away her racket and clapped her hands, caused comment. One reporter declared it was done to have both hands free to commiserate with her opponent, another considered it an exhibition of unrestrained glee.

Helen Jacobs made no excuses. "What a grand match," was her comment. At Forest Hills she created a record by a fourth successive win.

Helen staged her fifth Wimbledon final in 1936. Her opponent was Fru Sperling. In ninety nerve-racking minutes, Helen, ceaselessly attacking the world's arch-retriever, reached 6-5, 40-15 in the third set—only to lose both chances, one by a net-cord. Shaken, she double-faulted! Then controlling her nerves, Helen pursued her relentless pressure, and achieved her heart's desire, 6-2, 4-6, 7-5.

Tension over, the Centre Court rose in tumult to its favourite overseas woman player. Hordes of Americans—it was the 4th July—hurled hats into the air shouting "Helen!" Herr Sperling, after embracing his wife, was the first to congratulate the champion, who overcome with emotion and excitement, was assisted into the dressing room where Suzanne and Mrs. Lambert Chambers were waiting to greet her.

At the L.T.A. dinner that night Hilde Sperling wired Helen: "Sorry I can't be with you tonight. Even my husband's shoes don't fit me."

Alice Marble, recently recovered from a serious illness, was now back in American tennis. She led Helen, 2-1, 40-15 in the third set of the final at the Manchester (Massachusetts) tournament. An inspired bout of volleying saved the match, Helen winning 6-4, 0-6, 6-3.

At Forest Hills, Helen won her first round losing only two points. During practice she fell and sprained her thumb but managed to beat Kay Stammers in the semi-final 6-4, 6-3. Given a day's respite she faced Alice Marble with her hand strapped. Her great mobility won the first set but every backhand (her best stroke) was a labour. Alice then hit a wonderful streak and scored a sensational upset 4-6, 6-3, 6-2.

In 1937, Helen's father was seriously ill in California, during Wimbledon. Helen was not sure whether she could play out the tournament, and lost her title 6-4, 6-2 to Dorothy Round in the quarter-final.

She was in better form at Forest Hills. After defeating Kay Stammers 7-5, 6-3, Helen was the last American in the tournament, but lost in the semi-final to Jadwiga Jedzrejowska 6-4, 6-4.

Handicapped by a shoulder strain, Helen was unseeded at Wimbledon in 1938. Profiting from daily practice with Tilden, she established a record when, unseeded, she reached the final without losing a set.

Wearing an attractive new style of pleated shorts, Helen, stalwart and steady, claimed three seeded victims—Scriven, 6-3, 6-0, Jedzrejowska, 6-2, 6-3, and Marble, 6-4, 6-4.

In the fourth all-Helen final, the namesakes after eight desperate games reached 4-all, when a wrenched ankle finished the match for Helen II. Soon she was limping and could hardly cross over. Probably remembering Forest Hills in 1933, she refused to retire despite severe pain.

Mrs. Moody continued as though nothing had happened and hit her way to 6-4, 6-0. A dismal affair was relieved by her opponent's courage. Applause was perfunctory and press reports biting. The Helens had met for the last time. The battle of fifteen years was over.

At Forest Hills, Helen was beaten in the sensation of the tournament—and in a whirlwind. This took place in the third round when she lost 7-5, 6-2 to Margot Lumb.

In 1939, Helen went out 6-2, 6-2 to Kay Stammers in the Wimbledon quarter-final, but beat her 7-5, 6-0 in the U.S. semi-final, losing only four points in the second set. After a one-sided start, Alice Marble defeated Helen 6-0, 8-10, 6-4 in a thrilling final which one critic called "the greatest match in America".

Alice again beat Helen in the U.S. final in 1940. During World War II, Helen, commissioned in the W.A.V.E.S. reached Commander rank. Martial on court, she looked superb in uniform, and in 1943 was awarded the prize for America's best sportswoman.

Helen is now one of the most popular writers of girls' books in America—besides publishing many works on tennis. Early in 1954 she resigned her commission accepting an executive position with photographer Dorothy Wilding.

"Little Helen's" cut forehand—which she took lessons to improve even after winning international titles—prevented her becoming a model champion. But as America's unofficial ambassadress she was a universal success.

19

Beau Brummell of Tennis

IT was his two Davis Cup wins in 1932 against famous contemporaries that brought Gottfried Von Cramm into world prominence. Up to that time he had received little attention as Germany's second string. When, however, he beat Austin (the Wimbledon finalist) and then accounted for Frank Shields (Wimbledon finalist the year before) it was evident that a new force had arisen in European tennis.

Baron Von Cramm was born in Hanover on 7th July, 1909. His tennis delighted the purists. German courts helped to develop his deep, purposeful drives executed in classic style on both wings. He had a decisive touch on the volley, whilst his menacing service presented a problem to every opponent. Lithe, hard-working and full of endurance, the German had one weakness—his long swing-back made it difficult to disguise the direction of his drives—but few players were good enough to profit from this.

His good looks, good manners and good tennis drew huge crowds. Perfectly flannelled—Von Cramm never took to shorts—this tall blond sportsman proved one of the best ambassadors his country produced. In Paris, where he was the first German to win the title his victory was received enthusiastically.

George Lott crushed Von Cramm 6-3, 6-1, 6-0 in the fourth round of the French championships in 1931. That year the 21-year-old German paid his first visit to England, and although a stranger to grass, produced some promising tennis. With Jacques Brugnon, he won the doubles at Queen's Club, and in his first Wimbledon singles he caused a minor sensation by defeating the Hungarian champion Baron Von Kehrling 6-8, 6-1, 6-2, 6-3. Kehrling was a menace to anyone at that time and two years earlier had been seeded No. 8.

Von Cramm also disposed of Charles Kingsley, never an easy player to beat, and then lost 7-5, 6-2, 6-4 in the fourth round to a young English player, later his most famous rival—Fred Perry.

In 1932, Von Cramm was chosen with Daniel Prenn to represent Germany in the Davis Cup. In the fourth round they came to grips with Britain. Austin and Perry were expected to achieve a clear-cut victory. Prenn, however, won both singles and Von Cramm, although beaten by Perry, kept the rubber alive by accounting for an erratic Austin 5-7, 6-2, 6-3, 6-2.

A week later he defeated the top Italian players, Palmieri and A. del Bono to help Germany to a 5-0 win in the European Zone final.

Ellsworth Vines had just laid the Wimbledon field very low and it was anticipated that he would demolish the German team in a similar fashion. But although America won the rubber 3-2, Vines lost a set to Von Cramm 3-6, 6-3, 9-7, 6-3. The loser handled Vines's services with masterly skill and finished many rallies with carefully planned net attacks. In his second match, Von Cramm did even better when he defeated the great server Frank Shields 7-5, 5-7, 6-4, 8-6. He displayed much variety of shot and his mobile defence was a revelation.

When Hitler forbade Prenn to play in the Davis Cup, Von Cramm became Germany's leading representative. His best Davis Cup wins in 1933 were over H. Timmer (Holland) and R. Nunoi (Japan). He lost in the third round at Wimbledon to steady American Clifford Sutter (6-3, 6-4, 9-7) but with Hilde Krahwinkel gained an unexpected victory in the mixed doubles.

1934 . . . and Von Cramm was established as a player of world calibre. He played glorious tennis to win the French title from an entry that included Perry, Crawford and Austin. Four successive five-set encounters did not worry the German who was as fit as anyone in sport. Facile and fast-moving, he played fifteen sets in defeating Palmieri, Menzel and de Stefani to challenge Crawford in the final.

Crawford, running the German from corner to corner, led two sets to one. At his classical best, he was within a stroke of victory at 5-4 in the fourth set. A wonderful rally ended in a beautiful smash from Von Cramm whose nerve was never firmer. 5-all was called and then Germany led 6-5, and was helped to 7-5 by two Australian double-faults. The final set was gathered by the slimmer, fitter player. Von Cramm had served at top speed for two hours and this largely contributed to his victory 6-4, 7-9, 3-6, 7-5, 6-3.

The shadow of the Swastika was already moving towards him. When he reached the singles final Von Cramm was bidden by Berlin to conserve his energy and to withdraw from the mixed—much to the disappointment of his partner, Fraulein Horn.

Seeded No. 3 at the championships, Von Cramm developed "Wimbledon Throat" and lost in the fourth round to Vernon Kirby (6-2, 2-6, 6-4, 6-2). He played heroic Davis Cup tennis against France but his colleagues were too weak to avert a defeat. Von Cramm beat Boussus and Merlin, and with Denker he thoroughly extended Borotra and Brugnon. He finished the season with a third successive win in his national championship.

Only Perry could hold Von Cramm in 1935. He was hitting and serving even harder and the tempo of his dynamic tennis was too speedy for any other opponent.

In Paris his superior stamina outlasted Austin 6-2, 5-7, 6-1, 5-7, 6-0 in the semi-final. And in the final, hoping to unsettle Perry, he started with a Borotratic attack. But here was an opponent who flourished on such treatment. Von Cramm won one set but was forced to give up his title (6-3, 3-6, 6-1, 6-3).

The Wimbledon authorities seeded the German No. 2. His fiery tennis won three rounds without losing a set. Gene Mako captured one set but only two more games 6-0, 6-1, 3-6, 6-1. In the quarter-final, Vivian McGrath—who had beaten Allison by his unexpected double-handed backhand—won a set from Von Cramm (6-4, 6-2, 4-6, 6-1).

Budge had proved the dark horse of the championships having beaten Boussus and Austin. His powerful game won the first set off Von Cramm—but the latter, undismayed by Budge's crashing style, maintained his steadiness and triumphed by sound, if less spectacular, tennis (4-6, 6-4, 6-3, 6-2).

The final was played at tremendous pace as befitted the two speediest men in the game. Perry, never more determined, paid Von Cramm the compliment of continuous pressure. He won the first set and led 4-2 in the second. Von Cramm's storming pulled up to 4-all but the next two games went to Perry, tuned up to his greatest by the quality of the opposition. And with slightly greater speed on drive and volley, he gained a rousing success 6-2, 6-4, 6-4. Both men were warmly applauded as they came off court. No German had been so near to becoming champion before.

Almost single-handed, Von Cramm brought Germany to the Inter-Zone final of the Davis Cup in 1935. His victims included Crawford, McGrath and Allison.

It was his ambition to beat Perry and this he achieved dramatically in the French final of 1936. Daring and dynamic, he attacked with such fury that he captured the first eight games. Perry was not at his best, but Von Cramm had never performed better. He could not, however, maintain such a rarified standard and Perry then took six successive games. In the third set Von Cramm broke through a bitterly fought sixth game to lead 4-2—and the set went to Germany 6-2.

Back to the fight came his rival who swamped Von Cramm in the fourth set. But with hopes raised for a thrilling finish, Von Cramm unleashed an amazing brand of aggression. He broke service in the first game and when Perry served a fatal double-fault to trail 0-3 he could not win another game. Von Cramm had regained his title 6-2, 2-6, 6-2, 2-6, 6-0.

This match promised an exciting Wimbledon final. Von Cramm proved too nimble on a damp court for Crawford (6-1, 7-5, 6-4)— and he then won a beautiful semi-final from Austin (8-6, 6-3, 2-6, 6-3).

But his last match was a great disappointment. After eight minutes of thrilling tennis, Perry led 1-0. The first game contained ten deuces —the second saw Von Cramm a helpless spectator. Handicapped by a pulled thigh muscle, the German could not move and was defeated 6-1, 6-1, 6-0.

In 1937, Von Cramm did not defend in Paris—he was concentrating on grass court tennis hoping to win Wimbledon and the Davis Cup.

Again those classic artists, Crawford and Austin, blocked his way to the Wimbledon final. Von Cramm fought off Crawford in five sets (6-3, 8-6, 3-6, 2-6, 6-2). Austin expended his stamina in saving a third set and could resist little further (8-6, 6-3, 12-14, 6-1). Thousands came to cheer the German to better fortune this year. But he found Budge in implacable mood. The Californian relying on a "Tildenesque" defence resisted all onslaughts (6-3, 6-4, 6-2).

But in the Inter-Zone final, Von Cramm rose to superlative heights. In the deciding rubber he led Budge 4-1 in a memorable fifth set. 12,000 spectators witnessed, perhaps, the greatest-ever Davis Cup drama as Budge reached 4-all. In a glorious finish, after he had been pulled back from victory five times, the Californian triumphed 6-8, 5-7, 6-4, 6-2, 8-6.

This victory virtually decided the fate of the Davis Cup—it also decided Von Cramm's fate. Had he won, even Hitler would not have risked imprisoning such a popular hero.

The German lost the U.S. final to his friend Budge 6-1, 7-9, 6-1, 3-6, 6-1. They failed to meet in the 1938 Australian final, the somewhat stale Von Cramm losing his semi-final to Bromwich 6-3, 7-5, 6-1.

He never pretended to have any Nazi sympathy. In 1938, he was imprisoned and it was later discovered the court had been instructed to convict him. News of the Baron trickled to the world occasionally. It was said he had tried suicide, and that his aged mother had appealed personally to Hitler.

Released in 1939 his entry was refused at Wimbledon. He played at Queen's crushing Riggs 6-1, 6-0. Two weeks later Riggs became triple Wimbledon champion!

He survived three Nazi interrogations during World War II. After hostilities Von Cramm recommenced first class tennis but did not reappear at Wimbledon until 1951. Absent twelve years from grass, he met in the first round—Drobny! He played brilliantly to great applause but at forty-two could not give away twelve years to such opposition and lost 9-7, 6-4, 6-4.

Von Cramm was born under an unlucky star. His drive and daring deserved the world championship, his dress and demeanour established him as the Beau Brummell of Tennis.

Famous Red-Head of Tennis

DONALD BUDGE always denied waving to Queen Mary. "The press boys were kidding," he declared. "I did what Austin did; we both bowed." Nevertheless, the story that he had greeted Her Majesty in that fashion, receiving in return a kindly smile, caught fire in 1935 and added to his rapidly growing popularity.

Son of a Scot who migrated to California to start a laundry business, Budge had crimson hair and a pink complexion. Cartoonists were grateful for a prominent nose and receding chin. Tennis authorities were equally pleased by his willingness to always co-operate.

In adolescence, this 6 ft. 1 in. Californian was painfully shy. But thanks to his buddy, Gene Mako (also born in 1916), Budge expanded and learnt self-reliance. Mako, completely poised and older than his years, also transmitted to Budge an interest in jazz and practical jokes.

As a boy, Don preferred even marbles to tennis. Then, partly joking, partly appeasing elder brother, tennis-coach Lloyd Budge, he entered the Californian boys' junior championship of 1930—and won the singles after one week's practice.

His appetite whetted, Don improved by leaps and bounds. His first big win came in the 1934 U.S. Clay Court semi-final where he met Parker in the semi-final. Parker was defending champion and seemed sure of a place in the final again when he led Budge by two sets and 3-1. Feeling the match was won and easing his concentration, Parker slackened in his relentless retrieving—to let Budge in with a torrent of hurricane shots. The red-head stormed through the next eleven games and in a terrific finish hit himself to victory, 2-6, 3-6, 6-3, 6-0, 9-7.

He lost his final to the sterling defence of Grant, but with Mako won his first important doubles championship. Forest Hills provided an opportunity for revenge and in the third round he overcame Grant 6-3, 3-6, 4-6, 8-6, 6-3. 10,000 people saw Budge then oppose Vernon Kirby who had beaten Shields in an earlier round. Left-handed, Kirby disguised the direction of his forehand too well for the 17-year-old Californian and won 4-6, 6-4, 6-4, 6-4.

The highlight of Budge's 1934 tennis was at the Pacific Coast championship where in the final he made Perry throw all his reserves of brilliance into their match before the Englishman could win 3-6,

6-4, 7-5, 1-6, 7-5. The team of Budge-Mako, too, was rapidly ascending. Victorious at Rye and Southampton, they won the Pacific Coast doubles and finished the season in glorious fashion, when at Los Angeles they overthrew in succession Lott and Stoeffen (the Wimbledon champions) and then the formidable and famous Allison and Van Ryn.

Budge and Mako could no longer be ignored, and as a reward they were chosen for a European trip in 1935.

Aided by Sydney Wood, Budge now relinquished a "Western" forehand for an "Eastern" grip—but not until 1937 was he completely satisfied. "My backhand is my forte," was no exaggeration. Hit with body swing and simplicity, it remains one of the great shots of tennis.

At first, the leisurely Vines was his hero. "Then I saw Perry bounding, and I saw him take the ball on the rise. I immediately began to walk faster." A combination of Perry and Vines was discernible in Budge's wonderful attacking game, a game he never ceased to enjoy.

Budge was an immediate success in England—and, indeed, throughout his career his popularity was phenomenal. If he lost, a wide smile acknowledged defeat and offered congratulations—if he were victorious, alibis for his opponent and a sympathetic grin were forthcoming.

By 1935, Budge had developed a compact, confident game. His volleying improved after studying Fred Perry—from Mako he learnt the drive-volley. A somewhat cramped forehand was, nevertheless, quite safe. A peerless backhand and a scintillating overhead soon made him one of the world's most formidable players. But, despite his interest in tennis, Budge asserts, "When the game ceases to be fun, a player should cut the guts out of his rackets and put them in storage." It was his delight in tennis that appealed to so many admirers.

At his first Wimbledon in 1935 Budge showed his mettle by reaching the semi-final and beating two seeded men. He draw a large crowd when disposing of Britain's Frank Wilde—he then beat South African Max Bertram—and next accounted for Australian Adrian Quist. So far, Budge had not lost a set. He then tackled the seeded Frenchman Boussus. Budge opened with a devastating attack. The artistic Boussus won one rally in the first three games of the first set and only three rallies in the first four games of the second. He was soon down 6-3, 6-2. But he found his touch and with Budge taking a breather, Boussus captured the third set 6-3 with some elegant net play—only for Budge to crash through the next set with such power that he won it to love.

In the quarter-final, Austin in perfect volleying touch, led Budge by a set and 5-2. He paid too much attention, however, to his opponent's backhand which strengthened under pressure. Budge pulled out several stunning passing shots and the score reached 5-all. As the match lengthened, Austin's chances of victory receded. With greater speed and stamina, the Californian, who did not feel the heat as much as his opponent, survived a tough battle lasting over two hours (3-6, 10-8, 6-4, 7-5).

In the semi-final, Von Cramm's powerful cross-court forehands defeated Budge 4-6, 6-4, 6-3, 6-2. In 1932 people said of Vines "Another Tilden"—now, three years later, Budge was labelled "Another Vines".

Although beaten by Grant 6-4, 6-4, 5-7, 6-3 on a damp court in the U.S. quarter-final, Budge achieved a No. 2 ranking in America in 1935. He won at Newport after Frank Shields had nearly aced his way to victory (6-3, 5-7, 3-6, 8-6, 6-1). Another win over Shields was recorded in the Los Angeles semi-final (7-5, 6-4, 6-4)—and Budge went on to win the title from Menzel. The red-haired Californian finished a wonderful streak of successes by a triple win in the Pacific Coast championships, where in the singles final, his victim was Riggs 6-0, 6-2, 7-9, 6-4.

Budge's Davis Cup wins in 1936 over Crawford (13-11 in the fifth set) and Quist, proved he was Von Cramm's equal. And indeed only Perry now had the beating of this 20-year-old Californian.

At Queen's Club, Budge won a two-set final from American David Jones (6-4, 6-3). Jones had a mighty service but could not hope to hold Budge in ground strokes. In this match Jones served twenty-two aces and eight double-faults, whereas Budge contributed fifteen aces and one double-fault.

Seeded No. 5 at Wimbledon, Budge's severity forfeited only thirty-one games in five matches. In the semi-final Perry led Budge 5-3, only to lose the next four games. He then decided to attack Budge from the back of the court. This won him two sets. Budge reached 4-2 in the fourth set, but his spurt only invited another assault from the Englishman who won 5-7, 6-4, 6-3, 6-4.

But in the U.S. final that autumn, Perry was twice within two points of defeat. In their greatest match the Englishman beat Budge 2-6, 6-2, 8-6, 1-6, 10-8. Budge's backhand passes left the most agile volleyer in the world stranded at the net. His withering attack produced a 5-3 lead in the fifth set, but Perry's steadiness and superb physique just survived a thrilling finish.

In their last meeting as amateurs, Budge was revenged on Perry at Los Angeles 6-2, 4-6, 6-2, 6-3. Perry, however, was not keyed up to his usual buoyancy. In was the Englishman who advising a shorter swing now helped Budge to eradicate the last weakness on his fore-hand.

Critics confidently forecast that Budge, not Von Cramm, would

125

be next Wimbledon champion and in 1937 the Californian towered above tennis. In the Davis Cup he won all his matches (eight singles and four doubles with Mako). At Queen's Club, he gave a demonstration of his devastating power when he overwhelmed Austin in the final 6-1, 6-2.

Frank Parker was the only contestant who could take a set off Budge at Wimbledon. This was in the semi-final, Budge having stormed through five rounds losing thirty-five games. Parker's stabbing service returns won the first set. At 4-all in the second Budge was looking anxious—once he was on level terms his assurance flooded back. There was only one man in the match at the finish (2-6, 6-4, 6-4, 6-1).

In the final, even Von Cramm's brilliance failed to shake Budge's all-court efficiency. The German led 3-1 in the first set and was within a stroke of 5-4 in the second. But Budge was faultless—he had a reply to every move. "What could I do against such tennis?" asked Von Cramm, who collected only nine games (6-3, 6-4, 6-2).

But Budge was to play even greater tennis soon after, for in the Davis Cup Inter-Zone final, with the score two rubbers all, he and Von Cramm met again.

The brilliant German, producing his best-ever tennis, led 4-1 in the final set, and not one of the 12,000 spectators gave Budge a chance. Drama reached its greatest height when Von Cramm, straining every sinew for victory, was met by a Californian counter-attack.

"I did have to take desperate chances." These tactics twice pulled Von Cramm back from 5-3, and before an audience worked up to an almost unbearable climax, America beat Germany 6-8, 5-7, 6-4, 6-2, 8-6.

Tilden, witness of the exploits of Norman Brookes, Bill Johnston and the "Musketeers", declared this the finest Davis Cup tennis he had seen. In the Challenge Round, Budge beat Charles Hare 15-13, 6-1, 6-2 and Austin 8-6, 3-6, 6-4, 6-3, America triumphing 4-1.

By defeating Von Cramm in the American final 6-1, 7-9, 6-1, 3-6, 6-1 Budge equalled the feats of H. L. Doherty, Vines and Perry, by holding the U.S. and Wimbledon crowns simultaneously. The German's backhand passing shots were breath-taking, but he was fighting a man whom he felt he could never now beat. Budge was then awarded the J. E. Sullivan trophy for the best American sportsman of 1937.

His professional value was soaring. A Budge-Vines tour was the wish of every would-be promoter. Although not wealthy, Budge refused 50,000 dollars. He wished to repay the U.S. L.T.A. for several European trips by defending the Davis Cup in 1938.

Neither tennis nor travel rendered the red-head stale. By defeating John Bromwich (victor over a tired Von Cramm) 6-4, 6-2, 6-1 in the

Australian final of 1938, and then winning the French championship at the expense of Menzel (6-3, 6-2, 6-4), Budge established a record. He now held, simultaneously, the four major championships in tennis.

Von Cramm and Budge had become close friends. The German had been divorced, and on his return from Australia, the Nazis imprisoned him. Budge had promised Von Cramm he would play in Germany in 1938, but now refused. Some prominent officials considered it unwise to mix politics with tennis, but Budge was adamant. He hated the Nazi way of life and resented his friend's imprisonment.

At Wimbledon in 1938, Budge was at his zenith. He lost only forty-eight games, crushing Austin in the final 6-1, 6-0, 6-3. When the match was completed Budge gave one of those demonstrations that made him so popular. Procedure demanded that the champion left the Centre Court first, but Budge requested his opponent, who was ten years older and England's No. 1, to accept this privilege. Austin, however, refused and they left the arena according to custom.

The Californian's brilliant career was drawing to its close. Although unwell, Budge beat Bromwich in the Davis Cup 6-2, 6-3, 4-6, 7-5, after saving four set points in the fourth set (one by a net cord) and then settled the issue by defeating Quist 8-6, 6-1, 6-2.

When Budge had added to his laurels by retaining the U.S. title with wins over Sydney Wood and Mako, the American authorities, mindful of his sacrifice in 1937, looked benevolently on his decision to play professional tennis. It was his Davis Cup captain who publicly announced Budge's exit from the amateur game on 9th November, 1938.

Budge beat Vines 6-3, 6-4, 6-2 at Madison Square Gardens in their first match, and won the series 22-17. Later he toured with Perry and then announced he would play only the piano for six months.

Despite a wonderful entry Budge won the French professional title in 1939. He beat Tilden (conqueror of Cochet) 8-6, 6-3, 7-5, and then Vines (victor over Stoeffen and Ramillon) 6-2, 7-5, 6-3.

In 1941, Budge defeated Riggs in a series, and in the U.S. professional final of 1942.

During hostilities Budge, commissioned in the army, injured his right shoulder. With added weight and lessened interest, he lost in the U.S. professional final to Riggs 6-3, 6-1, 6-1 in 1946. Next year, however, Riggs was forced to 3-6, 6-3, 10-8, 4-6, 6-3.

In 1948, Budge defeated Dinny Pails 4-6, 6-2, 6-3, 6-3, before losing the semi-final to Kramer 6-4, 8-10, 3-6, 6-4, 6-0. Fatigue helped to overcome the older player, who gave a great performance against the man who dominated amateur tennis after World War II.

California has produced many great champions, but none more distinctive than Donald Budge. His fiery head, popular personality and wonderful backhand have made indelible contributions to the game.

127

21

Triumph and Tragedy

WHEN Alice Marble arrived at Wimbledon in 1937 she drew attention not only by her tennis and boyish athletic figure. Her shorts—the briefest yet worn on the Centre Court—her pretty shirt blouses and a jaunty jockey cap under which nestled a cabbage leaf (a protection against sun-stroke) also caused considerable comment.

But most noticeable, perhaps, was her joy at playing in the championships. So long had she been in the shadow of insecurity and ill-health that she radiated happiness. Her story is as romantic as the adventures of her famous fictional namesake. As Alice went through a looking-glass into a new world, so did Miss Marble emerge from obscurity into fame.

The daughter of a lumberman, this long-legged, attractive Californian was born on 28th September, 1913. Her family moved to San Francisco where Mr. Marble died of pneumonia, leaving them penniless. "Mother got up at four every morning and cleaned office buildings so she could make ends meet."

It was Dan, her eldest brother and hero, who made Alice renounce baseball for that "silly cissy game, tennis". After four months Alice won her first cup. "I ran almost all the way home to show it to Dan but in the street I dropped it and both handles fell off."

To pay for tennis, Alice did baby sitting and worked in a canteen. In 1931, she was Californian junior champion. Her baseball activities helped to develop that lovely swinging service. Her volley and her stop-volleys were deadly in their efficiency and a joy to watch—her smash was, perhaps, the most decisive seen in women's tennis.

It was now that she met Eleanor Tennant who, unable to help her at that time, asked Howard Kinsey to coach Alice. Kinsey taught her spin and strategy and she won the Californian State title in 1932.

Alice provided an immediate sensation at her first appearance that year at Forest Hills by defeating Sarah Palfrey in the first round. In the third round, she led Joan Ridley 6-3, 4-1 and served an apparent ace for 5-1. Miss Ridley disputed the service, Alice lost concentration and was beaten 3-6, 6-4, 6-3.

By winning at San Francisco from Mrs. Harper 6-2, 6-2, Alice achieved a No. 7 U.S. ranking for 1932.

It was now that Eleanor Tennant really entered Alice's life. She

Partners at Wimbledon in 1949. Frederick R. "Ted" Schroeder (U.S.A.), who won the Championship that year, and American Doubles star Gardnar Mulloy.

Budge Patty. Elegant, economical, this popular American triumphed at Wimbledon in 1950.

Dick Savitt (U.S.A.).   A fluent backhand allied to all-round weight of shot secured the Wimbledon crown at his first appearance in 1951.

Miss Gertrude Moran, America's much publicized " Gorgeous Gussy "—and those equally famous panties!

got her a job in a sports firm and superintended her training. With Beese White, she re-modelled Alice's drives. Alice resisted their efforts at first, but finally gave way. The famous Marble backhand began to take shape, the forehand, if never so secure, was greatly strengthened. Few players have played tennis more naturally. Alice's grace, her supple body-swing and her resilience bore the hall-mark of a champion.

1933 . . . and Alice entered on her wonderful career, a career that suddenly collapsed and seemed doomed, but was pulled out of chaos by the courage of a girl of twenty.

All seemed well when Alice won at Essex and in the Longwood Singles. Many competitors and Committee members were, however, cold-shouldering the successful daughter of a lumberman. To justify selection for the Wightman Cup, Alice was the only player told to compete in singles and doubles at the Maidstone Club tournament. Her protest was curtly over-ruled. Fearful of jeopardising her career, Alice agreed. After playing 108 games in a temperature of 104°, Alice lost the doubles and the singles final to Betty Nuthall 5-7, 6-2, 6-0. She also lost twelve pounds in weight and contracted sunstroke.

Eleanor Tennant gave the Committee a piece of her mind. Incensed newspapers wrote up the incident. Alice gained a place in the Wightman Cup doubles but was exhausted at Forest Hills losing the quarter-final to Betty Nuthall 6-8, 6-0, 7-5. Alice led 5-1, 30-15 in the last set, but seemed to have no will to win. She was ill with fainting fits, and a bout of anaemia necessitated complete rest, but she joyfully sailed for Europe under the captaincy of Helen Jacobs in 1934.

Years of heartbreak were in store for her. Playing Mme. Henrotin in France, Alice collapsed. She remembered nothing of an agitated drive across Paris to the American Hospital at Neuilly. Tuberculosis was diagnosed. "No one, not even Helen Jacobs . . . could cheer me up . . . I spent hours crying."

Alice was sent home and Eleanor Tennant put her in a sanatorium slaving for the girl of whom she was so fond. With the help of Carole Lombard she kept Alice going mentally as her nerve, too, was cracking.

With care and rest, Alice struggled through. Eventually in 1936 she was allowed to re-enter tennis tournaments. She was not always fit and tired easily. Nevertheless, with Gene Mako she became American mixed champion. She took a set from Helen Jacobs in the Essex Club final, but seemed hardly likely to trouble her in the American final, where Helen, despite a bandaged thumb, led 6-4, 2-0.

Alice, too, was not well—"my legs felt like lead"—but she produced a wonder net attack of smashes, volleys and stop-volleys that

129

I

took ten of the next eleven games. Helen then won two games but could not prevent her opponent's victory 4-6, 6-3, 6-2. So overcome was Alice that she had to ask the umpire if she had really won.

So Alice came to Wimbledon at last in 1937. She arrived early to get acclimatised but lost three finals—at Beckenham, Weybridge and Surbiton. She still tired quickly, because lacking baseline control, she tried to win whole matches from the net, but the vital spark of the potential champion was discernible.

At Wimbledon she was the last American, achieving a remarkable victory against Fru Sperling 7-5, 2-6, 6-3, after the German led 3-0, 40-15 in the third set. Alice then forgot caution, six games of wonder volleying giving her victory.

In the semi-final, her forcing forecourt game held Jedrzejowska for one set. Then the Polish player's withering forehand began to extract errors and Alice, lapsing into wildness, was defeated 8-6, 6-2.

She was defeated in the U.S. quarter-final when "Dodo" Bundy, trailing by a set and 3-4, fought back against an over-confident opponent to win 1-6, 7-5, 6-1. Alice was worn out in the third set.

She never lost at Forest Hills again, but had to bide her time at Wimbledon. Although there was less wildness in her play from the baseline she could not yet counter a more varied defence.

Alice met Helen Jacobs in the Wimbledon semi-final in 1938. For once uncertain overhead, Alice, after missing some vital smashes, retired to the baseline. Here she could not deal with Helen's variation of spin and pace and had to yield 6-4, 6-4. This was her last defeat in important tennis by a fellow American. But in the U.S. semi-final, Sarah Palfrey nearly emulated Helen Jacobs's victory.

Down 1-5, Sarah routed Alice for the next nine games. At 5-2 in the second set she led 40-15 only for Alice to produce a great backhand volley and then force Sarah to net a return. It was now Alice who hit the lines with drives and volleys. From 3-5 she raced to 7-5 losing four rallies. Forest Hills was thrilled by their net play but Alice's overhead was more lethal. After both girls had scored 122 winners, she triumphed 5-7, 7-5, 7-5, to a tremendous ovation.

Next day she was superb. Here was the complete champion the critics had predicted. Australian Nancye Wynne was overwhelmed 6-0, 6-3.

It was known that Alice contemplated turning professional in 1938, but she realised the value of a win at Wimbledon. She continued her superb attractive tennis throughout 1939 and her serve-volley offensive (then a novelty in women's tennis) scattered the most stalwart opposition.

She revealed her superiority by defeating Kay Stammers at

130

Beckenham 6-3, 6-1. Her flat-hit volleys lost nineteen games in reaching the Wimbledon semi-final.

Now the Californian faced her greatest test. Fru Sperling had never won the championship but was a terror to champions. In an incredible display, Alice, attacking the most redoubtable retriever in tennis won the first set in nine minutes, losing nine points, and the second in eleven minutes losing five points.

Suzanne had never given the Centre Court such a sterling mixture of glorious power tennis. Fru Sperling only achieved one backhand passing shot. A storm threatened and Alice successfully raced the elements to win 6-0, 6-0.

In a 30-minute final she disposed of erratic Kay Stammers 6-2, 6-0, and to cement her superiority, Alice won the doubles with Sarah Fabyan and the mixed with Riggs.

Alice was the winner of a desperate final against Helen Jacobs at Forest Hills in 1939. She led 6-0, 3-1, but Helen drew level and did not submit until a third set 6-0, 8-10, 6-4.

During her convalescence Alice took up singing and entertained wounded soldiers in the war. After another victory over Helen Jacobs at Forest Hills in 1940, she signed a contract and immediately gave half her fortune to Eleanor Tennant.

She opposed Mary Hardwicke in more than three hundred exhibitions, and also coached professionally.

Despite financial security, her ill-luck followed her. Her friend lovely Carole Lombard was killed in an air crash. Later, Alice fell in love. "Joe was brown-haired and stocky, not terribly tall . . . he was the only one I saw." Their feelings were mutual, and she had never been happier. Then—"One night . . . the 'phone rang. It was Joe's commanding officer. The Colonel's voice trembled" . . . Joe had died in an air crash over Germany. Later the heart-broken tennis star had a recurrence of her illness necessitating an operation. She now lectures in America on the art of successful living.

Tragic yet triumphant, Alice's success story was dogged by disaster. Her flair for attacking tennis might never be equalled. By her wonderful skill, this thoroughly sporting American gave delight to thousands and started a new era in women's tennis.

22

"Bad Boy of Tennis"

PIGEON toes, a cocky grin and unlimited self-confidence. Add to this every stroke in tennis, mobility and supreme cunning, and the answer is Bobby Riggs, Wimbledon champion in 1939.

Nicknamed in America "The Bad Boy of Tennis", Riggs holds one supreme record—he was never beaten in any event at Wimbledon. In his only appearance there, this product of Los Angeles won the singles, the doubles with Elwood Cooke and the mixed with Alice Marble. Playing a beautifully controlled, fluent game—not hitting as hard as Vines but severely enough to win three championships—Riggs was the complete master. His rhythm and his balance were wonderful. His cleverness has been called "diabolical" and would have done credit to a veteran.

Riggs loved the big occasion—together with a bet on his ability to come through victorious. A satisfied grin did nothing to help a flustered opponent. He was never happier than when opposed to a baseliner who tried to outwit him. It was in these encounters that he could display his lovely stroke play and ability to make use of the whole court. The Californian often let opponents dictate to him the type of game that suited them best and he would then play—and beat them—at it.

Short, but of sound physique, his lack of inches was a sore point with Riggs—for reasons more valid than vanity. The Californian tennis authorities accustomed to athletes built on the lines of Vines and Budge—and forgetting Cochet's years of supremacy—consistently ignored Riggs declaring he was too small to ever become a world champion.

Lacking the physique and the temperament for cannon-balls, Riggs, nevertheless, could return a ball from anywhere to anywhere on court. Like Cochet, he liked to make a meal of his matches. This so annoyed one critic, a warm advocate of the Vines "hitting" school, that he called Riggs "the best Frenchman produced by America since the days of Cochet".

Born on 25th February, 1918, Robert L. Riggs was the son of a minister, being the youngest of seven children with a seven-year difference in age between him and the next child. His first love was table tennis—at eleven he started tennis. At fourteen, he was thrilled when 16-year-old prodigy Frank Parker—already a name in American tennis—spoke to him saying "Some day you're going to be a good player, kid". Parker then walked off engrossed by his book—"Tarzan of the Apes".

Riggs was coached by Dr. Esther Bartosh and his improvement was phenomenal. In 1935, he was unbeaten in junior tennis. He registered seventeen wins over Joseph Hunt (American champion of 1943) and conquered him in the National Junior Championship final 6-3, 1-6, 4-6, 6-0, 6-4. The winner felt himself ready for senior competitive tennis—the prospect of Wimbledon and the Davis Cup holding particular appeal.

Every potential champion from California was sent "East"—to compete in the Eastern seaboard grass court tournaments. Riggs was not given this chance. He and officialdom had little time for one another.

Riggs and his great friend Wayne Sabin found a backer and toured privately. Riggs won five tournaments. And although he went down to John Van Ryn in the second round of the 1936 American championships—it was Rigg's first season on grass—the junior won a set from Budge (now the top U.S. player) at Rye. A win at Newport over Frank Parker gained Riggs a No. 4 ranking in America for 1936.

Newspapers were now constantly writing him up as the "Bad Boy of Tennis" due to his quarrels with tennis authorities. The storm broke early in 1937. Riggs was mad keen on getting to Wimbledon. A group of friends agreed to finance him for the trip. They dropped the idea when he was invited to join the Davis Cup squad—to find out he was wanted for practice, only.

"I was raging mad . . . I got a well-placed kick in the teeth." Fuming at all tennis associations and determined to prove to the world that the U.S.L.T.A. had made a mistake, 19-year-old Riggs started the 1937 season in an unshakeable frame of mind. His most powerful rivals Budge, Mako, Parker and Grant were mopping up Wimbledon between them. They then captured the Davis Cup from Britain. All these triumphs were a source of annoyance to Riggs who felt, with justification that he was as good as Parker or Grant who were getting all the publicity plus the experience of tennis in Europe.

Meanwhile, Riggs was having things all his own way at home. He won at Seabright defeating the drop shots and volleying of the brilliant Japanese Yamagishi 6-4, 3-6, 6-1, 2-6, 6-3 in the semi-final; and then getting a walk-over from Allison in the final. A further success was at Southampton where he defeated Yamagishi 6-4, 6-3 (retired).

By this time the all-triumphant Davis Cup team were home and being welcomed as heroes—by all, except Riggs. Full of confidence, he was "gunning" for Parker and Grant. At Rye he beat Parker 6-3, 7-5, 7-5. He defeated Grant in a tournament next week and then at Newport gained a second victory over Parker in the semi-final 6-8, 6-4, 6-3, 4-6, 6-3. He won many rallies with clever drop shots in the final against Budge but could not achieve more than one set (6-4, 6-8, 6-1, 6-2).

Forest Hills was even more gratifying. Von Cramm was No. 2 in the world and had lost the Wimbledon final to Budge. In a thrilling semi-final, Riggs produced his best tennis to date when taking the first two sets off the German 6-0, 8-6. But ceaseless chasing of Von Cramm's widely-placed drives tired him and the German, rushing the net as much as possible, won the next three sets 6-3, 6-3, 6-2.

His defensive tactics sometimes exhausted the little Californian— but with a Lacoste-like ability to take stock of an opponent's game he had profited by his match with Von Cramm. And a month later in the semi-final at San Francisco, Riggs decided he was not going to let the German run him off his feet. To the astonishment and—in some quarters—annoyance of America, Riggs's inspired display defeated Von Cramm in straight sets.

He lost the final to Budge 4-6, 6-3, 6-2, 6-4 but had the satisfaction of being ranked second in America in 1937. Only Budge out of the Davis Cup nominees gained a higher position.

1938 started with another row—the authorities were frowning on Riggs's expenses account. A tirade from the Californian caused them to withdraw. He was dismayed by his omission from the team chosen for Wimbledon. In selecting Budge and Mako, the authorities announced they were financing only title-holders—Budge was Wimbledon champion and Budge-Mako held the doubles.

Despite his No. 2 ranking, Riggs was also told he must justify selection for the Davis Cup. Gritting his teeth, the Californian won at Seabright, the Longwood Bowl at Boston, Southampton and Rye and nothing could prevent his selection as No. 2 player to defend the Davis Cup in 1938.

In his opening rubber Riggs survived a weird match against Adrian Quist 4-6, 6-0, 8-6, 6-1. Quist pulled up from 5-1, 40-love down in the third set after which he was finished. In the final rubber with the cup already retained, Riggs was beaten by Bromwich 6-3, 4-6, 6-0, 6-2.

At Forest Hills Riggs lost unexpectedly to Gilbert Hall 6-2, 0-6, 9-7, 0-6, 6-4. But in 1939 with Budge now professional, Riggs was granted his cherished desire of a trip to Europe. With a new partner Elwood Cooke he sailed in the President Roosevelt.

At Paris, although dropping odd sets, Riggs reached the final easily enough. There he met a fellow American, Don McNeill, a competent

134

hard-hitter who had lost to Riggs in their ten matches in America. McNeill led 6-5 in the first set when Riggs had a very heavy fall. He seemed shaken, although it made no material difference to his play. McNeill, giving an alluring volleying display, ran his opponent about mercilessly to win the next ten games. Riggs rallied, but McNeill was champion at 7-5, 6-0, 6-3.

At Queen's Club, Riggs lost 6-1, 6-0 to Von Cramm (barred from Wimbledon because of his imprisonment). The surface was slippery and Riggs apparently feared another tumble.

Untroubled by these reverses, Riggs bet £10 on his chances at Wimbledon, where his compact game took him to the final. Here he met Cooke, and although the latter led by two sets to one, Riggs was not in real danger. Cooke had been kept on the move and was thoroughly weary, and Riggs showed his genius for match play by taking the offensive in the last two sets 2-6, 8-6, 3-6, 6-3, 6-2.

Another triumph awaited him at Forest Hills. In a championship noted for sensational upsets, Riggs won the final against Welby Van Horn (conqueror of John Bromwich) 6-4, 6-2, 6-4.

A contract for 25,000 dollars was lined up for Riggs if he retained his U.S. title in 1940. But after beating Talbert, Schroeder and Joseph Hunt he lost to McNeill (victor over Cooke and Jack Kramer) in a brilliant final 4-6, 6-8, 6-3, 6-3, 7-5.

25,000 dollars also awaited the champion of 1941, so Riggs concentrated on early nights, no beer and much beef. He got into wonderful form, beating Schroeder and Kramer for a fourth victory at Seabright and crushing Frank Kovacs in straight sets at Southampton.

Kovacs was rapidly ascending the U.S. ranking list. He and Riggs cordially disliked one another—at any rate on court Riggs found his fooling excessively annoying. Handsome and humorous, Kovacs was America's Danny Kaye of tennis. He once shocked Forest Hills by sitting on court drinking beer—but he could also produce marvellous tennis when he felt like training.

Although McNeill was defending champion, Riggs considered Kovacs the greatest danger at Forest Hills in 1941. They met in the final after Riggs had beaten Parker and survived a desperate battle against Schroeder (7-5 in the fifth set). Kovacs had dethroned McNeill.

Riggs lost the first set to Kovacs' storming. Then realising that retrieving was not going to pay, he attacked with such success that he lost only seven more games (5-7, 6-1, 6-3, 6-3). Both men then turned professional for 25,000 dollars.

Despite Pearl Harbour, 11,000 people attended the opening matches at Madison Square Garden on Boxing Day, 1941, to see

Budge, Kovacs, Riggs and Perry. A Budge-Riggs tour followed and Budge beat his rival in the U.S. professional final of 1942.

After thirty months in the U.S. Navy, Riggs, profiting from hard practice with Howard Kinsey, turned the tables on an out-of-condition Budge 6-3, 6-1, 6-1 in fifty-six minutes in the U.S. professional final of 1946. He again overcame Budge in the 1947 final.

In November, 1947, the professional ranks were joined by Jack Kramer, Wimbledon champion. Before 16,000 spectators Riggs won his opening match against Kramer 6-2, 10-8, 6-4 but in their series Kramer, dominated at first, emerged a comfortable victor. He abandoned trying to combat Riggs from the baseline, and his powerful net attack wrested the initiative from his older opponent. Kramer beat Riggs 14-12, 6-2, 3-6, 6-3 in the 1948 U.S. professional final and again at Wembley in 1949.

Riggs has a superb knowledge of tennis. Kramer sums up the difficulty of beating him when he admits "The pressure is never off. The heat is on all the time".

23

The Tricolour Again

YVON PETRA never expected to win Wimbledon in 1946. He had
already picked the champion. "I admire for the first time the
American Kramer and make him my favourite."

He always knew he could play super tennis and beat a great
player—on one of his own great days. When, therefore, his match-
winning form continued and he toppled a series of redoubtable
opponents, Petra became more and more delighted—and excited.

The Centre Court first saw Petra in 1936. This 6 ft. 5 in. sprightly
French Colonial was then twenty. Born in Indo-China, he had learnt
to play tennis in his bare feet and had developed a game based on the
trans-Atlantic serve-volley schools. Petra was built on American
lines and, emulating Vines, he sometimes wore a white peaked
cap.

His beautifully produced cannon-ball, hit from the very sky,
and a wide sweeping forehand also recalled Vines's tennis. Petra's
backhand weakened under pressure, but it took a great player to
profit from it.

Critics were not impressed in 1936, but Petra reached the third
round at Wimbledon before losing to Don Butler. Next year, he
failed to win a set from Austin in the French quarter-final (6-4, 6-2,
6-1) and at Wimbledon he was overcome in the first round by Frank
Wilde (7-5 in the final set).

Petra and Mme. Mathieu had won the French mixed doubles in
1937 and at Wimbledon they reached the final there to lose to Budge-
Alice Marble, 6-4, 6-1. Simonne Mathieu's gestures of despair were
world-famous and she transmitted many of them to her partner. The
Centre Court rocked at their antics, Simonne proclaiming the net
was English and Petra, all frenzied arms and legs, muttering and
hitting the ground with his racket, as though straightening out
imaginary weeds on the turf.

Although overwhelmed 6-0, 6-3, 6-1 in the fourth round at Forest
Hills by Budge in 1937, Petra's touring was tightening up his tennis.
He played brilliantly in the winter of 1937/38. Karl Schroder, the
hefty young Swede, armed with a great swinging service, was then
considered the strongest player on wood. He had several victories
over Borotra to his credit. Petra defeated Schroder after seventy

137

games, and then beat H. Bolelli to win the Coupe de Noel. By over-coming Paul Feret (victor over Borotra) Petra won the Paris All-Saints tournament, while his best triumph to date was in the French Covered Court championship when he beat Boussus 7-5, 8-6, 6-8, 6-3 and then volleyed his way past Schroder 9-7, 7-5, 3-6, 9-7.

France proclaimed a new Gobert, but Petra disappointed in the French championships of 1938, losing the first round to Spychala, the hard-working Pole. An inspired display in the doubles final made amends when with Destremau, Petra beat the famous Budge-Mako team 3-6, 6-3, 9-7, 6-1.

Davis Cup commitments on hard courts kept Petra from Wimbledon in 1938. He re-visited Indo-China that winter and was called up in 1939. Wounded, he underwent a delicate knee operation and was out of tennis until his release as a prisoner-of-war in North Africa in 1941.

Henri Cochet was running French tournaments in a limited form. Petra beat him in the "Tournoi de France" final in 1943 after five terrific sets. In 1944, on the eve of France's liberation, Petra defeated Bernard in five sets, to keep his title. Without losing a set, Petra captured the Paris championship in 1945 again overthrowing Bernard in the final—and he went on to win the French championship by a straight set defeat of Destremau.

These successes gained Petra some notice at Wimbledon in 1946, but not many critics took his chances of victory seriously. Neither, for that matter, did Petra. Kramer was strongly backed until his loss to Drobny left Dinny Pails top favourite.

The Centre Court was in for a series of dramatic matches all revolving around Yvon Petra. The Frenchman and Pails were scheduled for a quarter-final but Pails, missing his train, was an hour late on court. Petra refused a walk-over but both he and his opponent were highly agitated when play started.

Pails led 5-3 but Petra, despite the tension, hit and served with great accuracy and power to win 7-5, 7-5, 6-8, 6-4. Lapses of concentration caused Pails to miss some vital overheads but Henry Hopman admitted Petra won by his brilliance.

Tom Brown, last U.S. hope, and determined to uphold American prestige, led Petra by two sets in the semi-final. His strong whipped drives and beautiful net game dominated the match. Slackening somewhat in the heat, before the sustained pressure of a cannon-balling opponent, America allowed France to win the third set.

Excitement grew at 5-all in the fourth set. Petra then jumped in, crowded the net, and with some glorious power tennis drew level at two-sets all. He later admitted his service at this stage had saved the match. Brown re-acted and Petra, now all exuberance, stormed to

5-3 in the final thrilling set. Brown pulled himself together and made it 5-all.

Now the Centre Court witnessed some Tilden-like disputes with linesmen. Not crisis-proof, Petra declared that some decisions in the tenth game were unsatisfactory. Brown, un-nerved, lost his service and some furious French volleying finished the battle (4-6, 4-6, 6-3, 7-5, 8-6). In the opinion of many spectators, however, a great match had been ruined by Petra's protestations.

Another Brown—Geoffrey, of Australia—was Petra's last opponent. He had been advised to slow down the game and slow up the giant. When Petra refused to be shaken and led by two sets. Brown, in despair, reverted to his usual big hitting. Aces and a lusty two-handed shot won him the bitter third set. But Petra kept his head—his backhand remained firm under an intense assault—and he reached 5-4, 40-15, in the fourth set.

Brown's answer was to hit two outright winners off service, then to lead 6-5 and finally to take the set by breaking Petra's service to love!

Excited, Brown lost his opening service in the fifth set and this really cost him the match. A wonder half-volley from between his legs took Petra to 3-1. He was matching Brown for speed, and at 5-4 he had to serve for victory. He did so in glorious fashion, four dynamic aces proclaiming him champion by 6-2, 6-4, 7-9, 5-7, 6-4. The French flag had not flown over Wimbledon since Henri Cochet's 1929 victory—seventeen years before!

Hardly able to credit his fortune, Petra "threw" a kiss to his wife. He kissed his racket. He nearly kissed Geoff Brown.

Never before had he produced such continuous brilliant tennis. There were better players in the 1946 championship, but his terrific, if unorthodox, fighting spirit had dominated the whole scene.

That year, the French championship followed Wimbledon. Four men were seeded—Petra, Tom Brown, Drobny and Segura. But Marcel Bernard beat Segura and in the semi-final this left-hander exposed Petra's backhand weakness in a way nobody had been able to do at Wimbledon to win 5-7, 6-2, 6-3, 5-7, 6-2. Bernard went on to beat Drobny in the final.

Like Borotra, Petra never did his best in America. Discontented because his second round match against Patty was on a slippery outside court before a handful of spectators, Petra did not stir himself unduly. Losing the first set after he had led 4-2, the Frenchman discarded shoes to get a surer foothold. His big services were taken on the rise by the smooth-stroking Patty who tamed the towering Wimbledon champion to win 6-4, 9-7, 6-4.

Despite these defeats, Riggs was reported to have offered Petra

20,000 dollars to turn professional. But the French authorities persuaded Petra to refuse, promising him a position as manager of the Racing Club in Paris. This offer was verbal and Petra could never insist on its validity.

After a foot operation in 1947, he missed all Davis Cup singles. Nevertheless, Petra, beaten 4-6, 6-3, 6-2, 6-1 in the quarter-final, was the only man to take a set off Josef Asboth in the French championship.

At Wimbledon, hampered by his foot and harassed because his job had failed to materialise, Petra was hardly the Colossus of 1946. Tom Brown, too, was not at his best, but he won their quarter-final comfortably 7-5, 6-2, 6-4. He finished each set with a love game against a man who was now a shade of his former glory.

With a wife and child to support, Petra became a coach earning 1,000 francs an hour at the Hellios Covered Court Club in Brussels in January, 1948. The Centre Court has missed his picturesque personality. His sallies of wit, and sudden wide grin coloured many a battle, making him the most engaging Frenchman seen there since the heyday of the "Musketeers".

24

"Peerless Pauline"

HER family named her Bobbe . . . her friends called her "Peerless Pauline" . . . to her detractors she was "Big Match Betz". This attractive green-eyed daughter of Dayton, Ohio, was never invincible in small tournaments, but give her a major championship and her enthusiasm fired, Pauline Betz would reveal the spirit that gained her a No. 1 ranking in America for many years.

Very agile and vastly intelligent, Pauline was often called the "Lenglen of America". She had Suzanne's exquisite rhythm and co-ordination of movement. Like her, too, Pauline's lissom court covering and her grace possessed "ballerina" quality.

Pauline was born on 6th August, 1919. A tennis and table-tennis career might hardly have been expected of a girl who graduated as a B.A. Recognised as a scholar at Columbia University, Pauline was continually "dated" but nothing deterred this determined young woman from work . . . or Wimbledon.

Her net play and service were adequate, but Pauline was primarily a baseliner—here she revealed the beauty and genius of her tennis. Pauline's favourite and most formidable stroke was a backhand hit with flourish. She took frequent advice to strengthen her forehand drive and thrived on tournament play.

She was, also, a mistress of surprise, often sending over a very hard second service or a mild first delivery. And when she curbed, after 1941, a fondness for attempting far too many spectacular winners, Pauline was ahead of her net-rushing rivals Margaret Osborne and Louise Brough.

Refusing to take life—or tennis—desperately seriously, Pauline declared the greatest thrill of her career was when asked after an exhibition against Jack Kramer "Who won?" On another occasion, perhaps not thrilling, a man at a party—unaware of her identity—informed the tennis star he had seen Miss Betz win at Wimbledon, "A fine player but a big horse of a woman".

When Pauline became U.S. Covered Court champion in 1939, Bobby Riggs forecast that here was the national champion of 1941. Riggs gave her the racket with which he had won Wimbledon—and proved only one year incorrect in his prophecy. His gift whetted Pauline's appetite for gathering other match-winning rackets "Francesco Segura blanched when he saw me!"

Mrs. Betz was a source of constant encouragement to "Bobbe". A physical training instructress, this jovial woman started Pauline on tennis and could defeat her until she was sixteen.

Pauline was beaten 6-3, 6-4, in the first round at Forest Hills in 1939 by Freda James (Mrs. Hammersley) and next year lost the fourth round 5-7, 6-1, 6-2 to Mary Hardwicke.

About this time, Alice Marble turned professional and Helen Jacobs was soon to retire. This gave a fillip to all young Americans, but Sarah Cooke, the last of the old school, beat Pauline in the 1940 covered court final, 6-4, 1-6, 7-5, after leading 5-2 in the third set.

Pauline, however, showed more restraint in 1941. She regained her indoor title, added to it the clay court singles, and when she countered Sarah Cooke's attack at Rye to win 2-6, 8-6, 7-5, several critics backed her for Forest Hills.

Mrs. Cooke, however, was not in a yielding mood. Losing finalist to Helen Jacobs in 1934 and 1935, she had entered the final this time at Helen's expense. In a gale, her intensive volleying broke down Pauline's forehand. Under pressure, Pauline served eleven unusual double-faults to lose 7-5, 6-2.

The lesson was not lost. Pauline set out to remove weak and purposeless hitting against an opponent entrenched at the net.

With the retirement of Sarah Cooke, Pauline was her natural successor. At Forest Hills, she played some delightful, intelligent tennis and her form here in 1942 caused Alice Marble to declare "this is a new Pauline . . . a scrapper like Helen Jacobs . . . three women (Osborne, Brough and Hart) could beat her, but not at Forest Hills".

In America, no sooner has one menace disappeared than another looms. Osborne and Brough now threatened the Betz horizon. Louise startled Pauline's supporters by beating their heroine at Rye, while at Forest Hills, Margaret was only beaten off after Pauline had been within a stroke of defeat in the semi-final. The stoic Betz herself remained unshaken and in the final, she let the volleying fury of Louise Brough burn itself away in the first set. She then conducted a fluent, successful baseline defence to become American champion by 4-6, 6-1, 6-4.

Soon after, she swept Louise out of the final at Los Angeles 6-2, 6-3, by a display of rhythmic beauty.

Pauline was no complacent champion—moreover, she was a glutton for tournaments. 1943 provided her with a rich harvest of prizes. The Mexican, U.S. indoor and U.S. Clay Court titles were gathered by this swift-footed baseliner. She never lost more than three games in any match in the clay court meeting, while in the Tri-State championship final she overwhelmed Catherine Wolf without losing a point.

142

At Forest Hills, Pauline dropped a set to Doris Hart in the semi-final. Louise desperately pulled Pauline back from victory twice in the second set but in the third, the holder swept almost disdainfully to 5-1 and won her second title 6-3, 5-7, 6-3.

Success suited the champion. On and off court she developed a greater confidence. Her nickname "Peerless Pauline" aptly described her new sophisticated personality.

By beating Brough and Osborne, Pauline retained the U.S. trophy in 1944. She seemed to be getting a "Wills-Moody" grip on American tennis when Sarah Cooke, returning after four years absence from the game, surprisingly beat Pauline 6-3, 7-5 in the Clay Court final in 1945.

Betz's followers were not unduly worried by this result. "Bobbe" at Forest Hills was a much tougher proposition—and when she won the first set in the final from Sarah 6-3, and then pulled up from 2-5 to 5-all in the second by magnificent passing shots, the champion seemed certain to retain her title.

But Sarah had received a pep talk that morning. Dozing in a deck chair, she had suddenly awakened when a brown fist was thrust into her face and a firm, staccato voice had insisted, "Sarah, you must win today, you are the last of us". Us, being the old school of Wightman, Ryan, Wills, Jacobs, Marble, and—Molla Mallory, to whom the fist belonged.

So Sarah, "Not aware that I was exactly a hag, I did my best", crowded the net to save the second set 8-6, and launched a series of dainty stop-volleys that were too well-placed even for Pauline. In a feverish finish packed with glorious strokes, Sarah regained the title 3-6, 8-6, 6-4.

Subdued, Pauline realised her forehand was still susceptible to a sustained volleying attack. On Eleanor Tennant's advice, a shorter swing was encouraged. Hours of early morning tennis with "a yawning Budge Patty" plus her own determination, brought a new maturity to Pauline's game which was evident when she invaded Wimbledon in 1946.

Here she was in a class by herself, winning six matches for the loss of twenty games. Her facile base-lining was overwhelming and in a disappointing final Louise Brough could do no better than capture six games (6-2, 6-4).

Very keyed-up the night before the final, Pauline had benefited from a calming-down talk with Alice Marble.

The French championship was the American's next objective. Pauline lost four games in reaching the semi-final where she got past Dorothy Bundy, 6-3, 6-4. Her defeat in the final against Margaret Osborne knocked the critics sideways, more so as she led 6-1, 6-5,

40-15. Three heavy falls might have added to her difficulty as Margaret resolutely gained the net position and with a zealous volleying attack, triumphed 1-6, 8-6, 7-5.

This reversal of fortune did not endure. Soon after, Pauline was in the thick of another final. Down to Doris Hart 2-5 at Forest Hills, Pauline hung on and eventually turned the match in her favour 11-9, 6-3.

Early in 1947, Pauline competed on the Riviera. Rumours that she contemplated a professional tour with Sarah and Elwood Cooke— Pauline had always declared she would go out when on top—led to the U.S. authorities questioning her plans. Possibly they did not favour financing her at Wimbledon if she meant to renounce her amateur status.

Pauline seemed uncertain but finally joined the paid ranks. She toured with Sarah Cooke and later gave table tennis exhibitions.

50-year-old Jack Dempsey, hero of her college days, was reported to be engaged to Miss Betz. Later, a friend introduced her to reporter Bob Addie, saying, "You two ought to get acquainted". "We took his advice," was her laconic comment, and they married in 1949.

The mother of a flourishing family, Mrs. Addie and her children are frequent visitors to American tournaments. "Peerless Pauline" holds one record denied even to Suzanne—she never lost a set in singles at Wimbledon.

Frank Sedgman, Australia's " Golden Boy " of Tennis. His instinctive approach to the game won Wimbledon in 1952.

Vic Seixas (U.S.A.). His own favourite photograph. A very determined fighter, he was rewarded with the Championship in 1953.

Miss Doris Hart.   *Hailing from Florida, she overcame serious physical disabilities to become a very worthy Wimbledon Champion in 1951.*

Formerly a Czech, now an Egyptian, Jaroslav Drobny has a huge following on the Centre Court. He scored a sensational victory in 1954.

25

"King Kramer"

THE phrase "Every inch a champion" may well have been coined for Kramer. Lean, lithe, and long-legged, this Nevada-born athlete with the wonderful muscles displayed an imposing regality on court. Overpowering, but never overbearing, Jack Kramer exercised a benevolent despotism during his brief reign as world champion.

Forsaking his first love, baseball, for tennis, Kramer was U.S. boy champion in 1936 and inter-scholastic champion in 1938. Next year, Ellsworth Vines was officially invited to undertake 18-year-old Kramer's tennis education and before long it was evident that Vines had an ideal pupil.

Lacoste-like in his thoroughness, Kramer modelled his game on his instructor. Whilst he did not generate Vines's continuous crushing speed, Kramer's tennis was equally simple—to seek out his opponent's weakness and then attack it on service, drive and volley. If his rival came up, Kramer hit hard and low, and had at his command an aggressive well-placed spinning lob.

A kicking top-spin service started his attack—a cannon-ball was kept up his sleeve. To perfect a tennis machine, Kramer neither smoked nor drank and schooled himself to achieve complete mental peace before big matches.

. In 1939, although only ranked No. 15 in American tennis, Kramer (one of the youngest nominees since Vincent Richards) received Davis Cup colours. With Joseph Hunt, he won a set from Quist and Bromwich.

Hunt beat Kramer 6-2, 3-6, 5-7, 6-4, 6-3 in the second round at Forest Hills in 1939. Next year, however, Kramer after beating Parker in five sets, reached the semi-final—where he lost to McNeill, the ultimate champion.

Schroeder was Kramer's great friend. Teamed, they produced a Borotra-Brugnon understanding and were unbeaten for two years. At their first attempt they won at Forest Hills in 1940, beating Gardnar Mulloy-W. Sabin, a feat they repeated in 1941 with a win over Mulloy-H. Prussof. The mixed title in 1941 was also collected by Kramer, partnered by Sarah Cooke.

It was now that the famous Kramer "jinx" started to operate. Favourite for the U.S. title in 1942, he developed appendicitis and

145

left the field open to Schroeder. Later he toured South America and was unbeaten in any tournament.

In 1943, Kramer, training for coast guard duties, received permission from New London College, Connecticut, to compete at Forest Hills. Schroeder could not defend because of military duties, but Francesco Segura, who was having a wonderful season, was thought the greatest menace.

Although denied stern practice, Kramer's all-out offensive defeated Segura 2-6, 6-4, 7-5, 6-3 in the semi-final. This established him as top favourite, but a meal of clams made him violently ill just before the final. Suffering with gastric trouble, he lost his chances against Joseph Hunt (6-3, 6-8, 10-8, 6-0). In this last match in the 1943 meeting, neither finalist was included in America's first ten!

In exhibition matches for War Bonds, Kramer beat Budge 3-2. Sent to the Pacific in 1944, he took part in seven marine landings and hardly touched a racket during the next two years.

America, however, kept a close watch on Kramer—so, for that matter, did Australia (champion country). And in 1945, Harry Hopman warned Australia that despite the absence of Budge and Riggs, America was immensely strong because of her potential world-beater, 24-year-old Jack Kramer.

Demobilised in 1946, Kramer was top seed at Wimbledon. But the jinx, dormant since 1943, was not giving up easily. He power-charged his way through three rounds losing five games—only to develop a blister the size of a half-crown on his playing hand. Two fingers were also affected.

Kramer expected trouble in his next match—against the unknown Drobny. And after two and a half hours of brilliant, colourful tennis, the No. 1 seed was out 2-6, 17-15, 6-3, 3-6, 6-3. His previous short struggles had not aggravated his disability—Kramer had played throughout wearing a glove—but the 85-minute second set necessitated the American having medical attention while changing ends. Drobny played superbly, his fade-away volleys were gems, and Kramer generously asserted "A man can still run with a blister on his hand".

At Forest Hills, however, the ex-marine at last buried his bogy. His colossal speed of stroke and his immense service lost one set only—to McNeill in the quarter-final (6-3, 6-2, 1-6, 6-2). Falkenburg's cannon-balls were returned with interest (6-0, 6-4, 6-4) and in the final, Kramer out-steadied Tom Brown 9-7, 6-3, 6-0.

He now bestrode the tennis scene. Forming a two-man team with Schroeder he annihilated Australian opposition to win the Davis Cup in 1946. Playing in a temperature of 100°, Kramer beat Pails 8-6, 6-2, 9-7—Kramer-Schroeder levelled Quist-Bromwich setless—and finally, Kramer's 8-6, 6-4, 6-4 defeat of Bromwich was called "the finest exhibition of the game seen in Australia".

1947 . . . and Kramer was king of tennis, outstripping his rivals as confidently as ever Tilden had done. His physical perfection, his touch and his thunderbolts overwhelmed Wimbledon and, indeed, lessened interest in the men's singles.

The American lost thirty-one games (which included one set) in his quest for victory. Dynamic Geoff Brown was expected to prove an obstacle in the quarter-final but was slaughtered 6-0, 6-1, 6-3. Pails captured a set by running faster than he had ever done before. Kramer then paid him the compliment of ceaseless pressure and won 6-1, 3-6, 6-1, 6-0.

In the final, Tom Brown, convinced his one hope was to attack, tried to blast Kramer off court. The latter relied on sound defence and Brown's game collapsed (6-1, 6-3, 6-2). Throughout the championship, Kramer had played well within himself and had seldom served at more than half-speed.

Kramer never hid his intention of turning professional as soon as he received adequate compensation. At Forest Hills, he had revenge against Drobny in the semi-final. Dynamic, glorious aces gained Drobny the first set and a 3-2 lead in the second. This stirred Kramer who replied with raking drives landing within inches of the baseline. His services, too, produced as many aces as Drobny's. The American won the next ten games and proceeded to overwhelm his man in a display of unparalleled power tennis 3-6, 6-3, 6-0, 6-1.

Frank Parker, champion in 1944/45, was out to regain his title and he baffled Kramer at the start of the final. Reducing the pace of the match with drops that floated over the net followed by lobs that raised chalk, Parker won the first two sets. Showing his genius for match play, Kramer then volleyed all Parker's medium-paced shots —even from mid-court. Regaining the touch that had temporarily deserted him, under Parker's wizardry, Kramer recovered to win 4-6, 2-6, 6-1, 6-0, 6-3.

"I never played better tennis," was Budge's comment after watching Kramer help to retain the Davis Cup in 1947. The American levelled Pails 6-2, 6-1, 6-2 in fifty-two minutes and overwhelmed Bromwich 6-3, 6-2, 6-2.

A family man—he now has four boys—Kramer accepted the best professional offer yet made to a tennis player. This was in November, 1947, when he was reported to have received 70,000 dollars.

He was as dominating in professional tennis, winning an average of three out of four matches against Riggs. In an exhibition against Gonzales, Kramer recovered from love-40 in seven successive games.

Many consider him the greatest player since World War II—a claim supported by his flawless technique and fighting temperament.

147

26

"The Wizard of Oz"

Was Margaret (Osborne) du Pont the next best doubles player to Elizabeth Ryan? This is the claim made by her supporters and Margaret's record of ten successive years as America's doubles champion, certainly justifies this contention.

But unlike Elizabeth Ryan, Margaret also reaped a rich harvest of singles prizes. In six years as a top-line international—from 1946 to 1951—Margaret won at Wimbledon besides collecting three titles at Forest Hills and scoring two wins in the French championship.

Demure in dress and demeanour, Margaret Osborne was born on 14th March, 1918, in Joseph, Oregon. Although not a great personality, "Ozzie," or "The Wizard of Oz," as she was sometimes called in America, was a great favourite—and a great fighter.

Her game was based on a brilliant attack. Besides an enviable service and smash, Margaret's fluent touch on the volley revealed her greatest skill. For many years her drives were her weakness but when she cut out excessive spin, her ranking in singles soared several places.

At thirteen, she started tournaments. In 1940, she lost the third round at Forest Hills to Helen Bernhard, a match that revealed her ground stroke weakness. It was now that she remodelled her baseline game. She got much further at Forest Hills in 1941—the semi-final—but had to submit to Pauline Betz 6-4, 6-3.

1941, however, proved a vital year in her tennis. With Sarah Cooke she won the U.S. doubles and at Seabright she crossed rackets for the first time with Louise Brough.

When Sarah Cooke temporarily retired, the team of Osborne and Brough—a combination of names now world-famous—was born. They won their first tournament at the Philadelphia Cricket Club and lost only about a dozen times in over two hundred matches.

Inseparable friends, they admit to growing alike in outlook. Even Margaret's marriage to Will du Pont made no difference as he, too, was a friend of Louise—and it was his idea that Margaret should team up with her.

When the du Ponts went on honeymoon to Hawaii, Louise accompanied them causing the crack that she was now a "triples" partner.

Keen singles rivals, they went all out for victory. Although called the "Queens" and said to live a little in a world of their own, they never developed temperaments. Their understanding was surpassed only by the Lenglen-Ryan tandem.

Pauline Betz taught Margaret a lesson in the 1942 U.S. semi-final. At 5-3 in the third set Margaret, within a stroke of success, played for safety—against the swiftest court coverer produced by America! —and saw Pauline sweep to victory. A 6-4, 6-2 semi-final defeat from Louise Brough at Los Angeles was a reminder that America's best doubles player had yet to win an important singles tournament.

Margaret refuted this at Rye in 1943. Showing improved patience and a new ability to switch from attack to defence, she brought down Betz and Doris Hart. Her quarter-final defeat at Forest Hills by lusty Dorothy Bundy was a sobering blow.

A steadier Margaret revenged this result in the 1944 U.S. semi-final. But although she led Betz 5-3, 40-30 in the second set, Margaret was up against a mistress of the passing shot. In a fighting finish that revealed her wonderful base-lining, Pauline scrambled home in straight sets.

Doris Hart, hot on the heels of the leading Americans, gave a majestic display to beat Margaret 6-2, 6-3 in the quarter-final at Forest Hills in 1945—but the loser was chosen as America's No. 2 in the Wightman Cup next year.

Critics at Wimbledon, astonished by these new Americans, rated Margaret the most brilliant. After power-charging her way to the quarter-final, she had to fight for her life against Hart (5-7, 6-4, 6-4) —and then lost two bitter sets to Brough, 8-6, 7-5.

America then flocked to Paris. Nobody had a more gratifying visit than Margaret, who after beating Brough 7-5, 6-3, garnered her first major title at the expense of no less a contestant than the new Wimbledon Champion, Pauline Betz.

The game seemed over when "Peerless Pauline", leading 6-1, 6-5 was twice at match point. Margaret's stout-hearted rejoinder was to risk everything by attacking on a surface that responded best to defence, and to save the second set 8-6 by magnificent volleying.

Down 2-4 in the third set, Margaret fought back to level terms. Pauline had three falls and could not hold an opponent now in full cry. With a volley that would have done Borotra credit, Margaret was champion 1-6, 8-6, 7-5.

Back at Forest Hills, Margaret lost to Doris Hart 6-4, 5-7, 7-5 in the quarter-final. This decision was reversed at Wimbledon in 1947 when playing perfect tennis, Margaret became the first American to win the championship before gaining a victory at Forest Hills.

Her all-round versatility did not drop a set. Doris Hart (conqueror of Louise Brough) contested the final where Margaret, in a brilliant start, led 6-2, 2-0. Doris then got her sweeping strokes under control

149

to reach 4-2—only for Margaret to produce some sparkling tennis that won the next four games and the world championship.

The fate that befell Pauline Betz in Paris now awaited her successor. In the semi-final, Margaret won the first set easily against Pat Todd. Rain then stopped play and next day, Pat less well-equipped but steadiness itself, fought back to register an astounding winning decision, 2-6, 6-3, 6-4.

When Margaret won the U.S. Eastern grass court title with a victory over Louise 6-3, 4-6, 9-7, and then reached the U.S. final at Forest Hills, disposing of Hart 7-5, 7-5, it seemed as though nothing could stop her. But Louise surprised her friend in the final. After two hard sets, her volleying attack was irresistible, and she stormed through the last six games 8-6, 4-6, 6-1.

Margaret (Mrs. William du Pont since November, 1947), could not retain her Wimbledon title against the flowing, fluent display that Doris gave in the semi-final. Finding the corners with an impeccable length, Doris raced to 4-0 in the final set and clinched victory before Margaret could settle down to a counter-attack (6-4, 2-6, 6-3).

Louise won three titles at Wimbledon so when she and Margaret were due for another final at Forest Hills in 1948, few favoured the latter's chances. Margaret's father had just been killed and it was only at her mother's wish that she had continued playing.

After three tortuous hours of drama, twice interrupted by rain, Margaret defeated Louise 4-6, 6-4, 15-13. Her lobbing, deep and directed to the backhand, finally disrupted the great Brough smash. Margaret had been perilously close to defeat when her friend was within a stroke of victory at 6-5 in the final set.

The match was marked by scenes of tremendous emotional excitement and Alice Marble declared: "I have seen twelve final round matches, have participated in four myself, but never before went through such agonies". An overwhelming ovation, a tribute to such rare courage, greeted the new champion.

In 1949, Margaret all but won three major championships. She did not forfeit a set in France, beating the holder Nelly Adamson 7-5, 6-2 in the final.

She lost the Wimbledon final to Louise 10-8, 1-6, 10-8 after two hours. She led 5-4 and had four set points in the first set. And in the final set, she broke service for 6-5 and was within two points of victory. But Louise, slightly more mobile, anticipated Margaret's volleys to win an exciting, but not great match. Both girls were guilty of many mis-timed drives in their rushing forward.

Margaret was, however, supreme at Forest Hills. Thanks to a victory over Brough, Doris Hart was highly fancied, but in a brief

45-minute final she made many errors, a contrast to her strong, steady rival who hardly made a mistake in winning 6-4, 6-1.

It was rumoured that the ex-Miss Osborne would soon forsake tennis. In the spring of 1950, however, she again appeared in Paris accompanied by the faithful Louise, but lacking practice, she went down in the quarter-final 3-6, 6-0, 6-2 to Barbara Scofield, America's No. 7.

At Wimbledon, too, Margaret lost many chances through timing errors in the final against Brough and was defeated 6-1, 3-6, 6-1.

Although they had mopped-up Wimbledon between them, the reign of the "Queens" seemed to be ending. But at Forest Hills, Margaret came back with a vengeance. Her intelligent, versatile attack beat Doris Hart convincingly in the final 6-3, 6-3.

She retained the singles trophy and played wonder tennis to become triple champion for the first time. Partnered by Louise and Ken McGregor, she finished 1950 in glorious fashion.

By 1951, her career was closing. She lost to Shirley Fry 6-2, 9-7, in the French semi-final and lack of mobility hampered her greatly in her losing quarter-final at Wimbledon against Beverley Baker (6-1, 4-6, 6-3).

In July, 1952, was born William du Pont III. His mother made a comeback in 1954, when with Louise she saved two match points from Hart-Fry to win the Wimbledon doubles again. The U.S. title was also their prize in 1955 and 1956.

Forest Hills in 1950 really saw the finish of Margaret's splendid career. It was her last big singles win and it was, indeed, a wonderful sunset.

A Falling Star

"FALKENBURG lies down at home and on court, too." This caption under a photograph of Robert ("Bob") Falkenburg resting in his London hotel, was reported to have incensed the champion of 1948. And in turn, he blasted everything connected with Wimbledon, declaring that officials and spectators alike were the most prejudiced he had encountered.

All this uproar took place in 1948—eight years in advance of the tennis story of Falkenburg which started in 1940 when he became U.S. boy champion at the age of fourteen. Victor again in 1941, this prodigy of Los Angeles also won the American junior championship in 1943 and 1944.

In senior tennis too, 18-year-old A/C Robert Falkenburg won the American doubles championship in 1944 with Don McNeill, and the following year although beaten 6-2, 4-6, 6-1, 6-1 by the volatile Segura in an early round, Falkenburg reached both doubles finals. With J. Tuero he lost to Mulloy-Talbert 12-10, 8-10, 12-10, 6-2, while in the mixed Talbert-Margaret Osborne beat Falkenburg-Doris Hart, 6-4, 6-4.

Falkenburg's flat-hit cannon-ball was the fastest service in America. A fiery smash and deadly volleys made him a terror at the net, where he displayed much beauty and a touch of genius in his choice check-volleying. Accurate passing shots and a sound management of the lob decried the theory that this Californian's successes rested on the ferocity of his attack. Lacking stamina, Falkenburg, like Borotra, was frequently compelled to watch his reserves. He employed the same strategy of throwing sets, but, unfortunately, he lacked the Basque's gallery appeal and his "resting periods" provoked antagonism.

Brother of tennis-playing film star, Jinx Falkenburg, 6 ft. 2 in. Robert was without the compact self-assurance of Kramer or Mulloy. Angular and somewhat ungainly, he was slow and unhurried on court, taking particularly long to rise after his frequent tumbles. But, thanks to his fiery tennis and so-called stalling tactics, Falkenburg always packed the galleries.

He won forty-four out of fifty-six matches in the U.S. season of 1946. His victims included Talbert at Seabright and Petra (Wimbledon champion) at Newport. At Forest Hills, after beating Patty, 6-4. 6-4, 6-2, Falkenburg (aided by twenty aces) defeated Talbert 3-6, 6-1, 2-6, 6-2, 7-5. But the semi-final saw him go down in heavy defeat 6-0, 6-4, 6-4, before Jack Kramer.

He put up a sturdier struggle at Los Angeles. After beating Mulloy, Falkenburg took Kramer to 6-0, 3-6, 3-6, 6-4, 6-1, in the semi-final.

At Queen's Club in 1947, Falkenburg won his first European title, beating Australian Colin Long 6-4, 7-5. Seeded No. 7 at Wimbledon, Falkenburg caused interest and some amusement in his quarter-final meeting with Dinny Pails.

Pails led 4-2 in the first two sets, only to lose them both 6-4, 6-4 so when Falkenburg, serving magnificently and playing with beautiful control, led 3-2 in the third set, a sensational upset seemed certain.

At this stage the American developed cramp in his right hand. Unable to grip his racket, Falkenburg naturally caused some delay, while a peevish Pails raised laughter by sitting disconsolately on the rim of his up-turned racket.

Taking the next thirteen games, Pails led 3-0 in the final set. Falkenburg, shaking off his disability, pulled up to 3-2, but he could not regain complete concentration and Pails was out at 4-6, 4-6, 6-3, 6-0, 6-2.

The quarter-final also saw Falkenburg beaten in the American championships. Kramer, fresh from his Wimbledon victory, defeated his countryman, 6-2, 7-5, 6-1.

Kramer departed from amateur tennis in 1947. Nobody gave Bob Falkenburg an outside chance as his successor. At Wimbledon in 1948, Frank Parker was top seed but lost to Bergelin, who failed to reproduce that form and lost in turn to Falkenburg, 6-4, 6-2, 3-6, 6-4, in the quarter-final.

It was in the semi-final against Mulloy that the Centre Court saw the first instalment of the so-called Falkenburg stalling. Stumbling about all over the court, the young Californian took an inordinately long time in rising—often he got on his knees and then hoisted himself up. Mulloy, apart from once addressing the umpire (and it is not known whether he complained) did not speak. He looked thoroughly fed up and lost 6-4, 6-4, 8-6.

The Bromwich-Falkenburg final really set the seal on the latter's unpopularity—yet strategically his was a triumph for clever timing of pressure. The thrills started early when Bromwich led 5-4, 40-15, only to be cheated by two classical lobs. A set up, Falkenburg rested for six games. Backhand passing shots won him the third set; he made little effort in the fourth.

At this stage, however, Bromwich gained control and at 5-3 in the fifth set he reached match point three times. But the coolest person on the Centre Court was Robert Falkenburg. He revealed his marvellous match-winning temperament by two beautiful backhand passing shots, and at the third match point an Australian drive hit the net. With tension at fever heat, Falkenburg pulled up to 4-5, and realising that his opponent was near desperation, attacked him ferociously. Bromwich cracked, and could only win two of the last fourteen points. Falkenburg broke service to love to lead 6-5, and then captured the last game also to love. Two dynamite-laden aces made him the champion of 1948.

America had dramatically and suddenly snatched the prize from Australia to win 7-5, 0-6, 6-2, 3-6, 7-5.

There was considerable sympathy for Bromwich. The fact that Falkenburg would appear to be dying and then produced cannonballs evoked audible disapproval, making the final an uncomfortable affair.

In the midst of all this turmoil, no one recalled an incident in the semi-final of the mixed doubles of the Pan-American championships in 1946. Falkenburg and Louise Brough were awarded a vital point against Mottram and Mrs. Bostock, but Falkenburg requested this decision to be reversed, as (unseen by anyone) his racket had touched the net. This generosity had prompted a Mexican correspondent to declare its donor gave "a thrilling instance of the ethics of tennis".

Back home in 1948, Falkenburg lost in every tournament. Likas beat him at Seabright and at Newport, Schroeder defeated the champion at Orange, and in the U.S. quarter-final Falkenburg lost to Drobny 8-6, 6-1, 6-3. Drobny must have felt confident about handling the heaviest service in America, for although he won the toss he allowed his foe to open service. The Californian fell and sprawled all over the court but could not stem Drobny's powerful drives and volleys.

Following Falkenburg's seething remarks about Wimbledon, it was doubted whether he would return. But return he did in 1949, and in the third round was saved from defeat by his service, in his match against Asboth (6-4, 7-5, 2-6, 0-6, 6-4). And in the quarter-final, in a temperature of 88°, the Bromwich-Falkenburg drama was re-enacted.

A packed, expectant Centre Court crowd saw America win the first two sets 6-3, 11-9, by alert, aggressive tennis. But the length of the second set had raided Falkenburg's stamina, and he reverted to his old tactic of taking things easy—only this time he rested not for one set, but for two! It was a fatal error—the incentive for victory lessened, the initiative was now with Bromwich.

The final set, opening in great excitement, saw Falkenburg striving in desperation to re-assume his ascendancy. But Bromwich, scenting victory, broke service for a vital 5-3 lead. Falkenburg had enough strength left to ace his way to 4-5 but in the next game a great shout of "Bromwich" heralded an Australian revenge and that Wimbledon was without a champion.

There were no incidents. From a sitting position on court, Falkenburg acknowledged his opponent's last winning coup with a smile and a salute. Victor and vanquished were on the best of terms and left court arm-in-arm.

The sudden withdrawal of Falkenburg and Gussy Moran, a seeded team, from the mixed doubles, caused much comment. No explanation was given. Gussy denied a disagreement and soon afterwards visited the American Ice Revue with Falkenburg and his attractive Mexican wife.

Falkenburg, refusing to turn professional, now announced he was forsaking tennis for a business career. Possibly he was not taken seriously. Nevertheless, he was in earnest, and he settled down in Mexico, abandoning the game for many years.

He did not return to Wimbledon until 1954, when he lost the third round to Rosewall 6-2, 4-6, 6-1, 6-4. He still displayed much fire ln his tennis but showed marked deterioration in his lasting power.

One of the greatest-ever servers, this perplexing young Californian caused more controversy than any modern champion.

28

"Forever Ambling"

No wonder Americans called him "Lucky" Schroeder. He would not practise, he would not even compete at Forest Hills, yet year after year he was chosen for the Davis Cup—to the fury of less successful colleagues forced to undertake the arduous circuit of U.S. tournaments.

Why then did the authorities select Frederick R. "Ted" Schroeder? Not only for his wonderful backhand and ginger-laden net attack which recalled the agility and ability of Borotra. No, America realised that here was the man for a crisis; like that other great Californian, Billy Johnston, Schroeder had the heart of a lion.

Popular and taciturn, this muscular pipe-smoking refrigeration engineer possessed a peculiar stumbling "saddle-sore" walk. Australian spectators soon nicknamed him "Forever Ambling".

Twelve days older than his great friend Jack Kramer, Schroeder never joined the Kramer professional circus, much to America's surprise. Father of two boys, Schroeder was really interested in his career, and exhibition tennis had no appeal. There was, however, an elfin streak in his make-up that enjoyed keeping press and public guessing.

Schroeder was American junior champion in 1939. In 1940, Kramer and Schroeder, both nineteen, became the youngest-yet U.S. doubles title-holders. Next year they triumphed again and Schroeder went out in a desperate semi-final to Riggs, eventual champion. Saving seven match points in the fourth set, he fought his opponent to 7-5 in the fifth. Riggs laconically comments, "Ted told me . . . if I were smart I'd turn pro right away because next year he'd get me for sure . . . I took his advice."

1942 justified Schroeder's optimism when, despite a heavily bandaged arm, he beat top-favourite Frank Parker for the American title. But in 1943 Ensign Schroeder was unable to defend—nor did he play singles again at Forest Hills for seven years!

Although short of practice, Schroeder was chosen for the 1946 Davis Cup Challenge Round in preference to Parker. Australian hopes faltered when in a temperature of 100°, Schroeder overcame Bromwich 3-6, 6-1, 6-2, 0-6, 6-3. The winner's overhead was terrific, and in the doubles it was a mighty Schroeder smash to Bromwich's feet that won the trophy. Kramer and Schroeder, the tallest pair ever in a Challenge Round, overwhelmed the famous Quist-Bromwich tandem 6-2, 7-5, 6-4.

A third U.S. title was gathered with Kramer in 1947, but Schroeder still missed the singles. Hotheads who declared he feared defeat and consequent dropping from the team were silenced when he beat Bromwich 6-4, 5-7, 6-3, 6-3, and then, in spite of violent, protracted cramp in his playing hand, saved match point against Dinny Pails to retain the Cup after the bitterest battle of 1947 (6-3, 8-6, 4-6, 9-11, 10-8).

When Kramer turned professional, Schroeder was reported to have refused 35,000 dollars. He played, perhaps, his greatest tennis in the 1948 Challenge Round. At set-all against Quist he unleashed such a furious onslaught that the bewildered Australian won only twenty-three more points in two sets (6-3, 4-6, 6-0, 6-0). The slogging Sidwell received similar treatment (6-2, 6-1, 6-1).

1949 . . . and at last Schroeder visited Wimbledon where his pluck, brilliant tennis, running vest and tiny shorts all received outstanding notice. He opened by overthrowing his partner, the redoubtable Mulloy 3-6, 9-11, 6-1, 6-0, 7-5, and then declared he would sleep for the first time since seeing the draw.

The atmosphere became electric in a Schroeder-Sedgman epic quarter-final when the Californian, within a point of defeat, was foot-faulted. Unshaken, he came up on his second service, scoring a great volley. After salvaging another match-point, Schroeder's tireless aggression was rewarded, 3-6, 6-8, 6-3, 6-2, 9-7.

The Californian never doubted his ultimate victory. Sturgess (conqueror of Parker) surrendered 3-6, 7-5, 5-7, 6-1, 6-2; and the Drobny cannon-ball held no terrors for Schroeder, who stationed at the net, killed his opponent's sliced backhands. A racket hurtling into the sky announced another trans-Atlantic triumph, 3-6, 6-0, 6-3, 4-6, 6-4.

Interviewed on television, Schroeder gallantly declared every match had been difficult. Remember Gar Mulloy's fight? Pressed, he admitted Sedgman had proved the toughest problem. Would he return? Maybe, but in twenty years time and then as an umpire.

America was amazed when "Lucky" Schroeder challenged Gonzales at Forest Hills in 1949—and more so when Gonzales, beaten on their six previous meetings, retained his title 16-18, 2-6, 6-1, 6-2, 6-4. The tense 77-minute first set drained Schroeder's stamina, but the Tarzan-like Mexican, seven years younger, withstood the strain. Thereafter, Schroeder limited tournament play to a few Californian championships. Still a Davis Cup nominee, he beat Bergelin, Davidson and Mervyn Rose setless in 1951.

Of all modern champions, Schroeder played the least, Unlike many contemporaries, he could certainly claim "Tennis is not my business".

29

Playboy Turns Champion

A FORMER doubles champion was watching a sunburnt stripling in the U.S. Army Air Force making rings round one of France's most promising players. "That young man," he declared, "is a potential Vines or Budge."

The ex-champion was George Lott. The young Air Force representative was 21-year-old Budge Patty. The scene was the semi-final of the Inter-Allied Services tournament in 1945. Patty beat Robert Abdelessam 6-1, 6-0 and went on to win the singles final.

Lott was correct in his prophecy that here was a champion in the making. He was incorrect in declaring Patty was to be still another member of the American tennis power school.

Patty developed a game similar to Henri Cochet's. The same short swing back, disguising direction, the same easy genius in his "executions" at the net, and the same ability to handle a rising ball.

Patty's forehand volley is regarded as an all-time great shot in tennis. His approach to the game is instinctive, elegant, economical, and again like Cochet he prefers all shots on his forehand wing. Not a great hitter, the American can reduce the power of an opponent's game and absorb it into his own tennis.

He was born in 1924, coming from a land of champions—California. From a natural laziness and disinclination to move rose his nickname Budge—he was christened Gaius.

Helped financially by film stars Robert Taylor and Barbara Stanwyck, Budge appeared in junior championships. His natural fluent strokes were at once the subject of great interest—as was his capture of the U.S. national boys' title in 1939.

The mid-'forties saw Patty in the forces. At his first Wimbledon in 1946 where his play and personality drew comment, Patty lost the fourth round to Dinny Pails 6-2, 6-1, 7-5.

Marcel Bernard won the French title soon after Wimbledon with victories over Petra and Drobny. In the quarter-final he had been near defeat before overcoming Patty 2-6, 6-2, 6-1, 4-6, 7-5.

The first of Patty's many sensational wins—and losses—occurred in the second round of the American championship in 1946.

At Pauline Betz's cocktail party to celebrate her win at Wimbledon, he said he would beat Petra, Wimbledon champion, next day—and

158

did so on a slippery court, 6-4, 9-7, 6-4. By taking Petra's services on the rise he removed his rival's sting. At close quarters his skilful volleys evaded even this giant's telescopic reach.

To offset this win came his lackadaisical 6-4, 6-4, 6-2 loss to Falkenburg. Patty was domiciled in France and enjoyed the nickname of "Playboy", spending much time on parties and none on training. Recurring bouts of fatigue rendered every match a matter for speculation.

Wimbledon 1947 . . . and Patty was the unseeded sensation of the singles. His stamina survived fourteen sets while beating Sidwell, Man Mohan and Derek Barton—and he then decorated the Centre Court with a dream display of drives, drop-shots and volleys to subdue the guile of seeded John Bromwich, 6-4, 0-6, 6-4, 1-6, 6-4. It was the victor's timing of his efforts in the sets he won that turned the result in his favour.

Still another seeded victim awaited Patty. In their match, Drobny missed many first services. The American, standing into the second "kickers", handled them with magnificent classic returns and broke through six times for his 3-6, 6-4, 7-9, 6-2, 6-3 win.

Patty had led 6-5, 40-30 in the third set. Forced to a fifth set he found it a tremendous strain. His friends Tom Brown and Margaret Osborne were near the court to encourage him, Brown doing so by repeated fist-shaking.

Brown was his partner and next opponent. Patty, a spent force, offered only nominal resistance in his 6-3, 6-3, 6-3 semi-final defeat.

He could not survive the fourth round in Paris, losing to A. Stolpa 7-9, 6-3, 8-6, 6-2. It was then reported that he had overtaxed his strength and was suffering from a minor breakdown.

In 1948, Drobny and Bromwich were avenged. In the French semifinal Drobny beat Patty 2-6, 6-3, 4-6, 6-4, 6-3. Patty again attacked furiously and led 4-2 in the fourth set. Drobny kept the American on the move anticipating the physical reaction that would lead to Patty's ending. At Wimbledon, Bromwich was in no mood to let Patty inveigle him to defeat again, and in the quarter-final match he outplayed a somewhat jaded opponent 6-4, 7-5 6-1.

America complained that their former boy champion preferred European tennis to trans-Atlantic tournaments. This brought Alice Marble to his defence. She explained that due to his health, Patty lived in France, adding "Budge Patty, despite his lazy appearance, has worlds of ability".

In 1948, he did appear at Forest Hills losing a dramatic five-setter to Falkenburg 6-1, 4-6, 3-6, 6-4, 10-8 in the third round. An exciting finish terminated on a net cord from Falkenburg, who scored 170 winners to his rival's 161.

Some American sports writers were declaring Patty was on the wane. They asserted his nonchalant attitude to tennis was counteracting his obvious genius.

In Paris in 1949 Patty gave a smart reply to these detractors.

The new American champion Gonzales, armed with a mighty service was making his initial appearance in France. Patty, meeting this Colossus in the semi-final, handled those thunderbolts with remarkable control. Flashing to the net at every opportunity, he eclipsed his formidable foe 6-4, 6-3, 3-6, 6-3.

In the final, Parker, an opponent of completely different calibre, kept his careful passing shots so wide that Patty was at full stretch throughout the match. He won the second set but at great physical cost—yet came back to be within a stroke of 5-4 in the fourth before yielding 6-3, 1-6, 6-1, 6-4.

Wimbledon soon followed—a meeting that changed Patty's tennis life. By a strenuous and swift-moving net attack he led Drobny two sets to one. Feeling his stamina deserting him, Patty threw the fourth set—and to his dismay, could not re-gather enough energy for a fifth set volleying offensive.

After this third round 6-4, 6-8, 7-9, 6-0, 6-2 defeat and disappointment, Patty admitted he felt "a low down, no good heel"!

He realised that if he were to reach the top, parties would have to yield to serious training.

Living in France, he was naturally in close contact with the tennis-playing crowd. One of his great friends was Henri Cochet. Under Cochet's guidance, Patty gave up parties and cigarettes and set about increasing weight and muscle.

He ran miles every day and was rewarded with greater lasting power—which led to greater confidence. At his best in the forecourt, Patty was now able to launch a net attack for five sets.

The spark of genius responded immediately to the kindling of Cochet. In 1950, a weightier Patty survived three successive ordeals to register a magnificent victory in the French singles.

Fighting for his life, Patty disposed of Ivan Dorfman 0-6, 6-1, 3-6, 6-1, 11-9 in the quarter-final. Dorfman led 3-0 in the last set but Patty's perfect lobbing continually cheated Dorfman's overhead and wore him out in the final tussle.

Bill Talbert, three-set victor over Bromwich, next blocked Patty's path. His drives kept his opponent at the back of the court to lead by two sets to one and 4-3. After a break for rain Patty crowded the net, where his volleys flew to sudden death. Talbert hit back in spectacular fashion and in the fifth set needed a service game for victory when leading 9-8. Patty had an opportunity to test his newly-developed staying power and did so successfully to win 2-6, 6-4, 4-6, 6-4, 13-11.

The end of one of the greatest dramas staged on the Centre Court.   Drobny and Patty exchange weary smiles after that $4\frac{1}{4}$-hour marathon in 1953.   Drobny won 8–6, 16–18, 3–6, 8–6, 12–10
—after being six times within a stroke of defeat.

Tony Trabert, the versatile young American who captured the Wimbledon title in 1955 without the loss of a set (Picture Post).

He was hardly expected to take on Drobny with success. That he did so to become French champion 6-1, 6-2, 3-6, 5-7, 7-5, revealed his vastly improved confidence. The title had been within his grasp at 5-4 in the fourth set, but unruffled by its loss, the American played the fifth set stoically, several vicious volleys in the last two games giving him the verdict.

"I think I have as good a chance as anyone," was Patty's comment on seeing the Wimbledon draw. He must have felt his star was in the ascendant and from his first game displayed the répertoire of a champion.

Rain again interrupted his match with Talbert but this time, despite Talbert's adroitly angled returns, Patty, in glorious volleying touch, dominated from the net. One set was all Talbert—thought by many to be a certain finalist—could achieve (3-6, 6-4, 6-2, 6-3).

Seixas, footsore and somewhat weary, lost to Patty 6-3, 5-7, 6-2, 7-5, clearing the latter's path to the final. Patty had been a studious observer of Frank Sedgman, anticipating meeting him in his last match. He decided his only hope of victory was to wrest the net position from the Australian.

By storming at all costs, Patty gained his objective. His beautiful lobs kept Sedgman charging back to the baseline. Attacking on service and service return, Patty's wonder volleys won the first set, 6-1—he lost the wavering, thrilling second to the brilliant all-court game of his rival—and then re-assuming control of the net, guided his delightful volleys out of Sedgman's reach to win the game's most cherished prize, 6-1, 8-10, 6-2, 6-3.

The match finished on a particularly exciting rally leaving both players temporarily exhausted. Patty could not jump the net. After "my greatest thrill", the American and the Australian—close friends —left court, their arms entwined and the new champion's first award was a delighted hug from his attractive partner, Nancye Chaffee.

Patty's bid for victory at Forest Hills was cut short by an accident when partnering Schroeder at Newport against Talbert-Trabert. Leaping for a lob, he fell spraining an ankle.

Out of training and tennis for months, Patty's fourth-round defeat by Lennart Bergelin (3-6, 6-4, 6-2, 3-6, 6-3) in Paris was not entirely unexpected. His second-round defeat at Wimbledon by his almost unknown 17-year-old schoolboy partner, Hamilton Richardson was, however, totally unexpected.

Court 1 was thronged for this spectacular struggle in which Patty, believing that it pays to attack an opponent's strength, consistently directed his elegant volleys on to Richardson's backhand. But the youngster possessing one of the most solid, polished shots ever seen in tennis, parried his attack with glorious control.

161

L

As they battled desperately, producing supremely great strokes, excitement mounted—until eventually a mighty shout indicated the arrival of another new American wonder boy.

In the final suspense, Mrs. Richardson unable to restrain her tears saw her son triumph 4-6, 6-3, 4-6, 10-8, 6-4, and then receive the cordial congratulations of the beaten champion, the man who was piloting this 17-year-old through the doubles.

At Forest Hills, Patty lost the quarter-final 6-3, 1-6, 4-6, 6-1, 6-4, to Savitt, his successor at Wimbledon.

With less training and an inclination perhaps to rest on his past achievements, Patty's ranking took a decline in 1952. He won a remarkably long three-setter against Nielsen 6-4, 20-18, 7-5, to reach the semi-final of the U.S. covered court singles but was then overcome by Savitt, 6-2, 6-3, 6-2. He failed to win a set from Sedgman in the French quarter-final (6-4, 6-2, 6-2)—and at Wimbledon his progress was halted in an uninspired fourth-round match, 7-5, 4-6, 6-3, 7-5, by Seixas.

1953 . . . and Patty, although failing to win a major championship, re-established himself in tennis by helping to provide what was perhaps the greatest-ever match played on the Centre Court.

His form in the early part of the season was unconvincing, and he was beaten in the fourth round in Paris by little Felicissimo Ampon, 6-4, 6-2, 6-4.

At Wimbledon was staged a third-round epic. Patty and Drobny . . . old friends, close rivals, doubles partners. In a magnificent mammoth match which lasted from 4.45 p.m. until 9 p.m., the burly ex-Czech, six times within a stroke of defeat, saved the day against the slim American 8-6, 16-18, 3-6, 8-6, 12-10.

They had played one another so often that only a shot of superlative placement and power could gain any advantage. Drobny's cannon-balls and flashing forehands were perfectly matched by Patty with the unexpected ace, the disguised passing shot, the wonder volley.

In this tremendous drama, Patty hurt a groin muscle, and Drobny, after running up and down the baseline to ward off incipient cramp, pulled a thigh muscle. Patty gave an elegant display of all his talents to save the second set after trailing 3-5 and scored 112 winners to Drobny's 111.

At 5-4 in the fourth set he had a match point—again at 6-5, he was twice within a stroke of victory—and in the fifth set, he had three more chances at 6-5. But each crisis saw Drobny respond with fantastic skill and courage.

The end came with Patty struggling to keep on his feet, and Drobny equally dazed with pain. As they wearily shook hands, the Centre

Court rose to greet them in a display of overwhelming appreciation and emotion.

The L.T.A. gave them both a silver cigarette case on which were inscribed the details of the match. The Duchess of Kent presented the awards. Vic Seixas won the title but the 1953 championship has gone down in tennis history as the Patty-Drobny Wimbledon.

At Forest Hills, Patty defeated Rose 7-9, 6-4, 6-2, 6-3, but lost to Trabert who rose to great heights in his 6-4, 6-4, 6-2 win in the quarter-final. Next year in Paris, after Patty played a sound thoughtful game to dispose of sturdy Sven Davidson 6-4, 6-0, 6-4, he again failed to win a set (in the semi-final) against Trabert—6-1, 7-5, 6-4. Patty seemed anxious during this match, Trabert's deep drives robbing him of his favourite net attack.

By Wimbledon, however, he had played himself into form and his overthrow of Vic Seixas (holder) in the quarter-final 7-5, 4-6, 6-3, 6-2, revealed the accomplished power of his flexible forehand volley.

This brought him against—Drobny! Without reproducing the fireworks of 1953, they occupied the Centre Court this time for a mere two hours. Drobny avoided Patty's forehand drive and volley at all costs and with the latter's service not so lethal or so loyal, the ex-Czech won 6-2, 6-4, 4-6, 9-7.

During a winning five-set match against Flam at Wimbledon in 1955, Patty damaged his right elbow. Nevertheless, he played a vastly clever game to beat Hoad who was backed by many to win the title. By reducing the Australian's power completely Patty won 6-4, 6-4, 6-4. In the semi-final he fought Trabert on level terms for one set but could not keep it up against the latter's unyielding steadiness (8-6, 6-2, 6-2).

Effortless and elegant, Patty is a decoration to any championship, a danger to any champion. When completely fit, his class, his concentration—and the coaching of Henri Cochet—combined to carry off the game's most coveted prize.

30

Great Girl from Oklahoma

SHE has been known to practise her famous service five hundred times . . . she developed a game that has been called the nearest approach to masculine tennis . . . and from 1946 to 1950 she appeared in fourteen out of a possible fifteen finals at Wimbledon annexing eleven titles.

To Althea Louise Brough, the atmosphere of Wimbledon was an inspiration. Here, she played her most brilliant tennis. Her tremendously powerful play overhead, her touch on the volley, particularly those difficult shots taken close to the body, and her polished, natural hitting responded immediately to the speed of the Centre Court.

Like her closest friend Margaret du Pont, Louise was not a happy defender—unlike du Pont, Louise suffered greatly from nerves. This weakness marred many finals early in her career, and years later, when she had a surfeit of tennis, her game again deteriorated for the same reason. But in her heyday, at the height of her physical power, Louise was superb in singles and doubles, approaching Alice Marble in her brilliance as an exponent of the serve-volley game.

A junior star of the Dick Skeen school, Louise was born in Oklahoma on 11th March, 1923. She was American junior champion in 1940, a title she retained after a two-set battle against Doris Hart, 7-5, 6-2, in 1941. That year she caused a sensation by her play for one set against Sarah Cooke (ultimate champion) at Forest Hills. Down 2-4, Louise attacked with robust confidence to win the next four games. Then as was to happen so often again, Louise for no apparent reason changed her winning tactics, and panicked over errors. Floundering, she lost her zeal and the next two sets, 6-1, 6-1.

Critics asserted she lacked the flair for big match tennis. An important occasion seemed to upset her will to win. Against Sarah Cooke, Louise had lost control of her forehand.

1942 opened with more promise, Louise defeating Margaret Osborne, 7-5, 6-4, and then crushing Helen Bernhard, 6-2, 6-0, to win at Easthampton. She went from strength to strength and after beating Margaret 6-2, 6-1 in the Longwood Bowl final, Louise recorded two victories over Pauline Betz, to annex the Essex County Club singles title and to win at Rye.

Those who declared Louise lacked the calibre of a champion now admitted this hard-hitting Californian might step into Sarah Cooke's shoes at Forest Hills in 1942.

Polished Pauline Betz, a most persistent retriever, had other ideas. She had saved match point against Margaret Osborne in the U.S. semi-final and was in no mood to let the title drop through her competent fingers.

Louise, opening with a zestful exhibition, won the first set. Unsteadied by the prospect of victory, she lapsed into error. Pauline, fleet and forceful, took full advantage of this welcome gift and recovered to win 4-6, 6-1, 6-4.

In 1943, "Broughie" again challenged Betz for the American title. She fought frantically to salvage the match when Pauline was twice within a stroke of victory at 5-4 in the second set. But a stream of mistakes, indicating her reaction, then helped Pauline to 5-1 in the third set—and to victory, 6-3, 5-7, 6-3.

In a lesser championship, the Pacific South West meeting, Louise cantered through the singles without the loss of a set. She again demonstrated her liking for the less important type of tournament when a lusty display of hitting put Pauline Betz out of the Rye final 6-3, 6-1 in 1944.

A new force was rising in American singles—Margaret Osborne—who in 1944 was seeded No. 2 at Forest Hills. Brough and Betz were matched accordingly in the semi-final. At 3-all in the second set, Louise collapsed, completely un-nerved by Pauline's steadiness and her ability to convert defence into attack. The holder won in two confident sets 6-2, 6-3.

The semi-final was also fatal to Louise at Forest Hills in 1945 when she swapped her usual attacking tennis for spin shots against Sarah Cooke. The initiative switched to the latter, who resisting Louise's unhappy attempts to revert to hard hitting, won 6-3, 6-4.

Although she looked the picture of physical fitness, Louise tired in long matches. Although she smiled her sunny smile she was often under nervous stress. Far-seeing selectors realised that if these difficulties were overcome, Louise, still only twenty-two, could easily—with her wealth of talent—develop into a world-beater. Accordingly, she was nominated for the Wightman Cup in 1946.

Louise justified this confidence, and her victory as America's No. 3 against Joan Curry (8-6, 6-3) settled the fate of the trophy.

The first of many Osborne-Brough entertainments in England took place at the Queen's Club semi-final. Press and public were amazed by their masculine approach to tennis. Louise led 5-3 in the final set only to falter before her resolute opponent and go down 7-9, 6-4, 7-5.

She overcame her suspect temperament—and Pat Todd—in a fluctuating quarter-final (2-6, 9-7, 6-1) at Wimbledon saving two

165

match points. A display of all-round brilliance then defeated Margaret Osborne 8-6, 7-5—and drew the comment, "It takes an American to beat an American!"

But there was still another American to be beaten—Louise's old foe, Pauline Betz. In her first Wimbledon final, Louise's magnificent service refused to function and she was out of her depth against a cool, calculating defence. Pauline led 4-2 in the second set, when a stand by Louise brought the score to 4-all. That was the end of her efforts and the championship went to Pauline 6-2, 6-4.

Two doubles titles were gathered by Louise who in 1946 was a round-faced girl in shorts, resembling a college student. Later, shortening her hair and discarding shorts for smart tennis dresses, she managed to look more sophisticated. But shorts or skirts, hair short or long, "Broughie" has always been a favourite on the Centre Court.

Margaret Osborne turned the tables on Louise in the French semi-final 7-5, 6-3—after Louise had beaten Doris Hart 6-4, 4-6, 6-1. The Stade Roland Garros never saw Louise at her most overwhelming—she always found it difficult to put away her volleys on hard courts.

Her form at Forest Hills was most disappointing. Pugnacious Pat Todd wanted revenge for Wimbledon and claimed it emphatically in the quarter-final. Louise was guilty of an avalanche of errors and went down somewhat woefully, 6-2, 6-2.

1947 started brilliantly when Louise played a fiery final to beat Margaret 6-4, 6-0 at Queen's Club. But in a spectacular, speculative semi-final at Wimbledon she lost to the withering drives of Doris Hart, 2-6, 8-6, 6-4. Despite very great heat the match was conducted at surprising pace, Louise coming close to victory when leading 6-5 in the second set. At 3-all in the final set she weakened and wavered and Doris increased her attack for victory.

Doris duplicated this result in the French semi-final, this time in straight sets (6-2, 7-5). Consolation, however, was provided at Forest Hills—although Louise's hopes, facing a deficit of 2-5, love-40 in the third set against Australian Nancye Bolton, seemed doomed to perish in the semi-final. Reprieved, Louise played some wonder tennis in the final against Margaret Osborne who held her own for two sets. After the interval, Louise, unlike the girl who had so frequently flopped in the last set, gave a dazzling display to become American champion by 8-6, 4-6, 6-1.

This victory gave her a new confidence which was soon to overcome her nervous reactions. On her next birthday, Margaret presented Louise with a full-length film of their match.

Three championships at Wimbledon—and at the end of the season, the coveted Service Bowl presented yearly to America's outstanding sportswoman. These were some of Louise's prizes for 1948. Before the tennis season was under way, an operation was performed on her back. The result was greater staying power, and less of that sudden third-set wilting.

Doris Hart had assumed Pauline Betz's rôle as greatest menace to the Brough-du Pont hierarchy. Louise fell to Doris 6-4, 8-10, 6-1 in the Queen's Club semi-final in 1948. And when the latter upset Margaret at Wimbledon, she was strongly favoured to beat Louise when they crossed rackets in the final.

Doris was soon leading 3-1. But Louise, scrambling in agile fashion and never neglecting a chance to force mattters from the net, won the next five games. Doris came back into the fight to lead 5-4 in the second set. Both girls were tiring, but they produced many exhilarating rallies until Louise, aided by some sparkling volleys, shook off her countrywoman's challenge, 6-3, 8-6.

Margaret, asked during a B.B.C. interview whom she feared most had replied, "Louise . . . her very strong service." And it was against this formidable weapon that Margaret fought so magnificently to win the American title that year.

In a battle long remembered at Forest Hills, Louise reached match point at 6-5 in the third set. Margaret, however, revealed amazing tenacity. She lobbed and she drove faultlessly and after a feverish finish she emerged a weary, worthy winner 4-6, 6-4, 15-13. This was their thirtieth match and Margaret now led 16-14.

Despite a surprising defeat by Joan Curry 4-6, 9-7, 6-2 in the third round of the French championship in 1949, Louise's terrific speed carried her through to three finals at Wimbledon that year.

After another marathon against Margaret, Louise retained her title 10-8, 1-6, 10-8. They knew one another's game so completely that anticipation had ruled out the element of surprise. Both were inclined to hit the net too frequently by pressing too much. Louise was a fraction quicker and this guaranteed her victory.

No champion has faced a greater physical test than this Oklahoma-born girl did that sunny afternoon. When she and Margaret had defeated Todd-Moran 8-6, 7-5, Louise returned to lose, with Bromwich, the mixed final to Sturgess-Mrs. Summers 9-7, 9-11, 7-5. By the end of the afternoon she had played 117 games of "finals-day" tennis!

Doris Hart, always a trial to Louise, beat her convincingly in the U.S. semi-final 7-5, 6-1. They toured Australia together that winter and Louise had her revenge in the national final, but the trip did not benefit her tennis.

Her service was the chief sufferer. In Australia owing to wind conditions she was compelled to alter her throw-up of the ball and this gave her endless trouble afterwards.

Louise's service and overhead declined badly against Doris in the French semi-final of 1950 (6-2, 6-3). But in the Wimbledon semi-final it was Doris who went to pieces and lost 6-4, 6-3. Grateful for an unexpectedly easy victory, Louise improved in the final and beat Margaret 6-1, 3-6, 6-1.

She was, however, definitely overplayed and showed signs of nerves. Her form took a slump at Forest Hills where she succumbed to Nancye Chaffee in the third round 6-2, 7-5.

Whenever Louise now neared victory, she faltered. Her depression and deterioration, increased by a tearing of the muscle of her elbow, necessitated a complete rest. And at Wimbledon in 1951, she was a shadow of her former self.

With a painful arm and increasing nervous stress, Louise could not withstand the severity and steadiness of Shirley Fry in the semi-final. Trailing 0-5 she fought back to 4-5. When she lost the next game her resistance virtually collapsed, Shirley triumphing 6-4, 6-2.

In 1952, her elbow cured, Louise re-visited Wimbledon, this time teaming with Maureen Connolly.

She had not recovered her old power but could still give superb displays. One of these swept Pat Todd out of the semi-final 6-3, 3-6, 6-1. In a brilliant finish, Louise won the last three games losing three points.

She struggled desperately for one set against Maureen Connolly in the final. But she was facing a player who hit harder than anyone she had ever met. Her intelligent variation of pace took her to within a stroke of the first set but Maureen rose to the occasion, and in the second set, Louise wilted under a smothering attack (7-5, 6-3).

She had her chance when meeting her old nemesis Doris Hart in the U.S. semi-final. Leading 6-5, Louise lost a set point, and in the second set a lead of 4-2 dissolved. That old faulty throw-up unsettled her, and each time Doris stepped up the pace she forced a stream of errors to win 9-7, 8-6. It was Doris who again beat Louise at Forest Hills in 1953—a semi-final win of 6-2, 6-4.

1954 saw Louise back at Wimbledon, where summoning all her reserves of stroke and sinew, she outlasted Doris in the semi-final 2-6, 6-3, 6-3 recovering from 1-3 in the final set. But there was "Little Mo" to counter and although Louise, backed by a friendly crowd, chopped and altered her length and pace with amazing sagacity, her physique, not now so enduring, hastened her 6-2, 7-5 defeat.

After Maureen's riding accident, the U.S. title suddenly became wide open and the stalwarts of the old school were soon grappling for the crown. Hart and Brough fought a fluctuating final which

Louise was three times within a stroke of winning. She cracked on each occasion and Doris, "I could hardly believe it," emerged to win 6-8, 6-1, 8-6.

In 1955, Maureen was not defending at Wimbledon and no other woman was considered likely to upset a Doris-Louise final except Beverley Fleitz. And it was Beverley, who after crushing Doris, challenged Louise for the position of Maureen's successor.

She had beaten Louise several times recently, but with the experience of six Wimbledon finals behind her, Louise abandoned any idea of exchanging hard drives with Beverley. In a 90-minute thriller, Louise showed the hall-mark of a champion. With underspin shots she enticed her rival from her formidable baseline inviting her to overdrive.

Her policy had its risks. "Bev" hitting like fury, often beat Louise by half the court. Weary, the latter pursued her relentless, wonderful retrieving.

Her fortune swayed until after the dourest tennis she reached match point—double-faulted!—and then following a desperate exchange of shots was champion again 7-5, 8-6.

Playing an entire match in a foreign manner spoke volumes for her ability. She had won more often at Wimbledon than any of her great colleagues, Pauline, Margaret, Doris, Maureen.

"Margaret will be thrilled," smiled Louise on television. "How does it feel to be champion again?" asked Dan Maskell. "I must admit I'm awfully glad to have a fourth replica," replied one of the greatest girls from Oklahoma.

31

Too Tough, this Tennis

A BEAUTIFUL winning backhand ... a racket travels into the sky ...
a burly young Jew shouts delightedly, "I've done it!" . . . Dick
Savitt is champion.

Born in Orange, New Jersey on 4th March, 1927, Savitt always
admitted playing "purely by accident". At the age of fourteen, he
was knocking up on a public court near home when a stranger asked
Savitt if he would care to come along to his tennis club, adding that
it might improve his game. Young Dick agreed. His interest increased
after he saw some stars in action. "It would be fun to play like those
guys."

He achieved reasonable success in junior tennis but his progress
was halted by his naval training in 1946. Released from military
duties, this serious-minded young Jew entered Cornell University
to study economics. He was undecided whether to concentrate on
tennis or basketball for recreation, but a knee injury put the latter
out of question and tennis became his major sport.

Savitt won the Eastern Inter-Collegiate singles in 1949 and gained
a No. 16 ranking that year in America.

He had developed a massive baseline game. A laboured, but very
effective, forehand, a beautiful, powerful backhand and a heavy
service were his main weapons. Savitt was adequate on the volley,
but preferred the back of the court.

He was not light in weight, nor on his feet. When he became hot
and when he became harassed, he was heaviness itself. Tournament
play did not suit Savitt—so ridden was he by his emotions that it
controlled the fortunes of his tennis, rendering his standard of play
a matter of speculation always.

Beneath his fierce appearance lurked a rich sense of humour and
the ability to enjoy a laugh at himself—a contrast to some of his
incredible temperamental outbursts in the heat of battle.

It was in the U.S. championship of 1950 that Savitt started playing
the type of tennis that was to take him to the top. He reached the
semi-final, losing a tough four-setter to Larsen (the ultimate champion) 6-2, 10-8, 7-9, 6-2.

The outcome of this effort was an Australian tour as a partner to
Larsen in the winter of 1950/51. Savitt justified his choice with an

astounding victory in the Australian championship beating Sedgman and, in the final, McGregor 6-3, 2-6, 6-3, 6-1. This was a severe blow to Australian morale as that country had just won the Davis Cup from America and in the singles had been represented by Sedgman and McGregor!

After this great unexpected success, Savitt entered for the French championship prior to Wimbledon in 1951.

Not even the famous Tilden-Borotra matches provided as much drama as he did in Paris in 1951. In the quarter-final, he played brilliantly to lead Drobny by two sets and 4-2. A desperate counter-attack and Drobny saved the third set—only for Savitt to charge to 4-1 in the fourth. Again he lost his chances through over-hitting. Drobny caught him at 5-all, Savitt missed a sitter, and the ex-Czech pulled up to two sets-all.

His lost opportunities proved too much strain. The big, bulky Savitt burst into uncontrollable sobs. Most men would have retired but, at breaking point, he forced himself back on court.

Under the wondering gaze of thousands, Savitt, now a man in a dream, was beaten 1-6, 6-8, 6-4, 8-6, 6-3. In the changing room he collapsed completely and his partner Mulloy had to be summoned to help restore him to anything like normal.

By Wimbledon, however, Savitt had recovered control of his tennis and temperament and he assembled a menacing array of strong, steady shots. Nevertheless, he all but lost the third round to Kurt Nielsen 6-4, 1-6, 6-3, 8-10, 6-4, after the Dane led 4-2 in the last set.

Savitt faced Art Larsen in the quarter-final. The left-hander pursued a net attack but Savitt hit so hard and low that if Larsen caught the first passing shot he was usually left helpless by the second (6-1, 6-4, 6-4).

In the semi-final, however, Flam's profitable net attack and his control during rallies set up the formidable lead of 6-1, 5-1. Savitt frequently grinned at the bewildering mixture of wizardry that was relentlessly taking victory from him, and at this stage when Flam surprisingly missed an easy kill, he held his head and cried, "Oh, Herbie!" in mock despair.

A transformation came over the battle. Savitt pulled up to 5-all and the struggle waxed and waned until he finally secured that fateful second set, 15-13. Then gaining confidence and hitting with great power, he took the next two sets, 6-3, 6-2—a surprising change of fortune.

His next opponent was McGregor, so the Australian final was duplicated. McGregor pursued a net attack on Savitt's priceless back-hand but it paid no dividends. His service, too, was unusually un-

171

certain and the match ended as so many rallies had done—a magnificent backhand pass escaping a groping volleyer.

No racket has been hurled higher . . . no fallen rival has received greater sympathy. Tension over, Savitt let himself go in ecstasy after winning 6-4, 6-4, 6-4.

Forest Hills proved a disappointment. After beating Patty 6-3, 1-6, 4-6, 6-1, 6-4, Savitt went lame with a boil on his leg and could not do more than win a set from Seixas in the semi-final (6-0, 3-6, 6-3, 6-2).

He was awarded a place in the Davis Cup team. But from his point of view the trip to Australia was an unqualified failure. Savitt was forever sensitive and unhappily he received a lot of adverse comment in the Australian press, which tended to make him retire into a morose shell except for occasional witty, caustic comments.

He lost the Victorian final to Sedgman 8-6, 6-0, 6-4. Sedgman reverted to spiked shoes after one set but the American raised no voice of protest. This defeat, however, undoubtedly affected his position in the Davis Cup team, for Schroeder received the award of singles nominee against Australia.

It was declared that Savitt had exploded to his captain, Frank Shields, about his exclusion and he received much bitter criticism in Australia.

Defending his championship in the semi-final against McGregor, Savitt this time refused to continue because his opponent was wearing spiked shoes. It took all the urbane charm of Sir Norman Brookes to win him round. Savitt came back on court to lose 6-4, 6-4, 3-6, 6-4.

The strain of tournament tennis was obviously proving beyond this young American. When he arrived in Europe in 1952 he was in a state of extreme nervous tension.

Again in Paris, Savitt provided a never-forgotten spectacle. He lost a tremendous tempestuous tussle to Sturgess in the quarter-final, 6-2, 6-8, 4-6, 8-6, 6-3. At times almost unplayable, Savitt stormed his way to within a stroke of winning at 6-5 in the fourth set—to be clearly passed by an elegant forehand drive. His disappointment and an acute attack of cramp then finished the American.

He would not retire, although he could hardly contain himself for pain. Instead, he resolutely struggled on until Sturgess could claim a complete victory. Then the bewildered Savitt was helped off court and lay in a state of coma for an hour in the dressing room.

He was not the same Savitt who had finished last year's championship with a joyous shout. In the Wimbledon quarter-final he found Rose's imaginative tennis too exhausting to conquer. He tried to hit the Australian off court but was gradually succumbing to heat.

172

Rose, adroitly altering pace and length, continued a volleying campaign on short returns which Savitt, lumbering forward, repeatedly mistimed.

After four sets, it was obvious that Savitt was spent. In his service games unless he won the first two points he made no effort. The champion went down 6-4, 3-6, 6-4, 4-6, 6-2, and Rose declared his victory was due to his ability to judge Savitt's passing shots. The loser liked to make those deep drives from his baseline—moving forward when already hot and weary had hindered his accuracy.

It was Rose, too, who put Savitt out of the American championship—again in the quarter-final and this time in straight sets 6-3, 8-6, 8-6.

Savitt then decided he was through with the tennis circuit—and certainly wanted no more Davis Cup excitement! He started a career with an oil company and took to week-end tennis and two tournaments a year. Asked what period his schedule of play would cover, Savitt was reported to have replied with a dour grin "April!"

32

Frills ... and Thrills

So much was written about Gertrude Moran's clothes, comments and contours, that it condensed the fact that she was a tennis player of considerable talent. Gertrude, nicknamed "Gorgeous Gussy", was born in 1923 in Santa Monica. A fashion writer, this side of her activities caught up with her tennis—sometimes with disastrous results for her sports successes.

It was in the U.S. championship of 1946 that Gussy started to be mentioned as a possible annexe to America's big names, when she was the only player to take a set off Pauline Betz. This was in the quarter-final and Pauline was taken to 6-1, 3-6, 6-2.

There was no weakness in Gussy's competent hard-hitting game —except her inability to lose herself in it.

Dick Skeen, able producer of so many champions, now took a hand. Her errors were soon remedied, she was taught to vary depth and pace. A tendency to wildness was smoothed away and by the end of 1948 Gussy had achieved a No. 4 ranking in America.

She won at Seabright that year and caused a sensational upset at Forest Hills when Doris Hart, finalist at Wimbledon, bowed to her 6-4, 6-4 in the quarter-final. And against du Pont, Gussy, using the forecourt as frequently as her rival was twice within a stroke of the first set before submitting 10-8, 6-4.

Although determined to improve her tennis, Gussy never failed to debunk anyone—including herself. When delighted friends informed her that she had "arrived" by beating Doris Hart, Gussy asked "Arrived where?"

She joined in a record-creating mixed double semi-final when with Falkenburg she lost to Talbert-Margaret du Pont 27-25, 5-7, 6-1. Starting on Saturday evening, play was stopped when the score was 22-all—and the battle finished on Monday afternoon.

March 1949 saw Gussy annex three titles in the U.S. Covered Court championships. She overcame Nancye Chaffee easily 6-2, 6-3 and with Mrs. Buck and Gonzales won both doubles events.

Her first Wimbledon . . . and those priceless, perpetual parties! Nobody has been more publicised at any sporting venue as was Miss Moran at this torrid meeting. Gussy's glamour, her garments and her grin, however, failed to impress little Gem Hoahing when they met in the third round of the championships.

Camera-conscious—hundreds of films must have been used—Gussy floundered against the unruffled defence of Gem's tennis and could do no better than win one set (6-2, 5-7, 6-3).

She withdrew mysteriously from the mixed with Bob Falkenburg, but with Pat Todd reached the doubles final there to extend du Pont-Brough to 8-6, 7-5. Gussy's famous outfit had never decorated the Centre Court before this occasion, and the merriment she caused nearly won her the first set. Her opponents, completely thrown out of harmony, lost the first four games before fighting back to victory.

Her record in the American championship that season was better in doubles. In singles, she was beaten (after being within a stroke of a straight set victory) by Betty Hilton, but was involved in the longest match of both doubles. The semi-final saw Hart-Fry defeat Todd-Moran 12-10, 4-6, 6-4, while in an exhausting mixed "semi", Sturgess-Brough beat Gonzales-Moran 6-8, 6-3, 15-13. In the Eastern grass court championship, Todd-Moran beat Fry-Hart 6-4, 3-6, 6-4, but lost to them at Los Angeles 6-2, 6-4.

Then came the famous Eastern and European tour with Pat Todd. No film star received such fabulous press attention. When Gussy played in black shorts in Egypt it opened a deluge of discussion. When, more seriously, she did not appear—through illness—to receive a cup from ex-King Farouk, the matter was discreetly dropped.

News of engagements, near-engagements and engagements no longer invaded the press. Gussy won the All Indian Hard Court title and the Egyptian singles championships, but the interest in her tennis exploits seemed to have evaporated!

Before Wimbledon in 1950, whilst other women players were scanning the draw, hoping they were not placed near Hart or Brough, Gussy was holding press conferences—about her clothes!

She announced she would wear a ballerina outfit—and at the championships, she certainly wore some lovely costumes. What Gussy did not announce was that she was really going to concentrate on justifying her seeding. Playing attacking error-free tennis—despite the distraction of a vociferous crowd—Gussy reached the quarter-final losing to Margaret du Pont 6-4, 6-4.

Soon after, came the announcement, at first denied, that Gussy was going to join Riggs' troupe. She accepted £25,000 for a year's tour to oppose Pauline Betz. Her tennis could not match that of the ex-champion's and when Pauline had won fifty matches, Gussy could only claim eight victories. As a glamour parade, however, the rivals registered great gallery appeal.

175

Gussy became a baseball radio commentator. Later it was reported she wanted to re-enter the amateur game. Miss Moran, it was said, missed the tennis circuit. The tennis circuit certainly missed Miss Moran!

Gertrude Augusta was gay and amiable. Photogenic and photographer-generous, she achieved world publicity—but not for tennis.

33

Golden Boy of Tennis

IT seemed certain that Frank Sedgman would win Wimbledon in 1951. On his three previous visits he had gone down to the ultimate champion, each time getting nearer to the title. Beaten in the fourth round by Falkenburg in 1948, he had been twice within a stroke of victory in the quarter-final against Schroeder in 1949—only to fail in the final against Patty in 1950.

But in 1951 Herbie Flam, the darkest horse in tennis, had stepped in—and stopped the Australian. Then came 1952 and Sedgman, in perfect condition, justified his nickname of Australia's "Golden Boy of Tennis".

Son of a tennis club secretary, Sedgman was born on 29th October, 1927. Twelve years later, he crossed Hopman's path at the latter's coaching class. "I liked his spirit," declared Hopman. "He returned at seventeen, put on two stone in eighteen months and worked with great keenness."

A born athlete, Sedgman's physique, speed and stamina greatly enhanced his tennis. An indefatigable worker, he loved tournament play and developed an ideal power game together with much beauty of stroke production.

Aided by wonderful reflexes and a natural volleying instinct, this tall Australian could overcome the toughest adversaries by the rapidity of his net coverage. His attractive tennis, perfect court manner and fighting temperament drew huge crowds.

Australian junior champion in 1946, Sedgman visited Wimbledon two years later. He lost the fourth round to cannon-balling Falkenburg, but played brilliantly to win the doubles with Bromwich from Mulloy-Tom Brown 5-7, 7-5, 7-5, 9-7.

The 1949 Australian championship revealed a phenomenal improvement in Sedgman's game. He had never yet extended Bromwich, but showing a contemptuous disregard for wily tennis—a characteristic so noticeable later in his career—Sedgman hit the craftiest player on his continent out of the final 6-3, 6-3, 6-2.

At his second Wimbledon in 1949, Sedgman lost a glorious quarter-final to Schroeder 3-6, 6-8, 6-3, 6-2, 9-7. Despite torrid heat, both men kept up a non-stop attack and Court 1 was kept in delight and suspense by their array of lovely shots. Twice in the fifth set Sedgman

177

M

was within a stroke of success but Schroeder, fulfilling his reputation as the bravest man in tennis, summoned his fighting reserves to score a sensational victory.

They repeated this epic in the U.S. quarter-final before 13,000 spectators. Schroeder was again forced to the limit and it was only his unusual determination that overcame Sedgman's virile serve-volley attack, 6-3, 0-6, 6-4, 6-8, 6-4.

There was no holding Sedgman in Australia in 1950. He won four finals losing one set! His victims were McGregor (National championship) 6-3, 6-4, 3-6, 6-1; Worthington (Hard Court championship) 6-1, 6-0, 6-4; Drobny (South Australia) 6-1, 6-0, 6-2 and Wilderspin (Western Australia) 6-0, 6-2, 6-1.

His fourth round defeat in Paris by Ivan Dorfman (2-6, 6-1, 3-6, 6-4, 7-5) was a sobering set-back. The American's patient, thoughtful game extracted errors from his brilliant opponent.

A bigger disaster awaited Sedgman in London. Fooling about with his team-mates, he fell—and sprained his wrist. Top seed at Wimbledon, Sedgman played with wrist bandaged, but, nevertheless, reached the final.

A very tough quarter-final lasting two days owing to rain saw Sedgman defeat Larsen 8-10, 5-7, 7-5, 6-3, 7-5. Drobny, artistic and aggressive, led Sedgman by two sets and dictated the tempo of the match. A broken string, causing a change of racket, seemed to unsettle the ex-Czech. Sedgman saw his chance. He went for his rival like a fury, and came back to win magnificently 3-6, 3-6, 6-3, 7-5, 6-2.

These two five-setters, plus a four hour twenty minute double, in which Patty-Trabert beat McGregor-Sedgman 6-4, 31-29, 7-9, 6-2, were, perhaps, weakening for his wrist. It did not, however, appear to worry him in the final where he was outwitted by Patty 6-1, 8-10, 6-2, 6-3—and the Australian certainly offered no excuse.

Patty had studied Sedgman closely. The Australian did not follow up his second service, waiting instead to storm forward on his next shot. Patty, taking an early ball, forestalled Sedgman by invading the forecourt first, and the Australian, revealing a lack of resilience, which he later conquered, was forced to an unwelcome defensive game.

He made amends across the Atlantic. By defeating Schroeder and Tom Brown set-less and winning a double with Bromwich, Sedgman helped to capture the Davis Cup and created what sports writers called "America's blackest day".

Reacting at Forest Hills, he lost the third round in five sets to Cochell. Darkness was descending as Cochell risked everything on a successful, desperate attack. At Los Angeles, however, Sedgman was victorious with another win over Schroeder (9-7, 6-3, 6-2).

The French championships were never kind to Sedgman and in the 1951 semi-final Drobny was unkinder still. Revelling on a hard court, he drove and drop-shotted with deadly result to score an over-whelming victory against his opponent's power tennis 6-0, 6-3, 6-1.

When, however, Drobny and Patty both made unexpected early exits at Wimbledon, Sedgman was considered to have a great opportunity. He seemed sure of a semi-final when he won the first two sets from Flam. But the effort caused him to ease his attack. "Fighter Flam", by no means out of the match, continued retrieving impossible returns from impossible places and eventually got on level terms.

The fifth set saw Sedgman struggling to regain the initiative. His volleys took him to within two strokes of success but Flam still covered court with priceless agility and Sedgman was forced to defeat 2-6, 1-6, 6-3, 6-4, 7-5.

Convinced that he lacked the "killer instinct", Sedgman remedied this in the U.S. season of 1951 where he fulfilled his glorious promise. And until the end of his career his versatile, entertaining tennis was virtually unbeatable on grass courts.

After winning at Newport by crushing Rose 6-3, 6-4, 6-0, Sedgman routed Larsen (holder) in cyclonic fashion in the U.S. semi-final. Larsen went down 6-1, 6-2, 6-1 after a 46-minute hurricane.

The final took two minutes longer. In demolishing the robust Seixas 6-4, 6-1, 6-1, Sedgman lost eleven points in the second set and became the first Australian to win the U.S. title. Spectators, who had not seen such overwhelming tennis since Kramer's day, saluted Sedgman with an enthusiasm usually reserved for Americans.

Desperate attempts were made by Australia to keep Sedgman and his friend McGregor in amateur tennis. The climax was the renowned wedding present of over £5,000 from enthusiastic supporters which the tennis star received on his marriage on 30th January, 1952.

It was obvious that his amateur days were numbered. In 1952, he again failed to win the French title—again it was Drobny who provided the weapons to stop his advance. Sedgman had overcome Patty 6-4, 6-2, 6-2 and Sturgess 7-5, 6-2, 8-6, but was at a disadvantage on a court slowed down by heavy rain and was beaten by Drobny 6-2, 6-0, 3-6, 6-4, in the final.

With conditions favouring speed and all his glorious strokes in complete control, Sedgman was, however, at his brilliant best at Wimbledon. Sturgess received no quarter in the quarter-final 7-5, 6-1, 6-0. Rose made their semi-final an attractive affair, but despite many thrilling close-quarter rallies, Sedgman did not lose a set (6-4, 6-4, 7-5).

By a superlative game of delicacy and destruction, Sedgman beat Drobny 4-6, 6-2, 6-3, 6-2. Kept on the move, the ex-Czech could not

179

contain a rival in such full, confident cry. They were fairly level until 3-all in the third set, when Sedgman's added speed was signalled and seven successive games were his reward. Trailing 0-4 in the fourth set, Drobny made a desperate stand, but yielded in the eighth game to an opponent who rose to sovereign heights to become world champion.

In another savage assault at Forest Hills, Sedgman's phenomenal volleys from all parts of the court, at all kinds of heights and angles. were untakeable. Hoad lost 6-2, 6-1, 6-3, and in the semi-final Rose, aced fifteen times, surrendered 6-3, 6-3, 6-4. In a speedy 47-minute final, Mulloy was beaten 6-1, 6-2, 6-3, and in the first five games he won only five points.

After retaining the Davis Cup, Sedgman signed a contract to oppose Jack Kramer.

During his short career, Sedgman gave many sparkling displays. His conversion to professionalism was a body blow to Australia's tennis.

34

Adonis of Tennis

"HE is so handsome," sighed the pretty girl at the Centre Court, "just like an angry Greek God."

Her Guardee-type escort grunted. He was not so impressed by a male Adonis. "He'll have to change his name to Vexacious," was his comment.

Vic Seixas won at Wimbledon in 1953 because he refused to lose. When his greatest rivals Rosewall, Patty and Drobny fell out of the championship, Seixas realised—and took—his chances. His wonderful fighting spirit carried him through against Hoad, Rose and Nielsen but the nervous strain was terrific. Hence his frantic fury over mistakes and his exasperation at the vagaries of fortune.

Born in Philadelphia on 23rd August, 1923, Seixas presents a compact, virile game. Not a great genius, there is none the less a touch of this elfin quality in his alluring volleys and stop-volleys. His aggressive twisting service, his top-spin forehand and his beautiful lob, render him a formidable opponent. Tough and fit, Seixas will fight to the last ounce of his great strength.

Involved in several upsets with linesmen, Seixas is recognised as an authority on the rules of lawn tennis. In the heat of battle, he will remember that the balls need changing—but each little fracas is usually mollified by his easy smile and assuring manner.

"I started tournaments at ten and I won my first match. I don't think my (adult) opponent continued his tennis career," grinned Seixas. On the question of nervousness the Philadelphian admits to suffering when he comes on court. "Once play has started, I forget about it. The man who says he isn't nervous is no competitor," he declares, "or else he's a liar!"

He won the Bill Johnston award for America's best sportsman in 1948 and two years later made his mark in the French championship. In his first appearance, Seixas beat McGregor 6-4, 6-8, 12-10, 6-3, and lost the quarter-final to Drobny 7-5, 17-15, 5-7, 6-4. This colourful marathon revealed Seixas determined to harry Drobny out of the championship by a vitriolic net assault on the ex-Czech's backhand.

Drobny withstood the seige but had to assemble all his heavy artillery before overthrowing the tenacious American. The loser's virile tennis made a great impression on the French.

Seixas was not expected to go far at Wimbledon with Bromwich blocking his path in the fourth round. He not only beat the wily Australian 6-1, 7-5, 4-6, 6-3, but also brought down another highly-favoured star, Eric Sturgess. This 9-7, 6-8, 3-6, 6-2, 7-5 victory was a bitter-sweet success for Seixas who developed a sore foot and was never entirely happy in his losing semi-final against Patty (6-3, 5-7, 6-2, 7-5).

In the American championship in 1951, Seixas overcame the ubiquitous Flam 1-6, 9-7, 3-6, 6-2, 6-3, and then defeated an unfit Savitt, 6-0, 3-6, 6-3, 6-2. But six games were all he could collect in the final from Sedgman, tuned up to his superlative, overpowering best (6-4, 6-1, 6-1).

Flam was the cause of Seixas's downfall in the 1952 Wimbledon quarter-final. The eager volleyer found Flam's sinister passes too well placed. The winner was willing to wait his opportunity whereas Seixas pressed himself into defeat (6-4, 3-6, 6-3, 7-5).

Seixas partnered Rose for the first time in the U.S. doubles championship. Combining remarkably they stormed through to the final without losing a set—there they beat Sedgman-McGregor (undefeated for two years) in a desperate match (3-6, 10-8, 10-8, 6-8, 8-6).

The American singles championship provided a bitter disappointment to the U.S. public, 10,000 of whom watched Seixas lose the fourth round to Ken Rosewall 3-6, 6-2, 7-5, 5-7, 6-3. The Philadelphian battered Rosewall's backhand fruitlessly, and the little Australian brought into play his magnificent passing shot finishing his foe with a perfect specimen.

Seixas restored confidence in his capabilities by beating Sedgman 6-4, 6-4, 6-4, in the Pacific South-West final. This was Sedgman's first grass-court reverse for fifteen months.

Some formidable victims were claimed by Seixas in Paris in 1953. Sven Davidson failed to win a set (6-1, 6-4, 6-4)—Hoad suffered a similar fate (6-3, 6-3, 6-4)—and in an outstanding surprise, the Philadelphian overthrew Drobny, holder since 1951, and accepted as the world's No. 1 on hard courts.

Drobny faltered against non-stop net-rushing. He led 2-1 in the second set but was hustled off court for the next seven games. Down 0-2 in the third set, Drobny valiantly fought back, but could not again raise his game and was beaten 6-3, 6-2, 3-6, 6-3.

In the final, Seixas lost to Rosewall, his greatest stumbling-block in tennis. The Australian offset Seixas's zealous use of the forecort with dream backhands and won in four sets, 6-3, 6-4, 1-6, 6-2.

When Rosewall fell to Nielsen at Wimbledon, and Patty and

Drobny were both virtually eliminated by their famous marathon, Seixas's hopes soared.

He refused to accept defeat from Hoad in the quarter-final. Fighting, scrambling, volleying, Seixas was three times within a stroke of losing his service at 6-all in the last set, but his solid endurance survived, 5-7, 6-4, 6-3, 1-6, 9-7.

Mervyn Rose, intelligent, artistic, kept Seixas on court for two and three-quarter hours and for three-quarters of the match appeared the ultimate winner. At 4-all in the fourth set, Rose served two double-faults—and was met by a ferocious assault. Seixas won the fourth set and his pertinacity was rewarded with the fifth, 6-4, 10-12, 9-11, 6-4, 6-3.

Luckily for America, Danish Kurt Nielsen, of the cannon-ball service and crashing volley, was not the same self-assured man on finals day. With the aid of several beautiful passing shots, Seixas settled down smoothly and was four times within a stroke of 5-1. Nielsen staged a gallant recovery but the American made sure of the vital first set (9-7)—and won the second set with something to spare. Four great service returns forced a break of 2-1 in the third, and Seixas then bided his time until four dynamic services gave him victory 9-7, 6-3, 6-4.

This was his greatest thrill, Seixas admits, together with capturing the Davis Cup and his national title in 1954.

It looked as though he would also succeed at Forest Hills in 1953 when he repeated his Wimbledon victory over Nielsen 6-3, 7-9, 8-6, 6-4, and then beat Hoad 7-5, 6-4, 6-4 to reach the final. But he met Trabert on the crest of a wave and before an incredulous assembly Seixas was beaten 6-3, 6-2, 6-3.

The finalists teamed together and on form were, according to Kramer, "the strongest American pair since Allison and Van Ryn". In 1953, too, Seixas partnered Doris Hart. They won in Italy, France, Wimbledon and America. Never beaten, they retained the Wimbledon and American titles in 1954 and 1955.

Artistic Art Larsen eliminated Seixas 6-4, 1-6, 8-6, 6-1 from the French quarter-final in 1954, the latter having saved match point against Hartwig in an earlier round. The team of Trabert-Seixas won the doubles.

Although he fought like fury, Seixas had to surrender to Patty in the Wimbledon quarter-final 7-5, 4-6, 6-3, 6-2. It was Patty's volleying genius that triumphed over his opponent's lusty attack.

But Forest Hills brought the defeated champion great consolation. A polished display against Hartwig saw Seixas become champion in four sets (3-6, 6-2, 6-4, 6-4). Both doubles titles added to his triumph.

His 8-6, 6-8, 6-4, 6-3 defeat of Rosewall was the key to America's Davis Cup win that year. "I knew I would beat Ken. It is impossible for any man to beat me nine times running!'"

The major upset of the French quarter-final in 1955 was Seixas's defeat by Merlo 12-10, 6-3, 6-3. He had three successive chances to win the first set but found the wily Italian steering the ball quietly past him. At Wimbledon, too, his second-round eclipse by Gil Shea 3-6, 6-4, 6-4, 4-6, 6-4 made headlines. Shea showed a remarkably firm backhand and several times beat his opponent when he came in to attack that wing.

In the American semi-final, Seixas lost his title to Rosewall 6-4, 6-4, 7-5, but revealed his usual dourness and held a set point at 5-2 in the third set.

They met again in the Wimbledon "semi" in 1956 and provided the most dramatic match of the year. The game was stopped for two hours by a downpour and Seixas, fighting magnificently, led 5-2 in the fifth set after a bitter argument with a linesman. But the strain, mental and physical, was too much even for his tough reserves and Rosewall, playing inspired tennis, came back brilliantly to win 6-3, 3-6, 6-8, 6-3, 7-5.

Seixas gained some consolation by setting up a mixed doubles record—four successive wins. This time he partnered Shirley Fry.

His determination and his attractive game have established Seixas as one of the outstanding tennis personalities of the 'fifties.

35

She Walked ... and She Won

FROM wheel chair to world champion could summarise the career of Doris Hart. Born on 20th June, 1925, in St. Louis, Missouri, this frail, artistic tennis player might never have touched a racket, for at fifteen months a swollen knee cap caused a paralysis in her right leg. Poison set in, and amputation was feared. Instead, a minor knee operation was performed, the poison draining away, although very slowly.

Then incessant massage and the constant care of her parents and brothers Robert and Richard ("Bud") gradually restored strength.

Doris was four when her father moved for business reasons to Miami, Florida. Sunshine and salt water worked wonders with a girl who, nevertheless, throughout her childhood was subject to illness, having to undergo a mastoid operation and a bout of double pneumonia.

It was Bud who encouraged her tennis interest. All pocket-money went on court hire! And Doris admits "We lived and ate tennis".

By 1941, curly-haired Doris was a star in junior American tennis. Bud—himself a tennis ranker—was also a marvellous coach, keeping constant check on her weaknesses. Shot after shot received his special attention. Knowing Doris would always lack running power because of her leg, Bud concentrated on developing her anticipation.

The crashing Hart overhead, the swinging service, the ability to volley the hardest drive began to develop. Her style, her timing and the supreme beauty of her driving assured her a place in the history of the game's most classical performers.

Louise Brough, later one of Doris's most frequent opponents, beat her in the junior final 7-5, 6-2.

In her first appearance at Forest Hills in 1941, 16-year-old Doris met—Pauline Betz! She was beaten after a Herculean match 5-7, 6-0, 11-9 causing tremendous comment but she became close friends with her conqueror and this proved invaluable to her tennis.

Doris strived in the winter of 1941/42 to eliminate excessive spin from her backhand. In this she was aided by Bud and Pauline.

Milestones in her career were the capture of the junior title in 1942 and the start of a 5-year partnership with Pauline. They reached the U.S. final but in singles Doris could not get past Margaret Osborne in the "last eight" (7-5, 6-0).

In 1943, Doris lost the U.S. semi-final 9-7, 2-6, 6-1 to the fluent strength of Pauline.

The U.S. quarter-final two years later showed Doris to great advantage. Margaret Osborne had been finalist the previous year, yet could do little against the varied, elegant game that Doris presented that day and lost 6-2, 6-3. Pauline Betz was far more content to defend than Osborne had been and, thanks to her scrambling steadiness, she overcame Doris 6-3, 6-2.

But the Florida girl was rewarded by selection for the Wightman Cup team and in 1946, Doris paid the first of nine visits to Wimbledon.

There was little doubt which new American was favourite at Wimbledon. There is nothing the Centre Court respects greater than a player forgetting a disability. Doris's slight limp, her frail appearance and her gentle reserve at once established a happy union with everyone.

Spectators stood by her in every emergency. No British girl was more applauded. Doris became immediately the darling of the gallery.

In the best match of the quarter-finals, she lost to Margaret Osborne 5-7, 6-4, 6-4. The same round was fatal in Paris, this time Louise Brough providing Doris's exit 6-4, 4-6, 6-1.

Forest Hills, however, gave Doris a measure of revenge. Twelve aces, plus a stream of wonderful winning drives, were too much for Margaret who yielded 6-4, 5-7, 7-5. A victory over Mary Prentiss 6-3, 6-2 and Doris was in the final!

A flawless start took her to 5-2 against Pauline. Surprised at her own success. Doris re-acted. Her agile opponent pulled up to 5-all. When Pauline secured this set 11-9, fatigue affected Doris's timing and she was beaten 11-9, 6-3.

This losing final was followed by several more last-round failures—so many that Doris admitted considering herself the "bridesmaid of championship tennis".

In 1947, she played the Wimbledon semi-final brilliantly. Her classic drives overcame Brough, who after leading 6-2, 6-5 was gradually brought down by the pace of Doris's shots (2-6, 8-6, 6-4).

A victim of final-day nerves, Doris could not match Margaret Osborne's confidence and in two sets another title had eluded her (6-2, 6-4).

Her reward came in the doubles. Partnered by Pat Todd—Pauline was now professional—Doris defeated Brough-Osborne after they were leading 5-3, 40-love in the third set.

The French title seemed a certainty for Doris in 1947 when she again beat Louise 6-2, 7-5, and Pat Todd overcame Margaret. But Mrs. Todd, whose defence responded perfectly to hard court tennis, caused Doris's downfall 6-3, 3-6, 6-4.

Back home, Doris was beaten in the U.S. semi-final by Margaret Osborne 7-5, 7-5.

Another chance was lost in Paris in 1948. Hot favourite in the absence of Brough and Osborne, Doris was beaten 6-3, 4-6, 11-9, by Shirley Fry in the semi-final This two-and-a-half hours duel was the most wavering match of the championship.

Since Brough and Osborne were top seeds at most championships, it meant Doris had to overcome them both for victory. The effort of beating one would extract a heavy toll of her concentrating power and physical reserves—reducing her chances against the other.

Thus at Wimbledon after a brilliant spell of driving had deprived Margaret of her title in the semi-final 6-4, 2-6, 6-3, Doris was beaten by Louise, 6-3, 8-6. Louise had been her victim a fortnight earlier at Queen's. Doris put up hardy resistance in the second set, but just could not cope with her determined opponent.

Forest Hills provided a shock, Doris losing 6-4, 6-4 in the quarter-final to Gussy Moran, ranked No. 9 in America.

An eye operation kept Doris out of tennis until the American season in 1949. By breaking the famous Brough service three times, she beat Louise 7-5, 6-1 in the U.S. semi-final, only to re-act badly against Margaret and go down after a one-sided final (6-4, 6-1).

There was, however, a firm feeling in tennis circles that 1950 was to be Hart's year. This seemed confirmed when she at last won the French championship by beating Louise 6-2, 6-3, and then breaking through the defence of Pat Todd 6-4, 4-6, 6-2.

At Queen's, too, Doris was at her best. She saved match point against Louise and then gave a display of style and severity to beat Margaret in the final.

Her Wimbledon jinx remained alive. At 4-all in the semi-final against Louise, play was halted for the arrival of royalty. Doris lost concentration and Louise, putting up a robust resistance, swept to an unexpected triumph 6-4, 6-3.

Defeated but not downcast—"I left Wimbledon with a fierce determination"—Doris was in no mood to dwell on the past. Even though she lost the U.S. 1950 final to an inspired Margaret 6-3, 6-3— and then relinquished her French title in 1951 to the relentless steadiness of Shirley Fry 6-3, 3-6, 6-3—it was evident that the Hart challenge to the Centre Court would be very strong indeed in 1951.

Husbanding her reserves, she did not play singles at Queen's that year.

Wimbledon . . . and Doris became an immortal when she joined

Lenglen, Marble and Brough as triple champion. Her greatest worries, du Pont and Brough fell to Beverley Baker and Shirley respectively. Doris treated Beverley in cavalier fashion (6-3, 6-1) and in a brief 34-minute final, she crushed Shirley 6-1, 6-0.

Here was superlative Hart. Classic drives, devastating volleys, aces and wonderful control. And as Shirley hugged her in delight, the packed Centre Court's ringing applause held a special significance in saluting the courage of a new champion— the girl who doctors once feared "might never walk again".

Doris's joy was trebled. With Shirley she beat Margaret-Louise 6-3, 13-11 and with Frank Sedgman she captured the mixed doubles title.

Her heart was set on victory at Forest Hills. But a new star, 16-year-old Maureen Connolly was her conqueror in a disastrous semi-final. Doris led confidently 4-0. Rain then upset her concentration and, afraid to run on an increasingly slippery surface, she lost six games. As the deluge developed, play stopped. Next day Maureen, hitting with great power, was soon 5-1. Doris struggled up to within two strokes of 5-all but could not keep back her agile little rival, losing 6-4, 6-4.

The strain of an Indian tour after Forest Hills was reflected in Doris's tennis in 1952. She beat Shirley 6-4, 6-4, to regain the French title, but was making great demands on her physical reserves. In the Wimbledon quarter-final, on a very hot afternoon she could not hit enough winners to defeat Pat Todd and went down 6-8, 7-5, 6-4.

Pat lacked Doris's classic beauty of style but surpassed her in stamina. Her suspect forehand stood firm, her recoveries were amazing. The length and strain of their match compelled both girls to rest, in complete exhaustion, for over an hour.

At Forest Hills, Doris beat Louise 9-7, 8-6 but lost the final to Maureen Connolly, now the most formidable player in tennis, 6-3, 7-5.

In 1953 two women were outstanding in tennis—Doris and Maureen. Would the Florida star come back and outshine "Little Mo"? She did so, in the Italian final by a canny mixture of speed and spin (4-6, 9-7, 6-3). But in the French and American finals, Maureen's greater mobility and her pugnacious power won easily (6-2, 6-4 on each occasion).

It was for Wimbledon that they reserved their greatest display. In a sparkling, memorable final, Doris, superior overhead and on the volley, fought her rival in breath-taking fashion. She revealed the purity of her stroke production and it was only by marvellous tennis and magnificent temperament that Maureen retained her title after two thrilling sets 8-6, 7-5. This was Doris's last Wimbledon final and she went down in glorious, heroic defeat.

A repetition of this epic was anticipated by the Centre Court in 1954 but Doris lost her semi-final to Louise 2-6, 6-3, 6-3. She led 3-1 in the third set but Louise, although not her old confident self, kept up a remorseless, successful volley attack.

Just before Forest Hills, came Maureen's disastrous riding accident. Doris, too, was unwell—another eye operation was needed, but she carried on in the championship, beating Shirley 6-2, 6-0 to reach her sixth final. In a highly dramatic meeting during which she saved three match points against Louise, Doris achieved her last great tennis wish—she was American Champion at 6-8, 6-1, 8-6! Bud witnessed her triumph—and one of the first wires came from Maureen!

Although her eye trouble was righted, Doris felt herself physically unfit for much more tournament tennis. However, she was persuaded to visit England in 1955, and won at Manchester beating Louise 9-11, 6-2, 6-2. But the Wimbledon semi-final saw her crushed by Beverley Fleitz 6-3, 6-0. Doris had always handled Beverley successfully in the past but had no answer this time to her raking shots down the side lines.

Doris returned to form in America when she finished her famous career by a second splendid win at Forest Hills, after which she accepted a position as a coach.

Difficulty, to Doris, was never a set-back—merely a stepping stone on her journey to success.

36

The Drobny Saga

WHEN Bunny Austin beat 17-year-old Jaroslav Drobny at Wimbledon in 1939 it was no surprise. When 24-year-old Drobny beat top seed Jack Kramer in 1946 it was nothing short of a sensation.

One man, however, was not surprised—the beaten favourite, Kramer. He knew the strength of that colossal service and smash, the depth of that dynamic forehand. He had seen those killing volleys and those fantastic drop-shots. Kramer knew, furthermore, Drobny's ability to guard his weaker backhand with baffling lobs and strokes of sudden perplexing power and placement.

"If I beat Drobny, I shall win the title," was his comment before play started.

But he did not beat Drobny, although hampered by a blistered hand, the Californian stoically fought his foe for two hours twenty-five minutes. This pulsating entertainment, filled with delicate shots and devastating strokes from both men, was decided by the immense second set. Kramer led 9-8 with his service to come, only for Drobny to check him with a rich variety of spectacular shots.

Eventually Drobny's power prevailed, although Kramer had stubbornly saved six set points. On level terms at last—and Kramer's unfit fingers reacting to the length of the match—Drobny assembled enough winners to get through in five sets, 2-6, 17-15, 6-3, 3-6, 6-3.

He then hit his way through Pierre Pelizza, 6-4, 6-4, 6-4, but was thoroughly tired when tackling Geoff Brown in the semi-final and failed to win a set (6-4, 7-5, 6-2).

So as soon as tennis restarted after World War II, the world acknowledged Drobny—the man who looked so unlike a tennis champion—as one of the game's leading exponents.

Destiny directed Drobny to a tennis court. His father was groundsman at the first Czech Lawn Tennis Club, and had made his first racket for his 6-year-old son. At ten, Jaroslav was ball boy, thrilled by the series of famous players who came to perform prodigies at the club.

He was fascinated by Cochet and was given a racket by Tilden. However, he did not limit his sporting activities to tennis only. By 1938, Drobny was playing international ice hockey. That year, too, he made a notable advance in European tennis. Donald Budge was

190

at the height of his power establishing a record by annexing the four major championships in one year. One of the rare five-set matches he played in 1938 was against Drobny who held the omnipotent American to 6-4, 6-4, 4-6, 6-8, 6-2, in an early round of the Czech championship.

His first essay at Wimbledon in 1938 was terminated by A. Russell (Argentine) 10-8, 6-4, 7-9, 6-3. Next year, Drobny met top-seed Austin in the third round and retired when two sets down (7-5, 9-7), because of a damaged arm. In 1939, was recorded the first of his ten successive Czech championship titles.

In 1946, following their great impacts on Wimbledon, Drobny—or Petra—was certainly expected to triumph in Paris. Drobny reached the final by disposing of Tom Brown 7-5, 3-6, 6-4, 5-7, 6-2, but Petra fell to Marcel Bernard.

The final between two left-handers seemed virtually finished when a dominant Drobny led by two sets. He eased up in the third, displaying confident light-hearted indifference when missing some easy shots —and let go his concentration. Bernard attacked and swamped his opponent to pull off a surprising victory 3-6, 2-6, 6-1, 6-4, 6-3.

Wimbledon 1947 witnessed the first of many intriguing Patty-Drobny clashes on the Centre Court. This meeting in the quarter-final revealed the latter missing his first service—a failure that gave Patty the key to success. The astute American crashed down his rival's kicking second service with rare confidence throughout five sets.

Drobny, however, led two sets to one saving the third set after trailing 5-6, 30-40. Patty hung on tenaciously although he was bordering on collapse before his 3-6, 6-4, 7-9, 6-2, 6-3 victory.

A visit to America saw Drobny reach the semi-final at the expense of Tom Brown, 7-5, 6-3, 6-4. He led Kramer 6-3, 3-2 hitting with zestful exuberance. At this stage, the match was switched to a more important court. Drobny's concentration suffered whereas Kramer, in no way disturbed, proceeded to demolish a flustered opponent 3-6, 6-3, 6-0, 6-1.

The French championship in 1948 gave Drobny an opportunity to get the better of Patty. This took place in the semi-final and again took five sets (2-6, 6-3, 4-6, 6-4, 6-3).

In a desperately contested 3-hour final, interrupted twice by rain, Frank Parker led Drobny 6-4, 7-5, 4-2. Drobny then surged forward, caught Parker's beautiful passes and won six of the next seven games. His rush carried him to 5-2 in the fourth set only for the indomitable American to fight back to 5-all. At 6-5, Drobny was four times within a stroke of the set but was foiled by two superb volleys, a backhand pass and a net-cord. The match swung round and Parker smoothly stroked his way to success, 6-4, 7-5, 5-7, 8-6.

Few expected Giovanni Cucelli, a stranger to grass court play, to do more than give Drobny an interesting game in the second round at Wimbledon. The Italian's 6-4, 16-14, 1-6, 2-6, 6-3 victory was due to his acrobatic ability to cut off anything at the net in a manner he had never equalled before. Drobny had two chances to win the second set, only to be frustrated by his ubiquitous enemy.

Not content with this extended affair Drobny got involved in a 78-game Davis Cup match against Quist in the Inter-Zone final. He beat the Australian 6-8, 3-6, 18-16, 6-3, 7-5, saving five match points in the third set. Few players have taken part in so many gigantic battles as this burly European.

At Forest Hills, Drobny beat Seixas 6-4, 9-7, 6-4, and Wimbledon champion Falkenburg 8-6, 6-1, 6-3. He divided the first two sets with Gonzales but after contesting thirty-eight bitter games, Drobny's stamina waned and Gonzales went out in triumphant confidence 8-10, 11-9, 6-0, 6-3.

Drobny's superior physique proved invaluable in another five-set match with Budge Patty at Wimbledon in 1949. The American's attractive tennis gained a two set to one lead. Here his exertions finished him and Drobny was in complete command at the end (6-4, 6-8, 7-9, 6-0, 6-2).

Two formidable Australians, one full of punch, the other a master of placement, fell to Drobny on his way to his first final. Geoff Brown's storm tactics were upset by drop shots (2-6, 7-5, 1-6, 6-2, 6-4) and the scheming Bromwich was hit off court in summary style 6-1, 6-3, 6-2.

It was the fury of Schroeder's net assault on Drobny's backhand that settled the result of the final. Drobny fought courageously and at times brilliantly against an opponent comforted by the knowledge that if he could compel a backhand stroke it gave him an opening for his deadly volleying. Nevertheless, Schroeder was forced to five sets and they stood at 3-all in the final set before the American stormed to win 3-6, 6-0, 6-3, 4-6, 6-4.

Drobny was by no means happy in a police state. Soon after Wimbledon he was ordered to withdraw by his government from the Swiss championship because of the presence of Spanish and German competitors. Taking their courage in both hands Drobny and his partner Cernik refused to obey instructions and later toured America as stateless tennis players.

The vital decision, plus an uncertain future, did not help his tennis fortunes. At Forest Hills, his hopes were extinguished 6-4, 6-2, 6-2 in the quarter-final by Talbert who played "his greatest-ever tennis".

In 1950, Drobny's difficulties were partially solved when he accepted a job in Egypt and adopted Egyptian nationality. By now

Mrs. Norman Brinker (Maureen Connolly). America's fabulous " Little Mo," who but for a tragic riding accident might have broken all records. Champion in 1952, 1953 and 1954 (Picture Post).

Lew Hoad (Australia), whose power tennis won Wimbledon in 1956.

he enjoyed immense popularity at Wimbledon. His background, his flight to freedom and his solid middle-height—a marked contrast to the mass-produced inevitable Americans and Australians—evoked great interest.

Although completely happy on the Centre Court, Drobny's game responds better to hard-court tennis. His limited reach enables him to make contact with the ball more easily on that terrain, and his short-ness of leg, too, is not at such a disadvantage as on grass against hustling tactics.

By 1950 his supremacy on hard courts was accepted generally. When Drobny beat Eric Sturgess to reach the French final, few favoured Patty's chances of victory against him. Strict training had, however, worked wonders with the Californian's stamina and this new asset was invaluable in helping him to secure a rousing triumph, 6-1, 6-2, 3-6, 5-7, 7-5.

With one of the finest displays seen at Wimbledon for years, Drobny, in faultless touch, led Sedgman by two sets in the semi-final. Hitting his backhand with uncanny skill he found holes in Sedgman's net attack. In the third set a racket string snapped and his new racket seemed to unsettle the ex-Czech.

The ever-alert Sedgman, sensing Drobny's discomfort, multiplied the momentum of his volleying offensive. Tiring, Drobny started to miss his shots under intensified pressure and after an amazing trans-formation, Sedgman crashed his way to victory (3-6, 3-6, 6-3, 7-5, 6-2).

Another visit to Forest Hills proved a failure, Drobny seldom playing his best in this championship. Art Larsen and a slippery court provided his exit in four sets in an early round.

1951 seemed to be definitely Drobny's year when he disclosed such amazing form at the start of the season. He won the International Championship of Paris beating Savitt 6-1, 6-3, 7-5 and then overcame Bernard 8-6, 6-3, 6-4, to become French covered court champion. The Italian title fell to him by defeating Cucelli 6-1, 10-8, 6-0 and Drobny then retained the British Hard Court title demolishing Ampon, 6-4, 6-2, 6-0.

In Paris, Drobny—beaten in three previous finals—at last pre-vailed. He recovered from a losing position to beat Savitt 1-6, 6-8, 6-4, 8-6, 6-3, and then overwhelmed Sedgman 6-0, 6-3, 6-1. In the final, Sturgess fared little better (6-3, 6-3, 6-3).

Drobny had a run of ten games against Sedgman—and won seven successive games from Sturgess.

He had a slight shoulder strain at Wimbledon but was unconcerned about his early matches. In the third round, he was unlucky to meet Tony Mottram at the top of his form. And in the greatest upset of the meeting Drobny lost 5-7, 6-4, 2-6, 7-5, 8-6, bowing to a display of

193

wonder volleys and a remarkably sound backhand. It was one of these superb drives travelling at terrific speed past Drobny that gave Mottram his greatest victory.

This was heart-breaking for the loser but was alleviated by a new personal happiness. Having fallen in love with Rita Anderson (former Rita Jarvis) the ex-Czech at last felt he had some roots and could relinquish his previous nomadic existence.

Frank Sedgman was now one of Drobny's most frequent opponents. By 1952, they were regarded as the world's leading amateurs. Drobny was French title holder and Sedgman had won at Forest Hills in 1951. Savitt, Wimbledon champion, was not so greatly feared because of his explosive temperamental lapses.

Sedgman beat the ex-Czech in the Italian final of 1952, 7-5, 6-3, 1-6, 6-4. A week later, Drobny reversed the decision at Bournemouth 6-2, 6-4, 1-6, 6-4. In Paris, Drobny played some lovely tennis. He overwhelmed Mulloy, 6-1, 6-2, 6-2 and although dropping a set each to McGregor and Sedgman, his supremacy was evident. McGregor lost 6-3, 6-0, 4-6, 6-3, and Sedgman went out 6-2, 6-0, 3-6, 6-4.

Wimbledon proved very different. Here it was realised that if Sedgman raised the velocity of his volley attack, he could outpace his rival. Drobny, complete with wet handkerchief around his neck, survived a titanic tussle with McGregor in the quarter-final. Upset by foot-faults and feeling the great heat, Drobny was forced to produce every reserve of stroke and stamina to save the fourth set, in which McGregor was six times within a stroke of 6-all.

The fifth set was another desperate affair, at the end of which Drobny emerged a very limp victor, 6-0, 3-6, 2-6, 7-5, 7-5.

Flam, in the semi-final was equally exhausting. Drobny leading by two sets threw the third. The fourth developed into a bitter struggle, Flam, as always, achieving the unexpected and impossible. When he robbed his foe of the fourth set it seemed the American might prevail but he lost his opening service game in the fifth set. This proved decisive and Drobny, hanging on grimly, survived, after a breath-taking final rally to win 6-2, 6-4, 0-6, 8-10, 6-4.

Sedgman yielded the first set in the final. Then an Australian avalanche of volleys and half-volleys, swamped the less steady Drobny. His backhand received merciless attention, his lobs were stowed away by his brilliant adversary. Drobny made a fight of the match until 3-all in the third set when the cracking pace of the game proved too great a strain.

Sedgman reeled off seven successive power-laden games before Drobny made a last stand. He could not, however, stem the tide and lost his second final 4-6, 6-2, 6-3, 6-2.

When Sedgman turned professional in 1952, Drobny became auto-

The Trabert-Rosewall semi-final provided memorable tennis, evident from the first game which Trabert won after having been four times within a stroke of losing. His deep, solid drives were matched by Rosewall's anticipation in his net advances, several Australian volleys being wonder shots. Undeterred, Trabert won the first set but Rosewall increased the velocity of his attack to draw level. The tempo of the battle was brilliant as Trabert then led 4-2 in the third set and, amidst rising excitement, established a two set to one lead. The Rosewall reply was swift, scintillating. In the close-quarter rallies the "Little Master" produced a display of wizardry and Trabert, a great and gallant loser, bowed to the Australian 3-6, 6-3, 4-6, 6-1, 6-1, without making any mention of his disability.

Hartwig inflicted an unexpected defeat on Trabert 6-2, 8-6, 2-6, 6-2 in the U.S. quarter-final, but the American regained prestige when, with Seixas, he won back the Davis Cup from Australia at the at the end of the year. Here he registered a vital victory over Lew Hoad, 6-4, 2-6, 12-10, 6-3.

1955 was clearly destined to be Trabert's year in tennis. Paris showed the way to Wimbledon when he prevailed against Rose 6-2, 3-6, 6-3, 6-0. Richardson retired to Trabert, through injury, after losing a set and in the final Trabert's implacable drive and determination defeated Davidson, 2-6, 6-1, 6-4, 6-2.

Calm and thoroughly confident, Trabert exuded solid strength at Wimbledon. Swift-moving, supple and strong, he was yet never devastating, preferring rather to force opponents into error by his remorseless pressure. This was evident in the quarter-final. Drobny (holder) employed spin on his backhand to unsettle the American who trained his guns on to that spot. Down 5-6, Trabert took the next three games and then commanded play with his pounding offensive (8-6, 6-1, 6-4).

The highly intelligent Patty broke service for a 3-2 semi-final lead. Trabert's reply was a beautiful backhand down the line to draw up to 3-all. Patty held his own until 6-all when his elegant defence crumbled to lose 8-6, 6-2, 6-2.

The final against Nielsen only served to show Trabert's superiority. He handled the Dane's tremendous services with confidence. The first rally in which the American produced a perfect lob and a peerless drop-volley emphasised his command throughout the match.

Trabert lost one service game. This let Nielsen in to lead 4-2 in the second set. But the strain had been so great that he immediately reacted and scored only two more games in the struggle 6-3, 7-5, 6-1. By winning Wimbledon without the loss of a set, Trabert achieved what only Budge had previously done—in 1938.

The new champion did suffer one disastrous setback in America.

This was his Davis Cup loss to Hoad 4-6, 6-3, 6-3, 8-6, a defeat which virtually settled the fate of the trophy. In the U.S. championships, however, Trabert was supreme.

It took him fifty minutes in the semi-final to rout Hoad. The Australian's mighty service and hitting, set up a 3-0 lead—he had lost only two points in his first two service games. Trabert's reply was to take the offensive, to hit winners off Hoad's services and to get an unshakeable grip of the game. Hoad collapsed under this onslaught and lost three service games in the third set (6-4, 6-2, 6-1).

In the final, Rosewall held Trabert for one set. When, however, the American's powerful service and weighty service returns had secured the vital opening set, the match became a formality before Trabert's victory 9-7, 6-3, 6-3.

After achieving, in 1955, what no man had done since Donald Budge in 1938—the capture of the French, Wimbledon and American titles in one year, Trabert accepted a professional offer. Immensely popular, his departure as leader of America's tennis was a loss his country could ill afford.

38

Empress of Tennis

A TENNIS coach is giving a lesson in San Diego one spring afternoon. A diminutive 10-year-old girl on a nearby court starts merrily hitting some balls about with her left hand. The coach's gaze wanders . . . and he wonders. A star is born.

This was in 1945. Professional Wilbur Folsom, with his genius for discovering latent talent, realised that here was a rough diamond who could be hewn into a rare gem. But would little laughing Maureen Connolly accept the challenge and undergo the rigours of training necessary to ensure the thrilling prospect of world supremacy?

With a single-mindedness that has prevailed throughout her life, Maureen immediately placed herself under Folsom's tuition. Her first love had been for riding and she was already handling horses like a veteran. When her chance in tennis came, however, she accepted it gratefully—and docilely moved her racket over into her right hand.

Folsom laid the foundation. Maureen, aged ten, was a finalist in the La Jolla open tournament for the thirteen-year-old division. Then a meeting with Eleanor Tennant was arranged and "Little Mo's" second build-up commenced.

To Miss Tennant, Maureen was "a wonderful toddler with amazing adaptability. It took her only forty-five minutes to assimilate her new service." The girl who had become respected in junior tennis as a retriever developed a polished aggressive game, hitting wide and freely with plenty of pace.

When Helen Wills-Moody first saw this pint-sized prodigy she declared, "Maureen hits harder than I did at her age". And she further stated, "She has the stoicism, the quiet reserve and a greater tennis temperament at this stage than even Suzanne".

Maureen's marvellous concentration, her most mobile footwork and her magnificent physique all helped to produce a perfect tennis machine. Like Suzanne, she had an amazing stride. Like her, too, she was supremely steady—despite her phenomenal pace.

Her drives, landing on the line, carried immense power. It was claimed that a slow short shot to her forehand would ultimately unsteady her, but an opponent had to withstand a barrage of beautiful strokes before Maureen broke down. Later, when her volleying confidence improved, these half-court shots drew her forward to a devastating kill.

Tennis, however, did not entirely fill Maureen's life. Mr. Berste, her step-father, was a musician. Jazz-loving girl friends flocked to the house and Bing Crosby, Tommy Dorsey and Harry James were her heroes. Her best opponents were her "buddies".

"We're great friends although in tournaments we're blood-thirsty", Maureen admitted. None of them, however, practised so hard—and none achieved such success.

Her performances as American junior champion in 1949 and 1950, resulted in Maureen's selection for the 1951 Wightman Cup match where as third singles player she disposed of Kay Tuckey 6-3, 6-1. Soon after, a headline-making victory started Maureen's meteoric rise to success. This was in the U.S. semi-final where she downed Doris Hart, fresh from her Wimbledon triumph, in straight sets 6-4, 6-4.

In this sensational match, Maureen trailed 0-4. With a sprinkle of rain, Doris wavered—she mistrusted her foothold and Maureen hit through six games. Rain then stopped all further play. Next day, Maureen's fantastic speed set up a 5-1 lead. Doris, fighting valiantly, drew up to 4-5 but had to yield the tenth game to a stream of well-placed angled drives.

Maureen was made; and to prove that her win was no fluke, she then demonstrated her ability to handle an entirely different type of tennis. In the final Shirley Fry's insidious retrieving kept Maureen on court for one and a half hours. Her "road-block" tactics won the second set, but the greater staying power lay with Maureen and eventually Shirley's own stamina succumbed in a wearying struggle 6-3, 1-6, 6-4.

Champion at sixteen! American sports writers described her prodigious performance in superlatives. Here was their greatest player since Helen Wills. And until the end of her brief, brilliant career, Maureen hardly lost another match—indeed, her rare defeats caused more attention than her victories.

The arrival of the new American champion aroused tremendous interest at Wimbledon. A suspect shoulder strain was diagnosed as fibrositis and rumours that she might withdraw were strenuously opposed by the 17-year-old.

Maureen had some adventurous early rounds. Nevertheless, it was obvious that she possessed much latent power in reserve for, if any crisis presented itself, she could regain her poise and confidently hit out for victory.

In the fourth round, Susan Partridge (Mme. Chartrier) displayed an unsuspected array of attractive shots to combat the American storm. She had never played better and won a clever second set with a priceless backhand down the line. Moreover, her varied tennis took her to 3-1 in the final set. Here Maureen unleashed greater pressure and Susan was beaten 6-3, 5-7, 7-5.

Thelma Long made a fight of her quarter-final against Maureen for one set. Then her resistance collapsed and she won only two of the last fourteen games. By drawing Maureen up to overhit, the Australian won the first set, but the effort of concentration plus Maureen's augmented pace caused her to crack, and the end was something of a debacle (5-7, 6-2, 6-0).

The semi-final gave Maureen a win over Shirley Fry 6-4, 6-3. Down 1-4 she took the next seven games with a fierce attack.

So at her first Wimbledon "Little Mo" was a finalist—against her partner Louise Brough. A rich experience challenging a rising star. But although Louise had been a finalist four times before, she could not hold the furious drives that flowed from Maureen's racket. Louise, within a stroke of the first set, was outpaced from the back of the court—and if she tried to volley, her racket would often be nearly knocked out of her hand. At 7-5, 6-3 Maureen was champion—and those who thought her a ruthless machine were surprised to see the little American in a flood of tears when receiving Louise's congratulations.

Although there was appreciation of her skill and sportsmanship, Maureen never won the heart of the Centre Court. Wimbledon always helps a young player against an established star, but here was a case of dominant youth mowing down mature opposition. Her famous "nodding" head, her martial determination, and her unrelenting concentration antagonised many who resented her ability to lose herself so entirely in her tennis.

Doris Hart was out for Maureen's blood. At Forest Hills she watched every stroke of the Fry-Connolly semi-final, won by Maureen 4-6, 6-4, 6-1 (after Shirley led 4-2, 30-15 in the second set). But eight games were all Doris could collect from her opponent. Maureen, hitting with great confidence and often deceiving her opponent with her sudden drop shots, was unapproachable. Doris won those eight games at the expense of her stamina and yielded the match 6-3, 7-5.

By 1953, Maureen was empress of tennis and she achieved the record of four major titles in one year. No other woman had won such rare distinction. Maureen broke up her association with Miss Tennant and toured Australia under the care of Nell Hopman. In the Australian championship final she defeated Julie Sampson 6-3, 6-2.

Tennis with Harry Hopman eliminated any remaining imperfections in her net attack. Her volleys carried the same fabulous speed as her drives, her smashing took on an almost savage power.

Off court, she pursued her other various interests, and Nell Hopman declared "Maureen became almost my daughter. She is such a sweet kid, interested in clothes, boy friends and the cinema like any other teenager. I have played Helen Moody and I certainly think Maureen with her greater speed of foot would have beaten her."

Maureen lost the 1953 Italian championship to Doris Hart 4-6, 9-7, 6-3. In the French final, however, Maureen younger, fitter, much more mobile, gained an early revenge. She raced to 5-0 and triumphed 6-2, 6-4 leaving no doubt of her superiority.

At Wimbledon, however, there was every doubt. In a brief semi-final Maureen had crushed Fry 6-1, 6-1 by an amazing display of power tennis. But to beat Doris, who had not played so magnificently for two years, Maureen had to produce every shot in tennis, plus a few that she alone seemed to have in her répertoire.

In a thrilling spectacle, they provided a feast of beautiful all-court tennis. Ahead at 5-3, Maureen eventually won the first set, 8-6. She was within a point of 4-1 in the second set but Doris, who had seemed to weaken a little, raised her game to meet the challenge to come twice within a stroke of 5-4.

Unshaken, Maureen's reply was a series of shots that hit the line. The end came in the twelfth game and the Centre Court rose to both players as a reward for their superb courage and skill.

And Maureen? Ever seeking perfection, she was soon on court again declaring her volley was unsatisfactory!

Their next—and last—meeting at Forest Hills did not provide such glory. In terrific heat, Maureen lost only twenty games in twelve sets. Doris was affected by the weather and although she made a stand when 2-5 down in the second set, she was defeated 6-2, 6-4 in the final.

The French title was retained by Maureen in 1954 with a 6-4, 6-1 win over Mme. Bucaille. Louise challenged her in the Wimbledon final where, by mixing spin and flat shots she struggled up to 5-all in the second set—only to fall in exhaustion against even more destructive hitting (6-2, 7-5).

Shirley Fry had temporarily forsaken tennis, so Maureen teamed up with Doris. They won the American Clay Court title, establishing a happy understanding at once. Nobody could have believed that this 20-year-old champion's career would soon be closed. Then came the report that Maureen had been thrown from the horse given to her as a prize for winning Wimbledon. Later it was announced she would be out of tennis for an indefinite period.

When Maureen had her accident it was a world sensation . . . when she married Olympic horseman Norman Brinker it was world news . . . and when she said goodbye to tennis by turning professional, it was a world sorrow.

Maureen might have broken every record—had she not broken her leg.

39

Hurricane Hoad

THE world champion and his redoubtable partner are opposing a pair of 17-year-old youngsters. One dark, slim, short, the other not much taller but blonde, burly. Playing with the zeal of youth yet combining like veterans, the boys earn excited, repeated rounds of applause by their amazing brilliance as they win the first two sets.

Then the crowd saddens as experience begins to tell. The big men tower above their little rivals. They dominate the third set, the fourth set. The electric score board reflects the change in their fortunes as they reach match point in the fifth.

Then without warning, a wonder shot saves the day and in an irrepressible surge the boys are on top again—and go on to win! Beaten, but beaming, their older opponents offer congratulations while the crowd roars because Lew Hoad and Ken Rosewall have defeated Dick Savitt and Gardnar Mulloy, 6-4, 8-6, 1-6, 3-6, 7-5, at Wimbledon in 1952.

This was the first time the Australian colts really caused such a stir on the Centre Court but the fair-haired Hoad made his mark in singles also in 1952. It took all the experience and guile of Drobny to curtail his progress in the fourth round. By a fearless attack, Hoad's crashing volleys won the second set and held Drobny until 6-all in the third. It was the latter's ability to make Hoad stretch and dive for his shots at the net that won that vital third set and then finished a power-laden battle, 6-3, 3-6, 8-6, 6-3.

Critics remarked on Hoad's tremendous service hit with such easy swing and the violence of his volleying. His great forehand has, perhaps, the smoothest action in tennis. This shot and his very strong backhand carry top-spin. There is something disdainful in the assurance of his terrific strength and much beauty in his classic power.

Hoad trains with rigid thoroughness. Of burly physique, he never neglects his four-mile run every day. Hopman has declared that one of the chief reasons for Hoad's success is the determination he has revealed throughout his career.

Refusing to disturb his training schedule, Hoad missed almost the whole of the French final in 1953, when his friend Rosewall was battling Seixas, because he had to fit in his usual exercise.

Born in Glebe, New South Wales, on 21st November, 1934, Hoad is three weeks younger than Rosewall. Their first meeting as juniors in 1944 ended in a victory for Rosewall (6-0, 6-0). Since that time they admit it is impossible to remember the number of times they have met—or how often they have teamed together in doubles.

Both have caused considerable comment by their strained, unsmiling attitude on court. Hoad, despite his obvious physical strength, has at times exhibited a strange listlessness even in important matches. As he matured, however, this apparent indifference deteriorated on big occasions until 1956 saw him in his full glory, the champion of Australia, France and Wimbledon.

In 1952, besides his Wimbledon efforts, Hoad competed in Paris where he did very well to extend lissom Eric Sturgess to 9-7, 8-6, 6-4. In the American championships he struck a resolute blow for Australia by toppling Larsen, 6-3, 6-4, 6-4 in the fourth round before being put out by the volleying skill of Sedgman, 6-2, 6-1, 6-3.

1953 saw Rosewall and Hoad win the Australian, French and Wimbledon championships and prove worthy successors to Sedgman and McGregor. In the Australian Hard Court championships Hoad beat Bromwich 7-5, 6-3, 2-6, 8-6, in the final.

In singles elsewhere, however, American Vic Seixas proved Hoad's chief obstruction during 1953. In the French quarter-final, the Australian failed to win a set (6-3, 6-3, 6-4) but in the same round at Wimbledon, he put up terrific resistance to his more experienced opponent. Down two sets to one, he swamped Seixas by the fury of his attack to storm through the fourth set. They battled frantically for the fifth set and Hoad, cannon-balling with ease, was holding his services with less difficulty than the American. He had three chances to break through for 7-6 but Seixas shook off his challenge and in the sixteenth game Hoad weakened before his foe's vigour and went down 5-7, 6-4, 6-3, 1-6, 9-7.

They met again in the American semi-final. Hoad had reached the last four by beating Mulloy 6-4, 6-2, 11-9 but could not deal with Seixas's aggression and acknowledged defeat 7-5, 6-4, 6-4.

Seixas now seemed to have the beating of his young rival so Australia did not hold out much hope for Hoad when in his first Davis Cup match in the Challenge Round of 1953 his opponent was —Seixas!

Hopman, however, was confident that if Hoad maintained his concentration and attack for three sets he would overcome the Wimbledon champion. With Hopman at the sideline, Hoad pulled off the greatest win to date of his career to down Seixas 6-4, 6-2, 6-3.

He then became a Davis Cup immortal when his 13-11, 6-3, 2-6, 3-6, 7-5 defeat of Trabert kept the rubber alive. He revealed remarkable nerve control and despite the length of the match, served with great consistency and tremendous pace. When Rosewall defeated Seixas to retain the trophy, he and Hoad became national heroes.

1954 promised great events for them yet their results were a disappointment. They lost their French doubles title in the final to Seixas-Trabert and were defeated by the same pair in the Wimbledon semi-final.

In the French championships of 1954, Hoad played without zest against veteran Gardnar Mulloy and lost 6-2, 2-6, 7-5, 6-4 in the fourth round. Mulloy, belying his years, displayed great determination, a contrast to his almost bored-looking opponent.

The idea that Hoad and Rosewall were suffering from too rigorous a training was again raised at Wimbledon. Hoad's machine-like power tennis took him to the quarter-final, but here against Drobny he seemed unable to vary his big-hitting game and went down to an easy defeat 6-4, 6-3, 6-3. Drobny served with great punch, took Hoad's services with ease and guarded his suspect backhand with lobs that sailed over the young Australian's racket.

It took Hamilton Richardson two-and-a-half hours to beat Hoad in the quarter-final at Forest Hills that year, but beat him he did although when he sacrificed three match points in a tortuous third set, it seemed that the Australian's tougher constitution would turn the scale. It was Hoad's faulty policy of ceaselessly attacking Richardson's strong backhand that gave the American chances to provide so many glorious winners and to swing the match over to his favour after five desperate sets 6-4, 7-5, 11-13, 4-6, 6-3.

Australian discomfiture was completed when Hoad lost to Trabert 6-4, 2-6, 12-10, 6-3, a match that virtually decided the fate of the Davis Cup for 1954.

Just before Wimbledon in 1955, Hoad and Australian tennis player Jennefer Staley were married. On the first Saturday of the championships Hoad and Larsen performed a four-set entertainment on the Centre Court, won by the Australian 6-4, 6-4, 6-8, 6-3. Hoad led 4-1 in the third set and 5-0 in the fourth. Larsen wove his magic spells but Hoad, although made to run backwards and forwards, hit out for victory with crisp exuberance.

Against Patty in his next match in the quarter-final, however, Hoad found his power neutralised. By taking Hoad's services on the rise and keeping his service returns low, Patty had his opponent floundering. Hoad grew despondent and listless. The crisis came in the second set when after twelve deuces, Patty broke service for 4-3. The American proceeded quietly and Hoad went out of the championship to the tune of 6-4, 6-4, 6-4.

A new team of Hoad-Hartwig won the doubles beating Frazer-Rosewall in straight sets.

Although Hoad was crushed 6-4, 6-2, 6-1 in the Forest Hills semi-final by Trabert he had rendered Australia yeoman service a few weeks earlier. Nobody played as great a part as he had done to bring the Davis Cup back to Australia. He struck a vital blow against America by his defeat of Trabert 4-6, 6-3, 6-3, 8-6, his dynamic service helping to rescue the third set in which Trabert led 3-1. And in the doubles it was the team of Hoad-Hartwig that finally secured victory by a magnificent win over Seixas-Trabert 12-14, 6-4, 6-3, 3-6, 7-5.

In 1956, Hoad declared he would tour Europe and America with his wife and that his objective was to equal Don Budge's record and win the four major championships in one year—all of which had so far eluded him.

His first success was in Australia when after crushing Frazer 6-3, 6-2, 6-0 Hoad dispossessed Rosewall of his title, 6-4, 3-6, 6-4, 7-5.

Hoad was obviously not going to put everything into lesser championships—he intended to step up his attack only when after the most highly cherished prizes.

Thus at Bournemouth in 1956 he lost tamely in the semi-final to Hamilton Richardson. But in Paris, he found renewed fire and fame. Merlo, no easy problem on a hard court, was unable to win a set in the semi-final (6-4, 7-5, 6-4), while in the final, Davidson, although he battled for every shot, was overborne by the weight of Hoad's offensive (6-4, 8-6, 6-3).

Seeded No. 1 at Wimbledon, Hoad reserved his best displays for the latter stages of the championship, and then nobody could equal the grandeur of his glorious power. Richardson won a set in the semi-final but Hoad handed out enough fury on service and drive to triumph 3-6, 6-4, 6-2, 6-4.

He proved as agile as Rosewall in their quick-fire volleying duels in the final. His terrific deliveries kept Rosewall back while the latter's milder services invited Hoad forward. Rosewall's marvellous anticipation, his magnificent handling of cannon-ball services and his wonder tennis compelled Hoad to rise to even loftier heights.

Hoad hit through the first set—Rosewall's volleys won the second. Hoad retaliated to lead 4-2 in the third when a brilliant spell by his opponent left him trailing 4-5. Here Hoad rose to the occasion. A love game on his service made it 5-all. He then broke service to thirty and hurtling down more dynamic aces, gathered another love game and the set 7-5.

Rosewall fought back for a 4-1 lead in the fourth set, scoring several sparkling volleys—to be again confronted by an implacable power machine. Hoad pulled up to 4-all, hit a superb forehand for

Ken Rosewall.   Australia nicknamed him " Muscles " and " Little Master."   His enchanting tennis took him to the Wimbledon Final in 1954 and in 1956.

Miss Shirley Fry (U.S.A.). who made a great come back to capture the Wimbledon crown in 1956.

5-4 and then served himself out majestically to love—and to triumph 6-2, 4-6, 7-5, 6-4.

Despite his immense power, Hoad had hit with firmness and had maintained his control. His supreme skill and self-confidence deserved the highest honour in tennis.

He relaxed after this effort and lost the Welsh championship to F. Huber while in the Bavarian singles final Patty beat the Australian 1-6, 0-6, 6-2, 7-5, 6-4. In the German championship, however, Hoad smothered Pietrangeli 6-3, 6-4, 6-0 and Davidson, 6-4, 6-4, 6-2 and in the final beat the giant Sirola 6-2, 5-7, 6-4, 8-6.

With three major titles in his pocket and only Rosewall blocking his way in the U.S. final, it seemed certain that Hoad's quest for 1956 would succeed—and even more so when he took the first set 6-4. But "Muscles" had been playing great tennis. He succeeded with his first services and steered his service returns with fabulous control, frequently robbing Hoad of his favourite thundering volleys. Hoad seemed tired—he was not in the same form that won the Wimbledon final—and Rosewall's beautiful lobs encouraged some vital mistimed smashes. When he won the third set, Rosewall scented victory and Hoad was compelled to acknowledge defeat from his dynamic little adversary 4-6, 6-2, 6-3, 6-3.

Donald Budge's record was still unequalled—except in 1953 by great "Little Mo" Connolly.

40

Muscles from Australia

"THE best backhand of all time," enthused Sir Norman Brookes after seeing Ken Rosewall trample Mervyn Rose in the Australian final of 1953. This volume of praise was bestowed by a man, who with half a century of top-line international tennis behind him, had competed against such masters as the Dohertys, Wilding, Tilden, Crawford.

What did Mervyn Rose think of his conqueror? "I have never been passed so often," was his admission after going down, 6-0, 6-3, 6-4, to a stream of deadly strokes and devastating volleys.

Nothing short of a calamity could have kept Rosewall from a tennis court—which would have been a catastrophe for tennis.

He was born on 2nd November, 1934, and was often taken by his parents in his pram to watch tennis. He enjoyed wielding a racket with both hands as a plaything, and while still a tiny boy had his own miniature practice wall.

Small, but strong, Ken was nicknamed "Muscles" in Australia, while the completeness of his tennis equipment also gained him the title of "Little Master". In 1944, he started his series of matches against Lew Hoad with a 6-0, 6-0, victory.

Rosewall was Australian junior champion in 1950. He regained his title in 1952—and gained a trip to Europe where his quiet, thoughtful self-confidence and brilliant volleys, backed by polished security of ground stroke, proclaimed a potential world-beater.

A quick-moving, instinctive player, Rosewall reveals great skill in handling a rising ball. His ability to switch direction in mid-stroke and the rapidity of his reflexes have seldom been surpassed.

The fiercest shot is met on a nonchalant half-volley. Even a smash can be volleyed, almost impudently, from the baseline. Rosewall produces great beauty in his tennis, his facile management of the lob recalling the game of Lacoste. Only on service, does the Australian fail to find perfection.

The consistent volleying of Gardnar Mulloy defeated Rosewall, 9-7, 6-3, 8-6, in the second round of his first Wimbledon in 1952, after the loser's beautiful lobs had achieved a 5-3 lead in the first set. Twelve net-cords (five to Rosewall) were recorded in their match.

It was Mulloy, too, who staging a gallant recovery from 1-4 in the fourth set, dismissed Rosewall from the American quarter-final that year. Although rocking on his heels, the Miami veteran held on tenaciously for his 6-4, 3-6, 4-6, 7-5, 7-5 victory.

Rosewall had, however, produced a fourth-round surprise when, with a series of backhands of unparalleled beauty, he defeated Vic Seixas 3-6, 6-2, 7-5, 5-7, 6-3.

After Sedgman relinquished amateur tennis, Australian leadership passed to Rosewall and Hoad. In the 1953 Italian championship, Rosewall defeated V. Skonecki, 4-6, 6-1, 6-0, 6-2 and Patty 8-6, 6-3, 6-2.

Only one man now stood between "Muscles" and the final—but the man was Drobny! In perfect form, the ex-Czech trounced his little rival, 6-1, 6-4, 6-2.

However, in the French championship, Drobny fell in the semi-final before Seixas. Rosewall, meanwhile, playing flawless tennis had won five matches without surrendering more than three games in any set—and in the semi-final although Enrique Morea of the thundering service and terrific stretch did win two sets, the Australian never lost his self-assurance (2-6, 6-2, 6-4, 0-6, 6-2).

Everything Seixas tried in the final meeting served to emphasise the genius of Rosewall. Endless beautiful passing shots escaped the net-rushing American, while on every possible chance Rosewall was up in a flash to volley, where his anticipation and his delightful angled shots were nothing short of uncanny. All Seixas could claim was one set (6-3, 6-4, 1-6, 6-2).

Rosewall's classic tennis received "rave" attention in the French press. After the singles final, René Lacoste—himself the possessor of a dream backhand that had withstood the test of Tilden for many years—was seen comparing grips with the "Little Master".

Seeded No. 1 at Wimbledon after his display in Paris, Rosewall was now considered the wonder boy of the year. Yet he seemed already somewhat tennis tired and it was asserted his training was too severe.

A remarkable quarter-final saw Rosewall lose to unseeded Kurt Nielsen, 7-5, 4-6, 6-8, 6-0, 6-2. After the third set came an astonishing metamorphosis and Rosewall, who had been handling Nielsen's cannon-balls with competence, completely collapsed.

Again reference was made to his very serious attitude to tennis and it was also reported he was ill with stomach trouble.

The U.S. singles quarter-final also saw Rosewall in a terrific match in which he saved himself—only by a stroke—from defeat at the hands of Davidson (6-0, 8-10, 2-6, 6-0, 11-9).

Trabert, hitting solidly through Rosewall's mixture of pace and placement, provided his downfall (7-5, 6-3, 6-3), in the semi-final.

O*

It did not take the resilient Rosewall long to resume his former high estate. In the 1953 Davis Cup Challenge Round, he thrilled Australia by beating Seixas 6-2, 2-6, 6-3, 6-4, to retain the trophy.

The Australian, however, failed to reproduce such form when defending the French title in 1954. His 6-3, 3-6, 6-3, 6-3, loss to Davidson in the fourth round was aided by his own errors. Rosewall's copybook brilliance was missing, and the tentative game he substituted could not contain the hard-hitting Swede.

A string of menacing names confronted Rosewall at Wimbledon in 1954. He beat Flam 6-2, 8-6, 6-4, and lost a set to Falkenburg (6-2, 4-6, 6-1, 6-4). In the quarter-final, Hartwig led Rosewall two sets to one. Roused, Rosewall sprang to life and volleyed his opponent's shots to death, winning 6-3, 3-6, 3-6, 6-3, 6-1.

His semi-final against Trabert was replete with thrills. Despite a blistered hand, Trabert won two of the first three sets. Then Rosewall, defiant against a man who had often got the better of him, raided the net to give an alluring volleying display.

With an attack that recalled the volleying glory of Henri Cochet, Rosewall unfolded a stream of exquisite wonder shots. Some of Trabert's smashes were returned on the volley and the gallant American yielded to the Australian avalanche 3-6, 6-3, 4-6, 6-1, 6-1

Rosewall and Drobny presented a fascinating final. Drobny gave away thirteen years but had the comfort of vaster experience and the backing of most spectators.

Rosewall handled Drobny's service with priceless ability but even his consistent lobbing could not always evade Drobny's dramatic, devastating smash. His flatter, deeper backhand took him to 11-10, 40-30, in the pulsating first set—only for his rival to brilliantly avert danger and win the set, 13-11.

Delightful tennis gave Australia the second set, 6-4. Back thundered Drobny to win the third, 6-2.

In the fourth set, the pace was fierce, the excitement almost frantic as Drobny broke through for 8-7, and then served to win a sensational final.

After defeating Larsen 9-7, 4-6, 4-6, 6-3, 6-4 in the most entertaining match of the U.S. championship, Rosewall was surprisingly robbed of a place in the final by the overhead severity of Hartwig (6-4, 6-3, 6-4).

Rosewall and Trabert occupied opposite ends of Wimbledon draw in 1955. The Australian was merciless in dealing with Davidson in the quarter-final (6-4, 6-1, 6-2).

His next opponent was Nielsen, determined to prove his 1953 victory was no fluke. His cannon-ball, his speed and a persistent net attack forced Rosewall on the defensive.

Nevertheless, Rosewall's intelligent responses took him to 6-5, 30-love. Here the Dane stepped up the velocity of his game and with Rosewall's lobs losing accuracy, the first set went to Nielsen, 11-9.

Rosewall faltered in the second set but his resilience came to the rescue in the third. They struggled desperately until 4-all in the fourth when a dynamic service return from Nielsen took him to 5-4. Rosewall made frantic efforts in the tenth game coming within a stroke of 5-all, but more crashing services and volleys gave Denmark victory at 11-9, 6-2, 2-6, 6-4.

At Forest Hills, the match that Wimbledon had hoped would materialise (Rosewall-Trabert) took place in the final. This time Rosewall, unable to subdue the heavy artillery of the American, lost 9-7, 6-3, 6-3.

Rosewall reached his second Wimbledon final in 1956 by beating Seixas in the greatest drama of the year. Down 2-5 in the fifth set against the fighting American, Rosewall revealed rare championship quality. Strokes, smooth and sparkling, flowed from his racket to obtain a magnificent victory 6-3, 3-6, 6-8, 6-3, 7-5.

Hoad, however, proved unapproachable in the final. Rosewall led 5-4 in the third set and 4-1 in the fourth—but on both occasions he met a ruthless machine. He played lovely tennis and to beat him 6-2, 4-6, 7-5, 6-4, Hoad had to use the full rhythmic fury of his dynamic game.

When they contested the 1956 U.S. final, Rosewall's most ardent supporters did not give him a chance. But after losing the first set, he started returning services with a flawless touch. Hoad was not at his best and rally after rally ended with a wonder shot by Rosewall, who gaining the lead and fresh confidence attempted—and achieved —amazing angles.

At 4-6, 6-2, 6-3, 6-3, Rosewall was American champion—a comforting revenge after several defeats by his partner.

After helping to retain the Davis Cup for Australia, Rosewall signed a professional contract to oppose Gonzales over a series of matches.

The little Australian is a delight to the connoisseur. His facile, fascinating interpretation of tennis deserves the highest praise—and did deserve Wimbledon's highest prize.

41

The Girl Who Came Back

ON 30th June, 1927, at Akron, Ohio, was born Shirley Fry who might well be regarded as the last of the great Americans—that band of famous women warriors who made such succesful raids on Wimbledon after World War II.

Unlike so many of her countrywomen, Shirley possesses a mild service. She lacks the happiness of style that characterises Doris Hart's game, but makes amends with a decisive smash, an efficient volley and a very loyal backhand.

Her greatest asset, perhaps, is her undaunted fighting spirit and her determination to run herself to a standstill, if need be. These qualities drew from Maureen Connolly, "Shirley is the hardest girl in the world to beat."

Shirley was American junior title-holder in 1944 and 1945. Three years later, she came over to Europe on a tennis holiday and immediately made news.

In her first French championship, she caused the upset of no less a star than Doris Hart who was considered certain to reach the final. By chasing those paceful drives from corner to corner, Shirley emerged triumphant after two-and-a-half hours and won 6-3, 4-6, 11-9.

This was in the semi-final. France's No. 1, Nelly Adamson, was her next opponent and her long low-bounding, left-handed drive presented a formidable problem on the Stade Roland Garros surface. Nelly had the support, too, of the crowd and her Spanish coach, Estrabeau, who never ceased firing instructions at her during play. Shirley lost 6-2, 0-6, 6-0 but acquitted herself with fortitude under novel and noisy conditions.

Disaster awaited Shirley at her first Wimbledon. Meeting Louise Brough in the quarter-final, she sprained her ankle and spent her 21st birthday in a London hospital. Back at Forest Hills she lost the third round 6-2, 5-7, 6-4 to Mrs. Kovacs.

In 1949, she returned to Wimbledon where as a seeded player she lost unexpectedly 4-6, 6-1, 6-4 to Betty Hilton. In America, too, she achieved little success in singles beyond reaching the final of the Eastern grass court championship where she lost to Doris Hart 6-3, 6-4.

214

But 1949 was the year Shirley joined forces with Doris who was to become her greatest friend. A bond of sympathetic understanding was soon recognised between them and their potential ability was demonstrated by a sturdy resistance in the U.S. final to du Pont-Brough (6-4, 8-6).

Of this partnership Shirley said, "Doris natters to me all the time. I take no notice. It works!"

She could get no further than the quarter-finals of the three major championships of 1950. Beaten 6-3, 6-3 by Todd in Paris, Shirley lost 2-6, 6-3, 6-0 to Brough at Wimbledon, and went out 6-4, 6-4 to Hart in America. But critics were quick to emphasise the improvement in her play. Shirley, an acute and attentive leaner, had absorbed a lot of tennis knowledge from Doris. Her volleys were hit with greater snap, her forehand drive lengthened and strengthened and she was less prone to rely only upon her industrious defence.

They were recognised as the second best team in tennis when they toppled du Pont-Brough to win in Paris in 1950, 1-6, 7-5, 6-2. The "Queens" held match point in the second set, but the third set saw them routed.

1951 revealed Shirley as the World's No. 3. Doris may have regretted teaching her friend so much when Shirley beat her 6-3, 3-6, 6-3 to win her first major championship in Paris. Shirley went on to more glory when in the Wimbledon semi-final she un-horsed champion Louise Brough 6-4, 6-2. Louise, nursing a suspect elbow, was no longer the great serve-volley potentate and was down 0-5 in both sets. Her poor length and her slowness were in marked contrast to Shirley's deep resolute drives and her speed of foot. Most noticeable, perhaps, was the winner's calm, almost grim, concentration as against Louise's obvious nerves.

But nothing Shirley could do in the final was of any avail against Doris, who rose to great heights in her greatest hour. Shirley won the opening game, but lost the next twelve to a player from whom beautiful winners flowed in a stream of purity.

Forgetting her own defeat, Shirley, radiant with happiness over Doris's long-delayed win, overwhelmed her with congratulations— and returned that afternoon to win a first Wimbledon title when together they defeated Louise-Margaret, 6-3, 13-11.

Shirley was anxious to avenge Doris's defeat by Maureen Connolly at Forest Hills that autumn and in the final, she relied upon sound defence to out-steady Maureen. She put up a gallant stone-walling defence against those devastating shots and even Maureen grew weary after such prolonged rallies. But Shirley grew more weary still with her self-imposed retrieving. Ironically, her battle of attrition caused her own downfall (6-3, 1-6, 6-4).

A Far East tennis tour early in 1952 had a deleterious effect on Shirley and Doris. They returned laden with titles but lacking incentive. This was portrayed in the French final of 1952, when in two unimaginative sets Doris beat her friend, 6-4, 6-4.

Her early matches at Wimbledon tuned-up Shirley, and in the semi-final her intelligent defence built up a 4-1 lead against Connolly. Roused, Maureen produced a stunning attack to win the next seven games. Shirley was back in the battle at 3-all in the second set but Maureen hit even more vigorously and came through 6-4, 6-3.

At Forest Hills, Shirley offered Maureen her sternest challenge in the tournament. Down 1-4, she captured nine of the next eleven games to take her to 6-4, 4-2. But the effort of hitting back all those deep shots with high "floaters" drained her patience. Feeling she was safe, Shirley started to hit out—a gift to Maureen, who freed from the task of supplying her own pace, responded with a vitriolic attack. Failing to re-impose her slower type of tennis, Shirley re-acted winning only three of the last eleven games (4-6, 6-4, 6-1).

Just as Doris had always to face Brough and du Pont, it was now Shirley's turn to overcome Hart or Connolly. In Paris in 1953 she lost to Doris 8-6, 6-4, in the semi-final. And although Maureen openly admitted fearing to meet Shirley, she was determined not to fall into her rival's traps when they met at Wimbledon in the semi-final. A faultless and formidable 32-minute offensive during which Shirley was kept on a merciless run, saw Maureen overwhelm her rival 6-1, 6-1. The loser had provided tentative tennis until this round but had played herself into form. High deep shots, however, only invited Maureen to run in for the kill where she was devastatingly efficient.

They met again in the U.S. semi-final which Shirley reached with a 8-6, 7-5, win over Margaret du Pont. But again she met a super Maureen and was hit off court by a savage attack 6-1, 6-1.

Such non-stop tournament play was lessening Shirley's interest in tennis. This was reflected when she failed to take her usual place in the Wimbledon semi-final in 1954. Instead, she went down in an extended quarter-final 6-4, 9-11, 6-3 to Betty Pratt. Errors of timing on Shirley's forehand ended numerous rallies.

Depressed by her doubles defeat—she and Doris had lost their title after holding two match points against Louise and Margaret—Shirley decided to quit tennis for the rest of that summer. But Maureen's riding accident deprived Doris of a partner at Forest Hills, so Shirley came back into the team—to retain the title by a smart victory over Louise-Margaret 6-4, 6-4. In singles, Shirley lost the semi-final to Doris 6-2, 6-0 when the winner admitted she played "like a bomb".

In 1955, Shirley confined her tennis to America and in a quarter-final surprise lost to Dorothy Knode 9-7, 8-6. With Maureen out of tennis and Doris announcing that she, too, would soon retire, Shirley realised if she worked her game up to its former solidarity, a Wimbledon title would not be beyond her. Hard practice with Doris brought her up to form before she returned to the Centre Court in 1956 after an absence of two years.

Brough, Gibson and Fleitz were all considered to have better chances than the girl who had been a losing finalist five years before. And when Althea Gibson cannon-balled through the first set it seemed as though Shirley's hopes were to perish in the quarter-final. At this stage, her painstaking resistance started to unsettle Gibson. The pendulum swung over, and throwing in some clever volleys, Shirley wore down her rival 4-6, 6-3, 6-4.

Her next match was against Louise—her old rival, her new partner. Shirley's efforts from 0-4 in the second set turned the issue in her favour. Louise expended her energy to maintain her lead and her stamina wilted in a 6-4, 4-6, 6-3, defeat.

Shirley was in the final again! Her last opponent, Angela Buxton, had been within a stroke of winning their recent Wightman Cup match. Here it was a different story. Shirley presented an impregnable problem, and at 6-3, 6-1 the girl who had forsaken the game was back in tennis—as world champion!

Delighted and excited, Shirley told Maureen Connolly on television that Doris had cabled her on hearing she had reached the quarter-final, "Go . . . go . . . go." Shirley went—on to win.

42

"I'm Older than his Mother"

HE has never won a Wimbledon title . . . he has never got further than the semi-final in singles . . . yet without his picturesque, provocative personality, the Centre Court would be distinctly poorer.

His birthday was the 22nd November, 1914. His birthplace was Miami, Florida—where he now works as a lawyer. But tournament tennis fills his life and, at its best, his game drew from Tilden "Gardnar Mulloy has the finest strokes in tennis".

An aggressive service, a sudden cannon-ball, and a thundering spectacular smash build up his robust game. A long-armed proficiency at the net produces many winning volleys.

He will fight every inch of the way, but again, according to Tilden, it is Mulloy's inability to ignore mistakes that have prevented him reaching top singles honours. It is these minor uproars on court that have caused such merriment and such interest in this Tarzan-like Miami lawyer's tennis career.

In Australia, he centred in several controversial storms and has been known to hurl away his racket inviting a barracker to come on court and settle an argument—in other fashion!

Doubles are his forte. With Talbert, he made a great team winning the U.S. title four times besides playing Davis Cup Challenge Round tennis. Some experts consider Mulloy, along with John Bromwich, as the best doubles players since World War II.

Nevertheless, his singles record is remarkable. From 1939 to 1954 he was ranked in America's first ten missing only two years when he served in the U.S. Navy—where he reached the rank of Lieutenant Commander.

Mulloy-H. Prussof lost the U.S. doubles final in 1940 and Mulloy-W. Sabin did so again in 1941. On each occasion, Schroeder-Kramer proved too formidable. But in 1942, the team of Mulloy-Talbert came into prominence claiming the U.S. title by beating Schroeder-Sydney Wood.

They re-formed the partnership in 1945 and regained the title by beating R. Falkenburg-J. Tuero 12-10, 8-10, 12-10, 6-2. In 1946 they retained the treasured trophy after some Herculean matches. In the semi-final, they recovered to beat Parker-Falkenburg 3-6, 4-6, 6-3, 6-4, 6-4 and in a famous final, Mulloy-Talbert overcame McNeill-

218

Guernsey 3-6, 6-4, 2-6, 6-3, 20-18, after being seven times within a stroke of defeat!

Bill Talbert later declared this was the most thrilling and the most gratifying match of his career.

In 1946, after beating Segura 4-6, 6-4, 12-10, 6-3, Mulloy lost the U.S. semi-final to Tom Brown 6-4, 6-2, 6-4.

Wimbledon did not see Mulloy until 1948—when he was thirty-three. At his first attempt he lost a much-discussed semi-final to Falkenburg 6-4, 6-4, 8-6. Falkenburg indulged in his famous "stalling" and Mulloy although looking extremely bored, bore the situation extremely well.

With Tom Brown, he lost the doubles final to Bromwich-Sedgman 5-7, 7-5, 7-5, 9-7. In an unfortunate match the Australians received all the applause, the Americans hardly any at all. Indeed some ignorant sections of the crowd even cheered American mistakes—causing Mulloy and Brown to follow suit and clap their own errors.

The Americans had their chances. They led 4-2, 30-love on Mulloy's service in the third set and when they lost that opportunity, Mulloy signalled his fury by sending a ball over the stadium! Another lead of 4-2, 40-love again on Mulloy's service dissolved in the fourth set. Bromwich constantly out-manoeuvred Brown who was completely out of his depth.

At Forest Hills, Mulloy led Flam 3-1 in the fifth set of a fluctuating fight in the fourth round but tired before the uncanny retrieving of his opponent (6-4, 7-5, 3-6, 4-6, 6-3). He was compensated by a fourth victory in the doubles when with Talbert he defeated Schroeder-Parker 1-6, 9-7, 6-3, 3-6, 9-7.

It was said that the man who beat Mulloy always became the ultimate champion—or produced the best tennis of a championship.

Wimbledon 1949 . . . and the Centre Court witnessed a first round thriller when Mulloy, dynamic and decisive, led Schroeder by two sets. Schroeder came back like a fury and after a desperate finish emerged victorious (3-6, 9-11, 6-1, 6-0, 7-5)—and went on to become champion.

The stands were packed for the Mulloy-Parker clash in the U.S. quarter-final of 1949. Thrills were expected but the phlegmatic Parker gave a display of genius to upset his brilliant rival 6-4, 6-2, 6-4.

The quarter-final also proved fatal to Mulloy at Wimbledon in 1950 when he admitted Drobny's service was too much on that day and lost 6-3, 6-4, 6-4. However, he gave a sparkling exhibition to overthrow Earl Cochell in the same round at Forest Hills that year. By playing "the best tennis of the tournament" Mulloy won 6-3, 7-5, 6-2. Fatigue helped him to lose the semi-final against Flam 2-6, 6-2, 9-11, 6-1, 6-3. At 3-all in the fifth set Mulloy's stamina deserted him.

219

Mulloy was now regarded as one of Wimbledon's "characters". His magnificent physique, his nonchalant attitude, his dynamic tennis and his frequent annoyance over decisions, assured a large following. At Queen's Club, after he had made complaints, he was asked if he himself would like the thankless task of umpiring. He accepted with alacrity—and did a great job!

In 1951, he partnered Savitt in Europe. Described as the "grimmest-ever looking pair" they beat Drobny-Sturgess 4-6, 6-3, 2-6, 6-4, 6-4 to reach the French final, there losing to McGregor-Sedgman. At Wimbledon, Drobny-Sturgess reversed this decision in the semifinal 4-6, 6-4, 6-3, 6-4.

Mulloy could not get his service working in his third-round match with Gardini and his 7-5, 3-6, 6-4, 6-4 defeat was one of the surprises of Wimbledon. At Forest Hills, he lost the quarter-final to Larsen (holder) 6-8, 6-1, 6-2, 6-4.

The toughest match of the U.S. doubles saw the old warriors, Mulloy and Talbert, lose the semi-final to Rose-Candy 6-4, 6-8, 20-18, 9-7. The Americans were six times within a stroke of the third set and led 3-0 in the fourth.

Mulloy was involved in a third-round row with Steffan Stockenburg at Wimbledon in 1952. His complaints that the Swede was foot-faulting made their match an uncomfortable affair—and his unhappy young rival retired in the fifth set to give Mulloy victory by 7-5, 4-6, 3-6, 6-2, 4-2. Mulloy seemed to have little heart in his next match against Flam and played as though anticipating defeat (6-4, 7-5, 6-1).

Forest Hills revealed a different Mulloy, who for a veteran of thirty-eight played amazing tennis. Almost fit to drop, he gave twenty years and a beating to Rosewall (6-4, 3-6, 4-6, 7-5, 7-5). The loser was not born when Mulloy first appeared at Forest Hills!

Overcoming a handicap of nineteen years, Mulloy then defeated Richardson 10-8, 6-0, 8-6. He could not match Sedgman's speed in the final, losing 6-1, 6-2, 6-3, but received generous applause for his great courage.

He re-established himself at Wimbledon in 1953 when in the third round a lovely forehand return of service robbed Stockenburg of victory (4-6, 3-6, 6-3, 6-3, 9-7). This match was a much more friendly affair than their last meeting.

Mulloy injured himself but fought a gallant losing battle against Nielsen (10-8, 6-3, 7-5) in the fourth round.

1953 was almost his last year of serious singles. In 1954, he partnered Patty at Wimbledon. In their losing semi-final against Rose and Hartwig, Mulloy suddenly put on glasses. He was "helped" across court by Patty. On the first shot that appeared incorrect to him, Mulloy offered the linesman his spectacles!

Nickamed by his countrymen "Pappy" because he is one of the oldest playing Americans, Mulloy, a non-smoking teetotaller, keeps himself remarkably fit.

He hardly ever bothered with mixed doubles until 1955 when he partnered Shirley Fry at Forest Hills where they lost the final to Seixas-Doris Hart 7-5, 5-7, 6-2. Mulloy won the U.S. Hard Court mixed doubles with Pat Todd in 1956 beating Tom Brown-Darlene Hard 6-4, 3-6, 6-3, and at Wimbledon he partnered Althea Gibson where they lost the final to Seixas-Shirley Fry 2-6, 6-2, 7-5.

He introduced a new type of tennis to Wimbledon in 1956 by partnering his business associate Bud Robineau. Amusement and—in some cases—annoyance were the outcome of seeing on the Centre Court a man whose game scarcely rivalled that of a good club player. Thanks to the generosity of their opponents Nielsen and Ulrich, a match was made possible.

Mulloy's wisecracks and his personality colour every tournament.

Perhaps his most popular and most famous remark occurred at Queen's Club in 1956. After a bitter rally against Rosewall, during which the American was completely outpaced, Mulloy turned to the spectators and demanded truculently, "Do you know I'm older than his mother?"

INDEX

Abdelessam, Robert, 158
Adamson, Mme. Nelly, 150, 214
Addie, Robert, 144
Addie, Mrs. Robert. See Betz, Pauline
Aeschliman, Charles F., 58
Akhurst, Miss Daphne, 75, 113
Alfonso, King of Spain, 75
Allison, Wilmer L., 32, 33, 49, 70, 72, 78, 80, 89, 94, 105, 106, 110, 111, 121, 124, 133, 183
Alonso, Manuel, 13, 37, 51, 72
Ampon, Felicissimo, 162, 193
Anderson, F., 46
Anderson, Joe, 13, 36, 38, 46, 66, 92
Arnold, Mrs. E., 102
Asboth, Josef, 140, 154
Aussem, Fraulein Cilly, 32, 76, 82, 84, 114, 116
Austin, H. W. " Bunny," 48, 53, 61, 67, 71, 73, 78, 79, 87, 88, 90, 96, 101, 103-111, 119-127, 137, 190, 191

Babcock, Miss Carolyn, 114
Baker, Miss Beverley, 151, 169, 188, 189, 217
Barrett, H. Roper, 12, 51
Barron, Mrs. Shepherd, 22, 42, 101
Barton, Derek, 159
Bartosh, Dr. Esther, 133
Beamish, Mrs. A. E., 21
Beaux, Sandra, 112
Bell, Berkeley, 86
Bennett, Miss Eileen, 32, 59, 62, 68, 83, 93
Bergelin, Lennart, 153, 157, 161, 197
Bernard, Marcel, 71, 138, 139, 158, 191, 193
Bernhard, Miss Helen, 148, 164
Berste, Mr., 202
Bertram, Max, 124
Betz, Miss Pauline, 141-144, 148-150, 158, 164-167, 169, 174, 175, 185, 186
Blanchy, F., 66
Bolelli, H., 138
Bolton, Mrs. Nancye. See Wynne, Nancye

Borotra, Jean, 13, 14, 16, 22-24, 28-30, 32, 35, 38-40, 44-54, 61, 65-70, 72, 74, 78, 85, 87, 88, 92-94, 103, 104, 107, 109, 115, 120, 121, 138, 139, 145, 149, 156, 171
Bostock, Mrs. Jean, 154
Bouman, Mlle. Kea, 60
Boussus, C., 48, 69, 70, 93, 94, 96, 111, 120, 121, 124, 138
Bowden, F, 79
Brae, Count Della Corte, 84
Brae, Countess Della Corte. See Fraulein Cilly Aussem
Brinker, Mrs. Norman. See Connolly, Maureen
Brinker, Norman, 204
Bromwich, John, 122, 126, 127, 134, 135, 145-147, 153-157, 159, 160, 167, 177, 178, 182, 192, 197, 206, 218, 219
Brookes, Sir Norman, 11, 12, 92, 126, 172, 210
Brough, Miss Louise, 141-143, 148-151, 154, 164-169, 175, 185-189, 203, 204, 214-217
Brown, Geoffrey, 139, 147, 190, 192
Brown, Tom, 138-140, 146, 147, 159, 177, 178, 191, 219, 221
Browne, Miss Mary K., 22, 23, 29, 43
Brugnon, Jacques, 14, 24, 28, 30, 45, 49, 52, 54, 70, 103, 119, 120, 145
Bucaille, Mme., 204
Buck, Mrs. M., 174
Budge, Don, 33, 81, 85, 91, 106, 107, 112, 121-127, 132-134, 136-138, 146, 147, 158, 190, 199, 200, 208, 209
Bundy, Miss Dorothy, 130, 143, 149
Burrow, F. R., 22
Butler, Don, 137
Buxton, Miss Angela, 217

Campbell, Hon. Cecil, 13, 37, 51
Candy, Don, 220
Cernik, V., 49, 192
Chaffee, Miss Nancye, 161, 168, 174
Chambers, Mrs. Lambert, 17, 18, 57, 116, 117
Chaplin, Charles, 33

Chatrier, Mme. Susan. See Partridge, Susan
Cobb, Mrs., 17
Cochell, Earl, 178, 219
Cochet, Henri, 13, 14, 28-33, 39, 44, 45, 47, 48, 50-54, 65-74, 78-81, 83, 87-90, 92-96, 104, 105, 108-110, 132, 138, 139, 158, 160, 163, 190, 212
Cochet, Mme. H., 71
Coen, Wilbur, 69, 78
Colegate, Mrs. J. L., 57
Collins, Ian, 71, 87
Connolly, Miss Maureen, 168, 169, 188, 189, 201-204, 209, 214-217
Contostavlos, Mlle. Helene, 59
Cooke, Elwood, 107, 132, 134, 135, 144
Cooke, Mrs. Sarah. See Palfrey, Sarah
Cooper, Gary, 85
Covell, Mrs. P., 41, 57, 58
Craddock, Mrs. D. K., 17
Crawford, Jack, 73, 80, 81, 87, 89, 90, 92-98, 106, 107, 109-111, 120-122, 125, 210
Crawford, Mrs. Jack, 94-96
Crosby, Bing, 202
Cross, Miss Edith, 113
Cucelli, Giovanni, 192, 193
Culley, H. M., 81
Curry, Miss Joan, 165, 167

D'Alvarez, Senorita Lili, 16, 22, 43, 56, 59-61, 74-76, 82, 83, 99, 114
David, H. F., 93
Davidson, Sven, 157, 163, 182, 195, 198, 199, 208, 209, 211, 212
Decugis, Max, 18
De Gomar, Condé, 13, 66
De Joannis, Mons, 19, 20
Del Bono, A., 71, 120
De Morpurgo, H. L., 53, 58, 99, 108
Dempsey, Jack, 144
De Stefani, G., 71, 96, 110, 120
Destremau, B., 138
Doeg, John, 31, 33, 78, 79, 86
Doherty, H. L., 16, 103, 126, 210
Doherty, R. F., 92, 103, 210
Dorfman, Ivan, 160, 178
Dorsey, Tommy, 202
Doust, S. N., 12
Drobny, Jaroslav, 49, 122, 138, 139, 146, 147, 154, 157, 159-163, 171, 178-183, 190-196, 197, 199, 205, 207, 211, 212, 219, 220
Du Pont, Mrs. Margaret. See Osborne, Margaret
Du Pont, William, 148
Ellis, Miss Lumley, 59

Fabyan, Mrs. Sarah. See Palfrey, Sarah

Falkenburg, Robert, 152-155, 159, 174, 175, 177, 192, 212, 218, 219
Falkenburg, Miss Jinx, 152
Farquharson, Norman G., 110
Feret, Paul, 138
Flam, Herbert, 163, 171, 177, 179, 182, 194, 212, 219, 220
Fleitz, Mrs. J. See Baker, Beverley
Folsom, Wilbur, 201
Frazer, Neal, 207, 208
Friedman, Mrs. Barbara, 112
Fry, Miss Joan, 21, 22, 59, 60
Fry, Miss Shirley, 151, 168, 175, 184, 187-189, 202-204, 214-217, 221

Gardini, F., 220
Gentien, Antoine, 51
George V. King, 44, 49
Gibson, Miss Althea, 217, 221
Gilbert, C. J., 12
Gilbert, J. B., 42
Gillou, Pierre, 50
Giraud, General, 49
Gledhill, Keith, 86, 88, 94
Gobert, André, 12, 13, 138
Godfree, Mrs. L. A. See McKane, Kitty
Godfree, Leslie A., 40, 42, 43
Golding, Mme., 17, 58
Goldsack, Miss Elsie, 21, 59
Gonzales, Richard "Pancho", 147, 157, 160, 174, 175, 192
Gore, A. W., 108
Goss, Miss Eleanor, 19
Grant, B. M., 81, 90, 95, 125, 133, 134
Gravem, A. C., 13
Gregory, Dr. J. C., 93, 108
Griffin, C. J., 35

Hall, Gilbert, 134
Hammersley, Mrs. F. See James, Freda
Hard, Miss Darlene, 221
Hardwicke, Miss Mary, 131, 142
Harding, President, 26
Hardy, Sam, 79
Hare, Charles, 126
Harper, Mrs. L. A., 100, 128
Hart, Miss Doris, 142-144, 149-152, 164, 166-169, 174, 175, 183, 185-189, 202-204, 214-217, 221
Hart, Richard, 185
Hart, Robert, 185
Hartigan, Miss Joan, 101
Hartwig, Rex, 183, 195, 199, 207, 208, 212, 220
Harvey, Miss E., 42, 43
Hawkes, J. B., 14, 38, 41, 42, 46, 53, 92

Heeley, Miss Mary, 62
Heine, Miss E. L. " Bobby," 83
Henkel, H., 106, 107
Hennessey, John, 66, 68, 69
Henrotin, Mme., 129
Hilton, Mrs. Betty, 175, 214
Hoad, Lewis, 163, 180-183, 195, 196, 199, 200, 205-211, 213
Hoahing, Miss Gem, 175
Hopman, Harry, 87, 94, 138, 146, 177, 203, 205, 206
Hopman, Mrs. Nell, 203
Horn, Fraulein M. L., 120
Huber, F., 209
Hughes, G. P., 71, 96, 110
Hunt, Joseph, 133, 135, 145, 146
Hunter, Francis T., 14, 29-31, 37, 51, 52, 54, 67-69, 78, 103

Jacobs, Miss Helen H., 23, 43, 60-63, 76, 83, 84, 100-102, 113-118, 129-131, 142, 143, 196
James, Miss Freda, 99, 142
James, Harry, 202
Jarvis, Miss Rita, 194-196
Jedrzejowska, Mlle. Jadwiga, 84, 102, 117, 118, 130
Jessup, Mrs. J. B., 41
Johnson, Wallace, 27, 35
Johnston, W. M. " Little Bill," 12-14, 19, 26-30, 34-39, 46, 47, 51, 53, 67, 68, 85, 112, 126, 181
Jones, David, 125

Kaye, Danny, 135
Kingsley, C. H., 14, 103, 119
Kingscote, A. R. F., 12, 13, 26
Kinsey, Howard, 36, 37, 43, 46, 62, 128, 136
Kirby, Vernon, 80, 120, 123
Knode, Mrs. Dorothy, 217
Konstam, Miss Phyllis, 104
Kovacs, Frank, 33, 135, 136
Kovacs, Mrs., 214
Kozeluh, Karel, 33
Krahwinkel, Fraulein Hilde, 62, 63, 83, 93, 100, 102, 114, 116, 117, 120, 130, 131
Kramer, Jack, 91, 127, 135, 136-138, 141, 145-147, 152, 153, 156, 157, 179, 180, 183, 190, 191, 197, 198, 218

Lacoste, René, 11, 14, 19, 23, 28, 31, 33, 34, 37-39, 44-55, 65, 67-70, 77, 79, 87, 93, 103, 134, 145, 210, 211
Landry, Pierre, 78
Larcombe, Mrs. D. R., 17
Larsen, Art, 170, 171, 178, 179, 183, 195, 198, 206, 207, 212, 220

Lawson, Miss Mary, 110, 111
Lee, H. G. N., 55, 96
Lenglen, Charles, 17-22
Lenglen, Mlle. Suzanne, 13, 16-24, 26, 29, 35, 40, 41-43, 55, 56, 60, 62, 63, 65, 66, 73-75, 82, 83, 95, 99, 115-117, 131, 141, 144, 149, 188, 201
Likas, H., 154
Little, Mrs. Dorothy. See Round, Dorothy
Little, Dr. Leigh, 102
Lizana, Senorita Anita, 102
Lombard, Miss Carole, 129, 131
Long, Colin, 153
Long, Mrs. Thelma, 203
Lott, George, 48, 53, 70, 78, 86, 110, 116, 119, 124, 158
Lumb, Miss Margot, 118
Lycett, R., 13, 50

McGrath, Vivian, 80, 89, 94, 105, 121
McGregor, Ken, 151, 171, 172, 178, 179, 181, 182, 194, 197, 206, 220
McIlquham, Mrs. M., 61, 75
McKane, Miss K. " Biddy," 17, 20, 21, 40-43, 57, 58, 60, 62, 75
McLoughlin, Maurice, 16, 35
McNair, Mrs., 40
McNeill, Don, 134, 135, 145, 146, 152, 218
Maier, Enrique, 48, 49, 87, 94, 95, 111
Mako, Gene, 121, 123, 124, 126, 127, 129, 133, 134, 138
Malfroy, Cam, 78
Mallory, Mrs. Molla, 18-21, 23, 41-43, 57, 58, 61, 75, 115, 143
Mangin, Gregory, 69, 71, 81, 86, 104
Marble, Miss Alice, 33, 102, 117, 118, 128-132, 137, 142, 143, 150, 159, 164, 188
Marble, Dan, 128
Mary, Queen, 22, 49, 123
Maskell, Dan, 169
Mathieu, Mme. Simonne, 22, 23, 61, 62, 76, 82, 83, 100, 102, 114, 115, 137
Mavrogordato, T., 12
Melba, Dame Nellie, 11, 13, 25
Menzel, Roderic, 49, 89, 97, 98, 106, 109, 120, 125, 127
Menzies, Mrs. M. See Stammers, K. E.
Mercer, F., 69
Merlin, André, 23, 105, 110, 120
Merlo, G., 184, 208
Miki, Ryuki, 101, 104
Mohan, Man, 159
Moody, F. S. 59, 61
Moody, Mrs. F. S. See Wills, Helen
Moran, Miss G. A. " Gussy " 155, 167, 174-176, 187

Morea, Enrique, 211
Mottram, A. J., 154, 193, 194, 197
Mulloy, Gardnar, 81, 145, 152, 153, 157, 171, 177, 180, 194, 205-207, 210, 218-221
Murray, R. L., 26, 35

Nielsen, Kurt, 162, 171, 181-183, 195, 199, 211-213, 220, 221
Norton, Brian, 27, 28, 37, 45
Nunoi, R., 120
Nusslein, Hans, 90
Nuthall, Miss Betty, 43, 56, 60-63, 82-84, 99, 114, 129

Olliff, John, 93, 108
Osborne, Miss Margaret, 141-144, 148-152, 159, 164-169, 174, 175, 186-188, 215, 216
Oxford, Lady, 105

Pails, Dinny, 127, 138, 147, 153, 157, 158
Palfrey, Miss Sarah, 102, 128, 130, 131, 142-145, 148, 164, 165
Palmieri, G., 120
Parke, J. C., 26, 36
Parker, Frank, 81, 107, 123, 126, 133-135, 147, 153, 156, 160, 191, 218, 219
Partridge, Miss Susan, 202, 203
Patterson, Gerald, 11-15, 25, 26, 35-38, 45, 46, 92
Patty, Budge, 139, 143, 153, 158-163, 172, 177-179, 181-183, 191-193, 195-199, 207, 209
Payot, Mlle. L., 62
Peacock, Mrs., 20, 59
Pelizza, Pierre, 190
Perry, F. J., 23, 33, 48, 54, 71, 78-80, 86, 87, 90, 91, 93-97, 99, 104, 107-112, 119-127, 136
Peteri, Mme., 22
Petra, Yvon, 49, 73, 112, 137-140, 152, 158, 159, 191
Petra, Mme., 139
Pietrangeli, N., 209
Plaa, Martin, 90
Pratt, Mrs. Betty, 216
Prenn, Daniel, 93, 104, 109, 119, 120
Prentiss, Mrs. Mary, 186
Prussof, H., 145, 218

Quist, Adrian, 94, 97, 106, 110, 111, 124, 125, 127, 134, 145, 146, 157, 192, 197

Ramillon, R., 90, 127
Raymond, Louis, 46

Richards, Vincent, 14, 28, 29, 33, 34, 36, 37, 42, 43, 45, 47, 52, 53, 66, 67, 145
Richardson, Hamilton, 161, 162, 199, 207, 208, 220
Richardson, Mrs., 162
Ridley, Miss Joan, 83, 128
Riggs, R. L., 33, 122, 125, 127, 131-136, 139, 141, 146, 147, 156, 175
Ritchie, M. J. G., 12
Roark, Adrian, 64
Robineau, Bud, 221
Roc, Miss Patricia, 112
Rose, Mervyn, 157, 163, 172, 173, 179-183, 198, 199, 210, 220
Rosewall, Ken., 155, 181, 182, 184, 195, 196, 198-200, 205-213, 220, 221
Round, Miss Dorothy, 62, 63, 76, 99-102, 115-117
Russell, A., 191
Ruth, Babe, 14
Ryan, Miss Elizabeth, 13, 17-22, 32, 40-43, 59, 60, 62, 75, 82, 83, 93, 143, 148, 149

Sabin, Wayne, 133, 145, 218
Samazeuilh, J., 66
Sampson, Miss Julie, 203
Satoh, J., 48, 79, 87, 94, 95, 104, 105
Satterthwaite, Mrs. P., 17, 57, 58
Savitt, R., 162, 170-173, 182, 193, 194, 205, 220
Schroeder, F, R. " Ted," 81, 135, 145, 146, 154, 156, 157, 161, 172, 177, 178, 192, 218, 219
Schroder, Karl, 137, 138
Scofield, Miss Barbara, 151
Scriven, Miss M. C., 84, 115, 116, 118
Sedgman, Frank, 157, 161, 162, 171, 172, 177-180, 182, 188, 193, 194, 197, 198, 206, 211, 219, 220
Segura, Francisco, 139, 141, 146, 152, 219
Seixas, Vic., 163, 172, 179, 181-184, 192, 195, 198, 199, 205-208, 211, 212, 221
Sharpe, Nigel, 71, 78
Shaw, Bernard, 61
Shea, Gil, 184
Shields, Frank X., 31, 48, 69, 72, 77, 78, 80, 85-87, 90, 95, 96, 104-106, 111, 119, 120, 123, 125, 172
Shimidzu, Z., 26
Sidwell, O. W., 157, 159
Sirola, O., 209
Skeen, Dick, 174
Skonecki, V., 211
Sleem, Mohammed, 66, 96
Sperling, Fru H., See Krahwinkel, Hilde

Sperling, Herr, 117
Spychala, C., 138
Staley, Miss Jennefer, 207
Stammers, Miss K. E., 63, 84, 101, 117, 118, 130, 131
Stanwyck, Miss Barbara, 158
Sterry, Miss G., 59
Stockenburg, Steffan, 220
Stoeffen, Lester, 73, 80, 88, 91, 96, 110, 124, 127
Stolpa, A., 159
Sturgess, Eric, 157, 167, 172, 175, 179, 182, 193, 197 206, 220
Sullivan, J. E., 126
Summers, Mrs. Sheila, 167
Sutter, Clifford, 72, 80, 88, 95, 120

Talbert, Bill, 81, 135, 152, 153, 160, 161, 174, 192, 197, 218-220
Talmadge, Miss Norma, 74
Taylor, Robert, 158
Tennant, Miss Eleanor " Teach," 128, 129, 131, 201, 203
Tilden, W. T. " Big Bill," 11-14, 16, 18, 19, 25-39, 41, 42, 45-48, 50-55, 64-73, 77, 78, 82-87, 89-92, 96, 103, 112, 114, 117, 122, 125-127, 139, 147, 171, 190, 210, 211, 218
Timmer, H., 120
Todd, Mrs. Patricia, 165-168, 175, 186-188, 215, 221
Trabert, Mr., 197
Trabert, Tony, 161, 163, 178, 183, 196-200, 206-208, 211-213
Tuckey, Miss Kay, 202
Tuero, J., 152, 218
Turnbull, Don, 94, 96, 111

Ulrich, T., 221

Valdène, Comtesse de la. See d'Alvarez, Lili

Van Horn, Welby, 135
Van Ryn, John, 31, 52, 70, 72, 86, 89, 124, 133, 183
Vines, H. Ellsworth, 33, 49, 54, 71-73, 78, 80, 85-91, 94-96, 105, 107, 109, 110, 112, 120, 124-127, 132, 145, 158
Vines, Mrs. H. E., 91
Vinson, Miss Helen, 111
Vlasto, Mlle. Didi, 22, 42, 43, 58, 59
Von Cramm, Gottfried, 96-98, 106, 111, 112, 119-122, 125-127
Von Kehrling, Baron, 103, 119

Walsh, Mrs. Lorraine, 112
Washer, Jean, 27, 37, 51, 66
Watson, Mrs. Holcroft, 43, 60, 61, 82, 114
Webster, Tom, 113
White, Beese, 129
Whittingstall, Mrs. Eileen F. See Bennett, Eileen
Wightman, Mrs. Hazel, 35, 51, 57, 58, 68, 143
Wilde, Frank H. D., 124, 137
Wilderspin, Clive, 178
Wilding, A. F., 12, 210
Wilding, Dorothy, 118
Williams, R. N., 34-36, 46, 51, 66, 80, 85
Wills, Miss Helen, 21-24, 41-43, 56-64, 74, 75, 82, 83, 100, 101, 113-118, 143, 201, 202, 204
Wills, Mrs., 57, 58, 61
Wolf, Miss Catherine, 142
Wood, Pat O'Hara, 14, 51
Wood, Sydney B., 54, 69, 77-81, 85, 87, 95, 97, 104, 106-110, 124, 127, 218
Worthington, G., 178
Wynne, Miss Nancye, 130, 166

Yamagishi, J., 133

227